The Therapist's Starter Guide

THE

Therapist's Starter Guide

Setting Up AND Building Your Practice, Working with Clients, AND Managing Professional Growth

Mark Lanci and Anne Spreng

WILEY

John Wiley & Sons, Inc.

Library of Congress Cataloging-in-Publication Data:

Lanci, Mark.
   The therapist's starter guide : setting up and building your practice, working with clients, and managing professional growth / by Mark Lanci and Anne Spreng.
       p.   cm.
   Includes bibliographical references and index.
   ISBN 978-0-470-22892-0 (pbk.: alk. paper)
       1. Psychotherapy—Vocational guidance.   2. Psychotherapy—Practice.   I. Spreng, Anne.   II. Title.
[DNLM: 1. Psychotherapy—organization & administration.   2. Practice Management.   3. Professional-Patient Relations.   4. Psychotherapy—methods. WM 420 L249t 2008]

   RC440.8.L36 2008
   616.89′140068—dc22

                                                                                                    2008001497

Printed in the United States of America

10 9 8 7 6 5 4 3 2 1

Contents

Preface

You are a therapist—now what? Beginning practitioners are faced with many challenging questions:

- What kind of practitioner am I?
- How do I recognize ethical dilemmas and handle them when they occur?
- How do I protect myself legally and stay out of trouble?
- What about client charts? What do I include? What purpose do they serve?
- What kind of relationship do I want to have with my clients? How do I want to interact with them?
- How do I recognize when my clients are ready for change, and how do I best help them?
- What issues are important in the beginning of treatment? The middle? How do I end treatment with clients gracefully and inspire them to continue to develop in the future?
- How do I deal with clinical challenges? What if my client has a substance abuse problem or a personality disorder?
- What do I do if my client is suicidal? How do I get a client hospitalized? What if a client completes suicide?
- Do I know enough about medication to help my clients make decisions about their options?
- How do I get my practice established? What about working with insurance companies?
- What about my physical space? How do I generate referrals?
- How do I continue to grow as a practitioner?
- What are the trends on the psychotherapy horizon, and how do I position myself for success in a very competitive marketplace?

The practice of psychotherapy is a unique blend of science, art, and business. Most graduate school programs have a strong emphasis on the science aspect, less emphasis on the art of psychotherapy, and very little emphasis on the knowledge and skills practitioners need to survive in the business of psychotherapy. This book provides new practitioners with the basic skills needed to succeed, thrive, and grow professionally as well as personally. This book will give you the tools it takes to understand the science, practice the art, and thrive in the business of psychotherapy. We would not let our clients undertake the therapeutic journey without a road map; so why should we?

In this book, we demonstrate how to develop the skills you need to evaluate your client's mental health needs, create focused and efficient treatment plans, and document your interventions and effectiveness. Transforming yourself from a student of different theories of psychotherapy into a professional therapist with a thriving practice has too often been left to chance. Most therapists start out with good intentions, but it's easy to fall into bad habits and provide less than optimal treatment.

The fundamental purpose of this book is to provide new psychotherapists with a means of transitioning from graduate student interns to working practitioners at the start of their career. This book will benefit those training in programs of psychology, mental health counseling, clinical social work, marriage and family therapy, and similar disciplines. Clinicians in the first few years of establishing a practice and those who would like to revitalize their practice will also find it helpful.

It is our intention to expose you to concepts you should know in order to thrive in the real world of psychotherapy practice. We use a variety of methods to do this: reviewing the ideas and methods of prominent practitioners in the field, citing the professional literature, quoting practitioners and the general culture, and offering real-life clinical scenarios, exercises, and our own insights.

We have a wide variety of clinical experience: working with children, adults, and families; working in inpatient and outpatient settings; working with a variety of diagnoses, from depression and anxiety to personality disorders and psychosis; and working in private practice and in agencies. We have one more qualification: We have managed a network of behavioral health providers for a large, nonprofit insurance company.

In our roles in behavioral health care management, we have reviewed thousands of treatment reports, evaluations, and psychotherapy charts. We have seen it all! We have seen practitioners who quickly establish rapport, conceptualize the problem accurately, and design interventions to help the client change. We have seen practitioners who miss the diagnosis and concentrate on the wrong issue, and others who foster dependence in their clients (and then request additional sessions to support their dependence). We have consulted with therapists about how to provide excellent care to their clients. We have spoken with clients about how to improve their therapy experience. We believe there is a strong relationship between effective psychotherapy and organized, complete documentation.

We take seriously our responsibility to ensure that the members we serve in our organization receive the highest quality behavioral health care. We also take seriously our responsibility to be good stewards of our members' health care dollars. We find that these two responsibilities are more intertwined than most people think. Over the past several years, we have become aware of the need to train new practitioners who will be able to carry the therapeutic torch as the baby boomer practitioners start to retire. The industry needs clinically astute and compassionate practitioners who can communicate with clients in a language they can understand as well as with insurers who are paying for the treatment.

Good psychotherapy is effective, efficient, and ethical. Whether the costs of therapy are borne by the client, an agency, a government-funded program, or an insurance company, consumers of therapy have a right to the most effective, efficient, and ethical treatment possible. Too many psychotherapy clients endure years of meandering, unfocused, and unsuccessful treatment. This wastes the time and money of the client, the therapist, and society as a whole.

Organization

Section I covers the issues you must consider before you see your first client. The initial focus is developing your own philosophy of care and determining the type of practitioner you are. An in-depth discussion of relevant legal and ethical issues will make you aware of these very important topics by analyzing real-world scenarios. By increasing your awareness now, you will gain a thorough knowledge of these topics and be able to recognize ethical dilemmas and solutions as they are occurring rather than after the fact. Next we review the elements of a basic client chart. Setting up a coherent documentation system will help you efficiently record required clinical information as well as help keep your work with clients focused. We conclude this section by discussing what it takes to establish a thriving practice, including how to work effectively within a managed care environment.

In Section II we contemplate the process of actually working with the client. What is the nature of the therapeutic relationship? How will you interact with the client? This section involves the actual nuts and bolts of doing clinical work. Setting the stage for effective treatment starts by determining, with the client, the nature of the client's problems and how you will work together. Drawing up treatment plans, setting realistic goals, and establishing your relationship with the client are illustrated by references to the professional literature, real-life scenarios, and individual exercises. We follow the entire course of treatment, from the initial stage to the middle phase of treatment and then to termination. Issues that can enhance and impede the therapy experience are illustrated. We also cover common themes and strategies for working with challenging clients.

Section III concentrates on the personal side of practice. How do you deal with burnout and being exposed to traumatic experiences and intense emotions all day? How do you continue to grow and maintain excitement in your work over the long haul? Despite the fact that our clients come to us for answers to their problems, we as practitioners often learn a great deal about ourselves and the human experience along the path of helping others.

At the end of each chapter are a series of resources (suggested readings and web sites) and a series of exercises. These exercises are designed to help you to:

- Think in more depth about the concepts presented in the chapters
- Discuss your personal responses to these concepts with colleagues (or in a graduate school seminar if you are a therapist in training)
- Apply the concepts to your own practice, clinical situations, and professional struggles
- Formulate plans and activities to enhance your practice and your professional development, at whatever stage of your career you are

We invite you to engage with these exercises as much (or as little) as you like. Feel free to select exercises that meet your personal needs. You may find yourself returning to some of the exercises as you pass through the many phases of your career.

We have striven to give you clinical insight and practical understanding based on a real-world approach. We hope you find *The Therapist's Starter Guide* helpful as you begin your professional journey. This text is dedicated to helping you become an outstanding, effective, ethical, and satisfied professional. Welcome to an enormously challenging, humbling, and satisfying career in the mental health field.

Acknowledgments

No project of this magnitude can be completed without support and help from colleagues and family. Thanks to all of the practitioners in the mental health community in northwest Washington State for the countless consultations and conversations over the years that have truly enriched our lives. Thanks to Chris Portman, PhD, for his many years of professional friendship. His thoughtful suggestions regarding ethical and private practice issues and treating clients with chemical dependency problems have made significant contributions to this work. We would like to recognize Gina Thompson, MD, for her consultation on the chapter on understanding medications and Laura Ellis, PhD, for permission to use one of her case vignettes.

We would like to acknowledge Deborah Forgays, PhD, professor of psychology at Western Washington University, for her skillful review of this manuscript. Her insightful suggestions and encouragement were extremely helpful at many critical stages of this project's development. We would also like to thank J'May Rivara, MSS, Co-Director of Practicum at the Graduate School of Social Work, University of Washington, for her early manuscript review comments.

Not only does one have to write the book, but one then has to figure out how to get it published. Thanks to Ridley Enslow of Enslow Publishers, Inc. for helping some novice writers understand how the publishing world works. We would like to recognize Bob Pirtle for his help with the business aspects of this project and his connections that helped us find a publisher. We would also like to acknowledge Judy Spreng for her technical assistance and encouragement.

We would like to acknowledge the talented and skillful staff at John Wiley & Sons, especially Lisa Gebo for her early enthusiasm about our project and her ability to see its potential while still in its raw form. In addition, we are grateful to Peggy Alexander for her initial guidance, our editor, Isabel Pratt, for her care and support, and Marquita Flemming, who not only helped our book find a home but also guided it in its final stages of publication.

I am eternally grateful to Virginia Cappeller, PhD, mentor, colleague, and friend, for all of her guidance and wisdom. I can never pay her back, but this book has been my attempt to pay it forward.

I would not have been able to complete this project without the total dedication of my life partner, Tina Lanci. Your belief in me is a constant source of inspiration. Thanks for being so supportive and giving up lots of our personal time to give me time to write. Throughout this project, I have also discovered that you are an incredible editor and have an uncanny ability to know when even the smallest detail is not clear. You have always been my compass, not only on the written page but in life.

SECTION I

SETTING UP AND BUILDING YOUR PRACTICE

1

Defining Your Purpose

What You Will Learn
- The two main focal points of therapy
- The practitioner's challenges in working with each of the five reasons clients initiate therapy
- How to determine your own personal psychotherapy orientation
- How different therapists may bring out different information from their clients
- How psychotherapists' awareness of their own beliefs can assist in providing good care

A critical question that you must answer before beginning a psychotherapy practice is what you hope to accomplish for your clients. What is the purpose of therapy? What approach will I take in helping my clients? What is my therapeutic style? The answer to these questions will guide you in every interaction you have with your clients. The answer may be simplistic, or it may be overly technical and complex. In the end, you must choose a purpose that will focus your practice on helping your clients while also allowing you to have a meaningful and successful career. The purpose of this chapter is to help you define your style with the realization that no matter which approach you take, it will define how you view the client's problem as well as the solution.

What Is the Purpose of Therapy?

Most of us enter this field in order to help people. We may be the kind of person who seems to inspire others and is a natural problem solver. We may have had a therapeutic experience with someone who changed us for the better and want to pass along this gift. We choose to help clients with their most personal problems relating to their thoughts, emotions, and actions.

Psychotherapy has two main purposes: the treatment of mental illness and the fostering of personal growth. To treat mental illness you must be able to identify and diagnose mental illness in your clients. You must be able to identify symptoms, functional impairments, causes, and effective treatments for various mental illnesses and coordinate your efforts with other professionals. The purpose of this treatment is to decrease the severity and impact of your client's symptoms and sometimes, in less frequent cases, to eliminate them.

To foster personal growth you must be sensitive to your clients' sense of inner dissatisfaction that leads them to therapy. Do they lack meaning in their lives? Are they unhappy with their relationships? Are they feeling stuck or unmotivated in their work? Do they experience grief or anger that interferes with moving forward toward their goals? Your purpose here is to help your clients to take steps toward resolution of the problem they bring to therapy and to teach them how to successfully approach similar problems in the future.

Exercise 1: What Is Your Purpose?

Take some time to remember why you wanted to become a psychotherapist. Write down in one sentence the essence of your purpose.

_____

_____

_____

_____

_____

Exercise 2: Why Do Clients Seek Therapy?

Rank the following reasons clients seek therapy (1 is most important, 12 is least important):

_____ Find symptom relief
_____ Resolve problems
_____ Change behavior
_____ Change thought patterns
_____ Feel better
_____ Find opportunity to process
_____ Make healthy and responsible choices
_____ Make the unconscious conscious
_____ Achieve personal growth
_____ Develop insight
_____ Experience catharsis
_____ Other:_____

How did you rank these reasons? What is ranked the highest? What is ranked the lowest? What others have you added?

Exercise 3: The Purpose of Psychotherapy

Take a moment to complete the following statement. (Do not skip this section! Do not underestimate the importance of defining and truly understanding what you are doing!)

The purpose of psychotherapy is (in 25 words or fewer):

_____
_____
_____
_____
_____
_____
_____

The greatest discovery of my generation is that a human being can alter his life by altering his attitudes.
—William James

The Goals of Psychotherapy

The types of approaches to psychotherapy are broad and diverse. Each school of thought interprets the nature of the problem and the solution differently. A cognitive-behavioral therapist is interested in the client's thought patterns and how they affect behavior, whereas a process-oriented practitioner engages the client in an exploration of all facets of the problem so that the client arrives at his or her own conclusions.

Based on the various reasons clients initiate treatment, let us explore the purposes of psychotherapy.

To Provide Symptom Relief

Many clients make an appointment to see a mental health practitioner in order to relieve their symptoms, which have gotten to the point where they can no longer be tolerated. Things have gotten so bad that clients can no longer manage on their own. Anxiety has reached a point where it is interfering with their daily functioning. Perhaps they are depressed and no longer enjoy their favorite activities or have had excessive absences from work, or perhaps others have noticed that they cannot perform to the standards expected. They may have functional impairments in a variety of areas:

- Interpersonal relationships
- Work
- School
- Physical health
- Leisure activities

(See Chapter 9 for more on assessing functional impairments and functional goals.)

These clients would benefit greatly by the practitioner's finding the one symptom that would provide the most relief and setting up a plan to alleviate it. The client must perceive the change as achievable. The practitioner must work with the client to define a measurable goal (e.g., controlling anxiety so he or she can sleep through the night, or participating in a social event that previously he or she could not). For many clients with anxiety, the anticipation of facing the feared event is paralyzing. Most clients are very grateful when they can see tangible changes, and change opens the way for further and deeper work if they so choose. If the client's anxiety is high, it is unlikely that he or she will be able to actively participate in an insight-oriented approach; in that case, symptom relief is the first priority. For some clients, relief of their symptoms is all they want.

Challenges for the Practitioner

It is a challenge to work with the sometimes overwhelming number of symptoms clients present and to find the one solution that can provide the most relief. Some clients choose to end therapy even though the practitioner can clearly see the benefit of continuing and working through that barrier. Ask clients what issue is important to them and concentrate on that. Many other problems are often related to the core issue, so some change in one area often affects the others.

Clinical Considerations

Occasionally, a symptom that was just reduced is immediately replaced by another. Emotions can be layered like the skin of an onion: Once you peel back and remove one layer, another is revealed. A client may not be able to express an emotion because it is being overpowered by another, one not even in the client's conscious awareness. For example, a client is constantly worrying about the safety of another because his behavior puts him in danger. Once the worry is under control, the client becomes angry with that person for the behavior that caused the worry in the first place. This client may have no conscious awareness that she is angry. For the client, the worry was primary and was so all encompassing that no other emotion could be expressed. Once removed, the other emotion was brought to consciousness and expressed.

To Encourage Insight

Clients who seek psychotherapy to develop insight are often very intellectual and want to know the reason they are having a problem. Why do they always seem to have unsatisfying relationships? Why do they act the way they do? They seek treatment looking for answers to questions that may not have a definitive answer. They would prefer to spend many sessions exploring a variety of areas. For them, the journey is the destination.

Many clients take the insight they have gained and translate that into behavior change. Others do not: Their comfort zone is the process of gaining insight; actually doing something with this insight can produce anxiety and a flight back to gaining an even greater and deeper insight and avoiding having to do something. Then the cycle is repeated. Some of these clients may benefit from a referral to a body-oriented practitioner for massage, bodywork, or movement techniques in conjunction with mental health counseling. Integrating the intellectual and the somatic can sometimes jump-start a change process and move clients into insight-oriented action. They just need a little somatic push. If all of the time in therapy is spent exploring without ever applying any of the insights gained, clients are likely to tell their friends that although they enjoyed talking with you, you really did not help them much! Setting small goals based on their insight can help them move toward even greater insights based on results.

Challenges for the Practitioner

If the therapist is overly caught up in the interesting aspects of the client's intellectual quest, the therapy may ramble with no direction or purpose. It can be a challenge for these clients to define exactly what they want to get out of therapy. Some would argue that this process of definition *is* the therapy. The challenge for the practitioner is to help clients move from insight to action in ways that are meaningful to them.

Clinical Considerations

When you notice the therapy rambling with no sense of an end point, check in with the client and get some feedback about how therapy is going for him or her. This can be an opportunity to reassess the treatment plan according to the client's needs and get back on track.

To Resolve Problems and Encourage Behavior Change

Clients seeking behavior change come into therapy with the defined purpose of having you help solve a specific problem, such as "Why do I always have conflicts with others at work?" or "Why do I always feel so stressed out?" Through a series of negative experiences, these clients have learned not to trust their own judgment. They often repeat the same patterns without any insight into why the same problem keeps occurring. Exploring and gaining insight in order to change behavior is a very different experience from that of the client discussed previously, whose sole desire is to develop insight.

Challenges for the Practitioner

Identify ways your clients can feel confident. Increase their ability to solve their own problems.

Clinical Considerations

Watch for clients becoming increasingly dependent on the therapy process and less able to make decisions on their own. Sometimes more treatment can be a hindrance to their growth. They may benefit from a "therapy holiday" or homework to develop some of their own skills.

To Provide a Cathartic Experience

One of the most valuable aspects of psychotherapy is the provision of a safe environment for the client to discuss and release pent-up emotions related to the perceived problem. Many clients have no other venue for this expression. They may not want to burden their friends with what may be perceived as complaining or being negative. Common themes may be guilt, anger at self or others, and shame for what they have done in the past. These clients are usually stuck and are unable to fully process what has happened, or they are stuck in the processing stage and unable to move forward. Often this is because of some perceived fear or loss that occurs as a result of the resolution of the problem. Maintaining the status quo is unbearable, yet they are unable to move ahead because of the perception that the resolution of the problem may cause an equally unsatisfying outcome.

 George comes to therapy complaining of severe insomnia. He also notices that he is much more irritable with his family than usual. During the first few sessions, George mentions that he is a supervisor on construction sites. His company has just started construction of a 10-story office building, and he feels that this may have something to do with his new symptoms. Upon further questioning, George reveals that he has been working only on small residential projects for the past few years. This is the first large building he has worked on for several years. He recalls that at the last large building construction site he worked on, a worker he supervised fell off the eighth floor and died at the scene. As he tells the story, George is surprised to see that he is crying. At the time, he had focused on coping with the external effects of the accident but didn't really talk or think much about his own reaction. He did not want to burden his family and friends with details of the tragedy. After several sessions of talking about this intense experience and allowing himself to feel the grief, guilt, and anger he had been ignoring, George reported that his insomnia and irritability were resolving.

A cathartic experience can lead to initial emotional relief and the lifting of physical symptoms. It can also contribute to perception change, which can lead to other solutions. This change often leads to a satisfying resolution of the problem. (See Chapter 10 for more on "the two sides of catharsis.")

Challenges for the Practitioner

You need to deal with your own emotions when being exposed to a high degree of vicarious trauma while the client has the cathartic experience. Strive to achieve balance in your own life so that you bring an alert and relaxed attention to your sessions with clients.

Clinical Considerations

If treatment does not progress from the cathartic stage to a sense of acceptance and resolution, consider whether there is a barrier to moving forward. Is there a secondary gain present?

To Help Clients Feel Better

Many clients come to therapy with a sense that things are not going well for them in their personal or professional lives. They may have mood problems, issues of self-loathing, or difficulties with self-acceptance. Although they may not be sure of what they should do next, they do know that they do not want to stay in the same emotional state. They want to feel better.

The therapist's initial purpose here is to define what "feeling better" means to this particular client:

- What would the client be doing that he or she can't do now?
- What would the client be feeling that is different from the way he or she feels now?

The practitioner's job in these cases is to help these clients define the problem so they can determine their own solutions. Without defining what "feeling better" is, how will you know whether you have made any progress? (See Chapter 9 for more on how to determine what the client wants.)

Challenges for the Practitioner

Create a balance between giving these clients ample time to express themselves and defining a goal that the client feels is meaningful.

Clinical Considerations

If the client has a hard time defining what "feeling better" is and continues to focus on how terrible he or she feels now, gently redirect the client back to what life would be like if he or she did not have this problem so that the client can define what "feeling better" is.

As you can see from these examples, the purpose of psychotherapy can be quite different depending on the type of client you see.

Exercise 4: The Purpose of Psychotherapy Revisited

With the benefit of the previous client profiles, redo the earlier exercise:

The purpose of psychotherapy is (25 words or fewer):

_____

_____

_____

_____

Ultimately, the purpose of psychotherapy is twofold:

1. *To remove the barriers that prevent clients from achieving their stated goals:* This relates predominantly to growth-oriented clients who do not have a serious mental illness. Removing the emotional and psychological barriers provides clients with the opportunity and freedom to pursue a higher purpose for themselves and others.

2. *To help clients manage their symptoms in order to improve their daily functioning:* The purpose of psychotherapy with clients who do have a serious mental illness is to help them become aware of and manage their own symptoms. The goal is to minimize the disruption that the illness causes in their lives and improve daily functioning to maximize productivity, improve relationships, and enjoy life as much as possible.

TIP

The therapeutic journey is like going on a road trip. The client has defined the destination, has his foot on the gas pedal, and controls how fast he will get there. The practitioner has the steering wheel and directs the treatment so that the client can successfully get to his destination. Periodically pull to the side of the road and look at the map together. Is the destination still the same? Does it need to change?

Relationship-Oriented versus Evidence-Based Therapy

One of the major tensions in the field of psychotherapy is between relationship-oriented and evidence-based treatment. Your training has likely led you to be passionate about one side of this argument and perhaps critical of the other. Let's take a few moments to examine each orientation.

Relationship-oriented therapy focuses primarily on the healing nature of the relationship between client and psychotherapist. In *On Becoming a Person,* Carl Rogers (1961, p. 61) contends:

Personal change is facilitated when the psychotherapist is what he is, when in the relationship with his client he is genuine and without "front" or façade, openly being the feelings and attitudes, which at that moment are flowing in him.

The quality of the relationship is what really matters. Although Rogers was quite interested in the research on how this relationship could be most useful to the client, it was clear that specific techniques or procedures were antithetical to the genuineness of the connection between therapist and client. Since then, there have been numerous studies supporting the therapeutic alliance between client and therapist (Gaston, Thompson, Gallagher, Cournoyer, & Gagnon, 1998) and the therapist as a person (Lambert & Okiishi, 1997), suggesting that the therapeutic relationship is a major component of the therapy process and a strong factor in a positive therapeutic outcome. Since the advent of the importance of the therapeutic relationship as defined by Rogers, the field has evolved to also consider the more collaborative, interactive nature of the relationship between therapist and client. (See Chapter 6 for more on the therapeutic relationship.)

Evidence-based therapy is focused primarily on techniques and procedures that have been designed, implemented, and measured in a scientifically rigorous manner. Evidence-based practitioners are convinced that although the relationship between therapist and client may be useful, it is not in itself enough to produce lasting changes, particularly with regard to serious and persistent pathology.

Your best opportunity for providing effective, efficient, and ethical therapy is to stay current on the research. Base your treatment on best practices that have been tested and found effective in well-controlled studies. Learn how to understand research reports and to evaluate the quality of research. Approach this with both curiosity and a critical eye: Not all research is created equal. At the very least, understand what approaches to a particular problem have been tried and what studies have been attempted to evaluate their effectiveness. This can be a challenge in the field of psychotherapy, where theories and philosophies of care often go unchallenged and untested. Case studies are interesting to read but do not provide evidence of efficacy across a broad spectrum of clients. Although psychotherapy is often considered a "soft science," good research does exist.

Not all methods have been rigorously tested in double-blind studies. There are different levels of evidence, such as evidence of efficacy determined by others in reputable studies versus your experience of what works with your own clients. Always strive to perform at the highest level of evidence-based treatment, but in the absence of that, do what works and does not harm the client. The following is a hierarchy of evidence-based treatment:

1. Double-blind, placebo-controlled studies by reputable researchers that have been published in professional journals.
2. Single-case studies that have been published in professional journals.
3. Case studies published in trade publications.
4. Techniques, procedures, or approaches that are performed by vast numbers of practitioners in the field and are generally accepted as standard practice even though there have been no studies in that particular area.
5. Consultations and recommendations of methods used by other practitioners.
6. Personal observation of clients and what has worked best based on firsthand experience.

Your responsibility is to provide treatment that is likely to be of help to your clients. You should be able to explain the diagnosis to your clients, options for treatment and the research basis for them, and your reasoning for choosing one treatment over another in their particular situation. Using evidence-based treatment will improve your clients' trust in your ability to help them. Just as they would not want to take a medication that has not been rigorously tested, your clients would not be wise to embark on using a psychotherapy method that has not been evaluated. Your "toolbox" will be most useful to you and your clients if you keep handy a good variety of well-tested tools.

How do practitioners reconcile these two orientations? It is our contention that competent psychotherapists must be skilled in both approaches. One should not be exclusive of the other. A practitioner must build a relationship of trust, caring, and a free mutual exchange of information with each client. Likewise, the practitioner should rely on using proven techniques that are likely to help the client when appropriate. One key to providing effective therapy is to match the right treatment to the right client. For the "worried well" who function adequately in most areas of life, have no significant pathology, but are unhappy with the quality of their relationships, it is likely that evidence-based treatments would have little to offer. However, a skillful psychotherapist working with a client like this could use genuine communication to assist her in examining what she may be able to change about the quality of her interactions. In this case, relationship-oriented psychotherapy may be the best option.

Consider a different kind of client. This client comes to therapy with a paralyzing fear of spiders. He longs to go camping with friends, but knows that his fears will keep him from doing so. There is evidence that specific exposure, relaxation, and response-prevention techniques could have a relatively rapid and curative effect. A competent psychotherapist, recognizing the pathology of a specific phobia, would be wise to apply the evidence-based treatment rather than a relationship-based approach.

Of course, in both these situations, the therapist is likely to use aspects of each approach. For the client unhappy with her relationships, the therapist may well add some aspects of behavioral rehearsal and contingency procedures. For the spider-phobic, the therapist will likely need to build a genuine relationship with the client to establish a trusting environment in which to provide the evidence-based treatment.

Suggested Practice Guidelines
- Embrace your style, whatever it is! No matter what your style, it will be the perfect match for some clients and be extremely helpful to them. Embrace your style and do it well.
- As much as possible, develop your practice with clients who fit your style and approach. Not all clients will be suitable to and respond to your approach, so it is important to screen your clients for a good match. It is better to develop your practice with clients who are helped by your approach than to see many clients who don't respond and have a high dropout rate. Seeing clients who respond positively to your approach breeds success and more referrals! Know when to refer a client who is not a good match to a trusted colleague.
- Always strive to do your best, knowing that even that may not be sufficient to help everyone. Accept that, but continue learning.

• Continue to seek further training and education. Work to strengthen your natural style and supplement this with improving your skills in other areas. When in doubt, consult!

TIP

During the early stages of your career you will have some clients who view you as a savior for changing the course of their lives. Savor those moments and store them away, pulling them out when you need some inspiration. Other clients, however, will see you as the worst kind of practitioner for not understanding them and not being helpful at all. Use these moments as a learning experience. Congratulations! When you have experienced both, you have arrived and should consider yourself a bona fide member of the psychotherapy profession.

What Kind of Practitioner Are You?

In your classroom and clinical training you have undoubtedly learned a number of different theoretical psychotherapy approaches. You have studied the relevant research on empirically based therapy systems. You may also have developed your approach to psychotherapy through clinical internships and practical experience in related fields.

One important question you must thoughtfully consider before beginning your professional practice is simply "What kind of practitioner are you?" This will help you to integrate who you are as a person with what you have learned about psychotherapy. Understanding what your approach is, and why you have chosen it, will help you to discern how you can best use your skills with your clients. The ability to explain your approach clearly to clients and other colleagues will help you to build a practice that is consistent with your own values and strengths. In this section, we examine various continuums within the practice of psychotherapy to help you determine your own authentic "voice" as a therapist.

On the following pages we have listed some of the tensions present in contemporary psychotherapy models. Most psychotherapists' practices exist somewhere within each continuum. For the most part, there is no one right or wrong way to practice psychotherapy (aside from obvious ethical considerations). It is, however, imperative that you identify where you are on each continuum, and why you are there, and to integrate this with your own core values and therapy skills.

Exercise 5: What Kind of Psychotherapist Am I?

In the following continuums, identify with an "X" where you see yourself now and with an "O" where you think you'd like to be (if different).

Therapist characteristics:

Directive _ Nondirective
Intervening _ Observing
Technique-oriented _ _ _ _ _ _ _ _ _ _ Relationship-oriented
Secular-spiritual _ _ _ _ _ _ _ _ _ _ _ _ _ _ _ _ _ Religious
Brief _ Long-term
Psychoeducational _ _ _ _ _ _ _ _ _ _ _ _ Process-oriented
Nurturing _ Demanding

View of client problems:

Biological _ Psychosocial
Here and now _ _ _ _ _ _ _ _ _ _ _ _ _ _ _ Childhood origins
Diagnosis-based _ _ _ _ _ _ _ _ _ _ Personal growth–based

Therapeutic approaches: Rank from "none of the time" (1) to "all of the time" (5):

	1	2	3	4	5
Behavioral therapy	1 _ _ _ _ _ _ _ _ 5
Cognitive-behavioral therapy	1 _ _ _ _ _ _ _ _ 5
Dialectical behavioral therapy	1 _ _ _ _ _ _ _ _ 5
Mindfulness-based therapy	1 _ _ _ _ _ _ _ _ 5
Acceptance and commitment therapy	1 _ _ _ _ _ _ _ _ 5

Rational-emotive therapy	1 _ _ _ _ _ _ _ _ 5
Client-centered therapy	1 _ _ _ _ _ _ _ _ 5
Psychodynamic therapy	1 _ _ _ _ _ _ _ _ 5
Psychoanalytic therapy	1 _ _ _ _ _ _ _ _ 5
Narrative therapy	1 _ _ _ _ _ _ _ _ 5
Eye movement desensitization and reprocessing (EMDR)	1 _ _ _ _ _ _ _ _ 5
Energy psychology	1 _ _ _ _ _ _ _ _ 5
Solution-focused therapy	1 _ _ _ _ _ _ _ _ 5
Feminist therapy	1 _ _ _ _ _ _ _ _ 5
Functional analytic psychotherapy	1 _ _ _ _ _ _ _ _ 5
Neurolinguistic programming	1 _ _ _ _ _ _ _ _ 5
Family systems therapy	1 _ _ _ _ _ _ _ _ 5
Reality therapy	1 _ _ _ _ _ _ _ _ 5
Rational analytic therapy	1 _ _ _ _ _ _ _ _ 5
Others:	
_____	1 _ _ _ _ _ _ _ _ 5
_____	1 _ _ _ _ _ _ _ _ 5

A Trip to the Therapist's Couch . . .

Let's look for a moment at how a therapist's approach can influence the course of therapy. The following vignettes follow one client with one identified problem as she visits 11 different therapists.

Marcia is a 37-year-old woman. She has decided to seek therapy for some problems she's been having with anxiety. She's not sure what kind of therapy she wants, but luckily, she's found The Best Therapy Shop in the World in her local mall. For just $50, she can have a first session with any of 11 therapists, each representing a different therapeutic style. She is handed a menu, checks off the ones she would like to try, and walks into the first office.

A Nondirective Approach

Ms. Nondirective is the first therapist on Marcia's list. Ms. ND invites Marcia to sit down, offers her a cup of tea, and says gently, "What brings you here today?" Marcia, her hand shaking a bit as she holds her teacup, says, "I've been having some trouble with anxiety." Let's listen in:

Ms. ND: Mm-hm. Tell me more.

Marcia: Well, look at me; I am shaking all the time.

Ms. ND: I see.

Marcia: And I can't get to sleep at night. I just toss and turn.

Ms. ND: Mm-hm.

Marcia: Well, what are you going to do for me?

Ms. ND: Marcia, I think we should explore your feelings more. I think that as you have a chance to talk about your anxious feelings, you will find the answers you need.

Marcia: Okay. Well, it all started out when I was a child. . . .

A Psychoeducational Approach

Next, Marcia goes to visit Mr. Psycho-Ed. He has a whole wall of bookshelves in his office and several file cabinets with drawers marked "Handouts on Depression," "Handouts on Communication," and so on. He has several three-ring binders stacked on his desk.

Mr. PE: Hello, Marcia. What can I do for you today?

Marcia: I've been having some trouble with anxiety.

Mr. PE: Well, let's get to work on that. What kind of experiences of anxiety are you having?

Marcia: My hands shake whenever I have to talk with someone. And I'm having trouble getting to sleep at night.

Mr. PE: Well, I'm sure I can help you with the sleep problem. Here, I have a handout called "Getting a Good Night's Sleep." Let's go over it together and work out a plan. The physiology of sleep is quite interesting. Once we get your sleep under control, we can work on some of your social anxiety.

Marcia: Oh, okay. So you think I can get better? Do I have a serious diagnosis?

Mr. PE: We can worry about whether you have a diagnosis or not after we have helped you learn more about your symptoms. And I definitely think you can learn some much more helpful behaviors.

Marcia: Okay, let's get started.

A Solution-Focused Approach

An hour later, Marcia is ready for the next therapist on her list. She enters the office of Ms. Solution-Focused and sits down on the comfortable couch. The walls are painted a cheerful yellow, and sunlight is shining through the windows.

Ms. SF: Hello, Marcia. What brings you here today?

Marcia: Well, I've been having some problems with anxiety.

Ms. SF: Great! Anxiety can teach us a lot about what's working and not working in our lives. What does it feel like when you're not particularly anxious?

Marcia: Hmm . . . . I guess when I'm not feeling anxious I feel calm, secure, grounded. Like I did when I first graduated from college. I felt confident that I could do what I wanted to do and what was expected of me.

Ms. SF: Let's think more about that. What were you doing then? Tell me what a typical day was like.

Marcia: I remember I would wake up feeling refreshed every morning. I'd get up, go for a run, and sit down with my day planner. I'd go apply for jobs in the morning, and then hang out with some of my friends in the afternoon. We'd cook good, healthy meals and talk about all of our plans for the future.

Ms. SF: Wow. Sounds like you really know how to be relaxed and focused, how to keep a good balance in your life.

Marcia: Well, yes, I did then, but it's a lot different now with all this anxiety.

Ms. SF: Lets see if we can reclaim those things that worked well for you then. They'll probably be a big help to you now.

Marcia: Okay!

A Psychoanalytic Approach

Soon Marcia is on her way to the next office. This one has a big brass knocker on the door and a sign that says, "Dr. Psych (Analysis and Consultation)." When Marcia knocks, the door is opened by a kind older gentleman who invites her in.

Dr. P: So, Marcia, I see you have arrived. What would you like to talk to me about?

Marcia: Well, I'm having problems with anxiety.

Dr. P: I see.

Marcia: What do you want me to tell you?

Dr. P: Hmm . . . why don't you start at the beginning?

Marcia: The beginning? How long is this going to take?

Dr. P: It will take as long as it takes. It will be most productive if you can just talk as though I'm not even here . . . and if you tell me about your dreams. They can be very helpful in understanding what is going on in your subconscious. Once we have discovered the origins of your anxiety, you will be cured!

Marcia: Well . . . okay. I guess it started back when I was about 3. I remember . . .

Dr. P: Hmm.

A Family Systems Approach

Fifty minutes later (precisely), Marcia is ready for her next therapist. Ms. Family smiles and welcomes her into her comfortable office. There she sees a couch, a love seat, and several chairs arranged in a circle. She makes herself comfortable on the love seat, ready to begin.

Ms. Family: Hello, Marcia. What brings you here?

Marcia: Well, I've been having some problems with anxiety.

Ms. Family: Okay. Can you tell me a bit about your family?

Marcia: You mean now? Stanley and I have been married for 14 years, and we have two children. Little Stan is 12, and little Marcie is 10.

Ms. Family: And how does your family affect your feelings of anxiety?

Marcia: Hmm. It's always so crazy in the morning getting the kids off to school. Stanley used to help with that, but he's been so busy at work lately that he's out the door before I'm even out of bed. So I'm anxious in the morning, and it just seems to last all day.

Ms. Family: I see. Do you think that Stanley and the kids would be willing to come in with you to talk about this?

Marcia: Why? Do you think it would help?

Ms. Family: Yes, I do. Family members affect each other in many ways. Sometimes we can change patterns of communication and help everyone feel better.

Marcia: Well, then, I guess I could ask them to come in with me next time.

A Rational-Emotive Approach

Marcia makes a tentative appointment to bring her whole family in for a session with Ms. Family and moves on to Mr. Rational-Emotive. He greets her at the door and asks her to sit at the small table in his office and fill out a few forms. Fifteen minutes later, he reviews her responses.

Mr. RE: So, Marcia, I see that you are here to get some help with your anxiety.

Marcia: Yes. Can you help me?

Mr. RE: Yes, Marcia, I think I can. Now you say here that you feel most anxious in social situations, like when you are meeting new people. Are you feeling anxious now?

Marcia: Well, yes, now that you mention it, I am.

Mr. RE: Good. We have something to work with. Can you tell me what you are thinking about as you begin to feel anxious?

Marcia: Hmm. I guess I'm thinking that you probably think I'm not very smart if I can't figure this out myself, and that if I don't do something about my anxiety, my life will be just awful.

Mr. RE: Great! So we have two interesting thoughts to work with. "Other people will think I'm not smart if I can't figure things out myself," and "If I don't do something about my anxiety my life will be awful." Let's write those two thoughts down and see if we can come up with some more helpful thoughts.

Marcia: Well, okay, but why would that help?

Mr. RE: Our emotions are almost entirely caused by our thoughts. If you change your thoughts, your emotions will change, too.

Marcia: All right. I guess it is worth a try.

Eye Movement Desensitization and Reprocessing

Next, Marcia goes to the office of Ms. Eye. She sits down in a soft, comfortable chair in the corner. The office is a bit dark, and she sees an interesting-looking contraption next to her chair. Ms. Eye smiles and says, "Hello, Marcia."

Marcia: Hello. I'm looking for some help with my anxiety.

Ms. Eye: I see. Can you tell me when you started noticing this anxiety?

Marcia: Hmm. I guess I've always been a bit anxious, but it really got bad after I was in a car accident while taking the kids to school last fall. It was just a fender-bender, but it was really scary. After that, I started having problems sleeping at night.

Ms. Eye: So your anxiety got worse after the trauma of that accident?

Marcia: Yes.

Ms. Eye: I think you may have some unresolved trauma about the accident that is causing you to feel anxious; it may even remind you in some ways of other trauma you've experienced in the past.

Marcia: Well, yes, it does remind me of the time I was stuck on a Ferris wheel when I was 10 years old. I was so frightened I couldn't sleep for a month!

Ms. Eye: I see. Marcia, I think I can help you resolve and move past some of these traumatic experiences, and this should help to reduce your anxiety. Let me tell you about this process and give you some information to take home. If you decide to proceed with this treatment, we can probably work through your problems in two or three sessions.

Marcia: That sounds good!

A Dialectical Behavior Therapy Approach

Feeling quite hopeful, Marcia moves on to the next therapist on her list, Mr. Dialectic. His office is large and sunny, with a large whiteboard with colored markers on one wall. There are three-ring binders filling an entire bookshelf, and on the table she sees a brass bowl-shaped bell. Mr. Dialectic greets her warmly and invites her to sit down.

Mr. Dialectic: Hello, Marcia. I'm glad to see you. Let's start by talking about what behaviors are causing you problems.

Marcia: Behaviors? I don't have any problems with behaviors—it's just this feeling of anxiety.

Mr. Dialectic: Of course. That makes sense. You know, I think emotions can be thought of as a behavior, just like thoughts and actions.

Marcia: Oh. Well, how do we get started?

Mr. Dialectic: First, let's analyze your last bad anxiety experience from beginning to end. Then you can start learning and practicing some skills that can help you respond differently.

Marcia: Practicing?

Mr. Dialectic: Yes. If you choose to work with me on this, it will be really important for you to do homework assignments. I'll also teach you how to use a "diary card" to help you keep track of your anxiety behaviors and your skillful behaviors. And we'll work on finding the middle ground, to resolve things that seem to be opposing each other.

Marcia: That sounds like a lot of work.

Mr. Dialectic: You're right, it is. But I've seen remarkable results from this treatment. Are you willing to give it a try?

Marcia: Umm. Sure.

Mr. Dialectic: Great. Here's your notebook. Let's start with a behavioral analysis of your anxiety (picking up the marker and standing by the whiteboard). So, tell me about your last specific feeling of anxiety.

A Medical-Model Approach

An hour later, Marcia gathers up her notebook, behavior analysis, and homework, and moves on to the next therapist on her list, Ms. D. S. Manual. This office has white walls, a small bookshelf, and several somewhat uncomfortable-looking chairs. Ms. DSM turns from her neatly organized desk and invites Marcia to sit down across from her.

Ms. DSM: Hello, Marcia. How are you today?

Marcia: Hi. Actually, I'm feeling pretty anxious.

Ms. DSM: I see. Is that the major symptom you are experiencing?

Marcia: Yes, that and having a lot of trouble sleeping.

Ms. DSM: Let's go through this symptom checklist for anxiety. You know, insomnia can be one of the symptoms of anxiety disorders.

Marcia: Anxiety disorder? What's that?

Ms. DSM: Most problems that people experience with their mental health can be described as a disorder of some sort. Mental illnesses can be classified, diagnosed, and treated, very much like physicians diagnose and treat physical illnesses. We need to do a thorough mental status exam, identify your specific symptoms, and quantify how much these symptoms are interfering with your daily functioning.

Marcia: You mean I have a mental illness?

Ms. DSM: Well, we need to find out if you do. But don't worry, there are lots of effective treatments for mental illness these days to decrease your symptoms and improve your functioning. For example, you might want to consider medications at some point.

Marcia: Well, my doctor did say he thought some Prozac wouldn't hurt.

Ms. DSM: Sounds promising. So let us get back to this symptoms checklist.

An Alternative Approach

Marcia leaves the office after signing a release of information so Ms. DSM can consult with her primary care physician. Ah, now for the next therapist on her list. She moves on to Mr. Alter Native. His office seems to be in a suite with an acupuncturist, a naturopath, a massage practitioner, and a juice bar. Mr. Alter Native, dressed in blue jeans and some sort of long, flowing, vaguely ethnic shirt, invites her into his office. Candles, crystals, and a selection of herbal teas are on a low table in front of comfortable bamboo chairs. Marcia accepts a cup of tea, and Mr. Alter Native begins their session.

Mr. Alter Native: Welcome to this healing space. Marcia. How can I be of help?

Marcia: Well, I've been feeling pretty anxious lately, and have a hard time getting to sleep at night.

Mr. Alter Native: Ah. . . . So you are feeling like you are out of balance with yourself?

Marcia: Hmmm. Yes, I guess you could say I'm out of balance. It's so difficult lately to balance time for myself, time for my family, and time for work.

Mr. Alter Native: I see. We have a number of ways to help you rediscover your balance with nature. The natural world is full of healing traditions.

Marcia: What would you recommend?

Mr. Alter Native: For anxiety, I'd suggest we start with some meditations I can teach you. You might also consider acupuncture or massage treatment to help balance your mind and body. And we can start with some basic aromatherapy that you can use at home.

Marcia: Sounds very relaxing. Let's get started.

A Feminist Approach

Next, Marsha goes to the last therapist on her list. She walks next door to the office of Ms. Ms. "Call me Miz-Miz," she says to Marsha as they enter her office together. The office contains several comfortable chairs and couches arranged in an informal circle and some interesting posters on the walls. Marsha sits down in a chair next to Ms. Ms.

Ms. Ms.: Welcome, Marsha, to the Awakening Space. I hope we can do some helpful work here together. What brings you here today?

Marsha: Well, I've been awfully anxious lately, and I've been having trouble sleeping.

Ms. Ms.: Ah. I hear that from lots of women. Have you had any external pressures lately?

Marsha: Well, sometimes my family drives me crazy, and my husband's been working a lot lately, so he's not around much to help.

Ms. Ms.: So you're feeling some pressure to fulfill everyone else's needs but your own?

Marsha: Well, yes. But I'm a wife and mother, that's what I'm supposed to do, isn't it? It goes with the territory.

Ms. Ms.: I wonder if there are some ways you can empower yourself to pay more attention to your own needs. Do you have a supportive group of women friends?

Marsha: Uh . . . no, not really. My friends from college have all moved away and have families of their own. I do go to the PTA meetings at my kids' school—does that count?

Ms. Ms.: It can be hard to grow without a welcoming circle of friends or a consciousness-raising group of some sort. I do have an opening in my Thursday evening Power UP group. Perhaps you'd like to come and check it out next week.

Marsha: But how do you think that would help my anxiety and insomnia?

Ms. Ms.: I think that once you are able to pay more attention to your own needs, the solutions to your problems will arise from within you. I believe you have the strength within to grasp your own power and use it.

Marsha: Sounds like it might be worth a try. I'll come next Thursday. Thanks!

Exercise 6: Which Therapist Would You Pick?

- If you were Marcia, which therapist would you like to see?
- Which therapists did you most identify with positively?
- Which therapists did you dislike?
- What distinct sorts of information did the different therapists bring out from Marcia?
- How did each therapist see the problem? The cause? The solution?

Summing Up

So . . . what kind of practitioner are you? As you can see, different theoretical models can produce very different results for the same client. Your interpretation of the purpose of psychotherapy informs your approach to the therapy relationship. It is essential to become aware of your own philosophy of therapy and to be able to express it clearly. Skillful therapists listen carefully to their clients' formulations of the problems they bring and the kind of solutions they envision. This helps you to design and implement a therapy experience that draws on both your own philosophy of care and the client's expressed desires.

===**EXERCISES**===

1. Summarize your own personal psychotherapy philosophy.
2. What are your personal strengths as a psychotherapist?
3. What psychotherapy theories and practices do you most enjoy and embrace?
4. What is the relationship between your favorite theories and your personal strengths?
5. Complete the exercises in this chapter, and discuss your answers with a colleague or mentor.
6. What kind of therapy would you offer to Marcia? Why?
7. Write a one-page summary of the kind of therapist you'd like to be, explaining how you came to your values about psychotherapy. Include your fundamental beliefs about why people seek therapy and how you can help them. (It is a good idea to revisit this summary every year or two. You may find that your philosophy and style of therapy evolve throughout your career.)

2

Ethical Issues

What You Will Learn
- Why the study of ethics is important
- The source of the major professional ethical codes
- Practitioner behaviors that can cause ethical problems
- The appropriate uses of therapist self-disclosure
- The ethics of accurate diagnosis
- How to stay within your scope of practice
- The importance of knowing and respecting client rights
- How client complaints to the licensing board can affect your practice

We realize that some readers may have had a lot of exposure to ethical issues, while others have not. No matter what your level of exposure, dealing with ethical issues is an ongoing process. Throughout your long and productive career as a psychotherapist, you will invariably be faced with ethical dilemmas. Ethical dilemmas are not always obvious. That is why we study ethical issues now. The only thing that stands between you and potentially unethical behavior is studying these issues before they occur, the self-awareness to recognize them when they do, and your willingness to take action.

Why Study Ethics?

Studying ethical issues is relevant to all types of practitioners, no matter in what setting you work or populations you serve. It is often assumed in graduate schools that ethical training will occur during supervision at a practicum or internship. Handelsman (1986) points out that ethical training does not happen by osmosis and that training during supervision does not guarantee that a broad range of ethical issues will arise. Formal exposure and training in ethics is necessary to build decision-making skills. Many states now have mandatory ethical training built in to the continuing education requirement for licensure.

TIP

An ethical dilemma is like a virus. Sometimes you have it before you know you do.

The goal of this chapter on ethics is to increase awareness of the ethical dilemmas practitioners face in everyday practice. We hope that this exposure will help you in a real-life situation. If that does occur, pause, recognize there is a dilemma, reflect on what the issues are, and follow through with the proper action. Pope and Vetter (1992) surveyed a random sample of 1,319 members of the American Psychological Association (APA), asking them what areas they found ethically challenging or troubling. The areas where psychologists encountered the most frequent ethical dilemmas were the following:

Confidentiality

These dilemmas involved knowing confidential information regarding actual or potential risks to third parties. Practitioners surveyed by Pope and Vetter (1992) struggled with questions about whether to disclose and, if so, to whom. Also of concern was the careless or unintentional disclosure of confidential information by a colleague. Their survey and review of the literature revealed that although the incidents of confidentiality violations brought before the APA ethics committee are low, practitioners struggle with confidentiality issues more than any other.

Blurred, Dual, or Conflicted Relationships

These incidents involved maintaining clear, reasonable, and therapeutic boundaries with clients. The difficulties arose in interpreting just what constitutes a "dual relationship." This was a particular issue for therapists who practice in small towns, rural communities, and remote areas where choice of practitioners is limited and social networks are interconnected. These practitioners complained that the ethical principles did not address the unique and actual circumstances of their practice.

Payment Issues

This area involved incidents where there was inadequate insurance coverage for clients with urgent needs and therapists felt forced to either breach their responsibilities to the client or to be less than honest in their report to the insurer. Other issues included billing for no-shows, billing family therapy as if it were individual, distorting the description of a client's condition so that it qualifies for coverage, signing forms for unlicensed staff, and not collecting copayments.

Bernard and Jara (1986, p. 313) state that when faced with an ethical dilemma there are two distinct elements that must be recognized:

1. The extent to which the ethical principle applicable to the situation in question is understandable.
2. The degree of willingness to do what one understands should be done.

Bernard and Jara (1986) surveyed a nationwide sample of graduate students at APA-approved programs. The survey asked for anonymous cooperation and contained two scenarios of ethical violations. Also included were demographic questions that the student could decline to answer if they felt it would violate their confidentiality and a questionnaire that would get the students' reaction to the scenarios.

The first scenario involved a clinical graduate student who was involved sexually with a psychotherapy practicum client. To keep the surveys balanced, in half of the surveys the student therapist was male and in the other half, female. The second scenario was similarly balanced for gender. This time a clinical graduate student was demonstrating poor judgment and erratic behavior in a clinical practicum due to an alcohol problem and was concealing this from faculty. In each case, the subject uncovered the problem. The alleged violator was a friend as well as a fellow graduate student. The scenario involved one face-to-face confrontation that did not result in any change in behavior of the violator. The APA (2003) Code of Conduct regarding sexual involvement and exploitation of clients (Principle 2F) and substance use by practitioners affecting their interaction with clients (Principle 6A) were presented verbatim to provide consistency of information to assist the student's decision about how to respond to the survey questions. In this way, it was very clear that the scenarios presented were in conflict with the APA ethical principles.

Those surveyed were asked these questions:

1. According to the ethical principles, what should you do?
2. Speaking pragmatically, and recognizing that he (she) is a friend and a fellow graduate student, what do you think you would do? (p. 314)

The first question was designed to assess students' understanding that the violation described was indeed an ethical violation and that some action should be taken. The second question was used to determine students' willingness to take this action based on what they already had stated that they should do.

Each scenario had five possible responses:

1. Do nothing.
2. Suggest the student in question get help for his or her problem.
3. Keep trying to get the student to stop this behavior.
4. Tell the student that if he or she did not get this problem under control, the subject will mention this to the clinical supervisor.
5. Tell the student's clinical supervisor (p. 314).

Twenty-five graduate-level APA-approved programs were contacted, resulting in 170 responses. It was hypothesized that a very high proportion would recognize that an ethical violation occurred and that it was the student's responsibility to respond with a specific course of action. The investigators also hypothesized that the same students who recognized what they should do would probably be willing to do less. The results from the sexual scenario indicated that 50% would do what they said they should do, and 50% said they would do less. In the problem drinking scenario, 45% were consistent and stated they would do what they said they should do; however, 55% said they would do less. No one said they would do more than they said they should. In both cases, half or more of the students were essentially saying that although they understood what an ethical psychologist should do, they were not willing to do that!

The demographic variables between the two groups did not yield any significant differences, suggesting that how long students had been in training or whether they had been taking a course in ethics or substance abuse had no apparent influence on their willingness to put the ethical principles, which they knew were a standard of the profession, into action. The investigators concluded that although there is a strong emphasis on exposing students to the content of ethical principles, the follow-through in emphasizing how important it is to implement the proper action was lacking.

Baldick (1980) performed a similar scenario survey with psychology interns and found that those who had training in ethics scored significantly better at understanding ethical dilemmas than those who did not.

Ethical Codes

Before beginning a psychotherapy practice, and periodically throughout your career, you must identify, understand, and incorporate ethical principles into your practice. It is easy to get into trouble. Many experienced, well-seasoned practitioners do. For some, it is a temporary lapse of judgment; for others, it is a repeated pattern of behavior. Ethical violations can impede your effectiveness with your clients, threaten your reputation in the community, and put your professional license at risk.

Ethical codes such as those from the National Association of Social Workers (NASW) and the American Psychological Association (APA) are often used as a reference in cases of ethical violations. Ethical codes and standards are general, whereas real-life situations are usually very specific. The application of ethical principles to specific situations is often open to interpretation and subject to rationalization. You will be better equipped to cope effectively if you have had some exposure to real-life ethical dilemmas and worked through some possible actions beforehand. A psychotherapist often works with emotionally fragile and psychologically vulnerable clients behind closed doors. Becoming familiar with ethical principles will help you recognize when you may be putting yourself and your client at risk.

Practitioner Behavior

Boundary Issues

The line between what is reasonable and what is not can be moved so incrementally that a sea change can take place without being noticed.
—Elizabeth Kaye (1997)

Some practitioners have difficulty setting boundaries with their clients. A few of the common boundary problems in psychotherapy practice follow.

Setting Limits

Your client comes late to appointments or cancels at the last minute. Your client wants you to provide free crisis counseling by phone day or night. Your client gets very upset and loud during sessions, upsetting people in nearby offices. A child client rips up your magazines while in the waiting room, and his parent does nothing to intervene. In all of these situations, you are likely to feel uncomfortable. You may feel angry, frustrated, or frightened. You want the behavior to stop. You must be comfortable identifying and validating your own emotions, what you want the client to do differently, and what the consequences may be if your client refuses to change his or her behavior. Boundary issues are often an opportunity to identify problems that clients may have in other relationships that mirror what they are doing in these interactions with you. You may choose to question your client about the behavior. You may also tell your client what you want him or her to do differently, and why. For example: "I notice that you've been late to our last two appointments. When you are late, I worry that you are not taking our work together seriously. Since I have other clients waiting for me, when you are late, I cannot see you for our full appointment time. I would like you to work on being on time to your appointments. We can talk about how you can get here sooner. If you aren't able to come to sessions on time, we may need to stop working together for a while."

TIP

Notice your client's behavior and your feelings about it, without judging yourself or your client. Share what you are observing, how you are feeling, and what you would like the client to do differently. Let your client know the consequences of changing or not changing his or her behavior.

Receiving Gifts

Some clients may be genuinely grateful for your help and want to express their thanks to you with a gift. Others may be repeating unhealthy behaviors that they exhibit in other relationships. Some may be trying to influence your opinion. In general, receiving gifts of any real value is counterproductive and unethical. Get comfortable with saying "I'm sorry, but I don't accept gifts from my clients." If appropriate, thank your client for the thought behind the gift: "I appreciate that you value the work we do together." You can remind your clients that you are paid for your work with them and that their progress is the best gift you could receive. Sometimes accepting a small, inexpensive gift, such as a drawing from a child or a homemade ornament from an adult, is acceptable, and it can be kind to accept it graciously and genuinely. When in doubt, consult a colleague.

Touch

Giving or accepting touch from clients is an area with a great potential for problems. When considering touch in a certain situation, ask yourself these questions:

- Would it benefit the client therapeutically? Shaking clients' hands to congratulate them for their efforts and for success in changing a difficult behavior can anchor their success in an appropriate way. Shaking hands is also a generally accepted form of touch and in this case considered congratulatory.

- Would it be for my own benefit? Is there some personal need that is the driving force in your action?
- Would it be harmful to the client or to me? A touch that the practitioner considers innocent and appropriate may be interpreted by a needy client as "special treatment" and set the stage for misinterpretations and potential harm to the therapeutic process. A client may see the acceptance of a hug as signaling more than a therapeutic relationship. Knowing the issues related to your client will help to inform your decision. What might be right for one client may not be for the next.
- Would I do it in front of a colleague? This is often the best barometer to help you decide if the contact is appropriate or not.
- Would I feel uncomfortable with it?

TIP

Take the opportunity to set appropriate limits with your clients and use this mirror to bring up other issues related to touch. Is this an issue for them? Do they invade other people's personal space and make them feel uncomfortable? How do they approach others for appropriate touch?

The most common form of touch requested from a client is a hug, often held for longer than would be considered socially appropriate. Being a surrogate for the touch that clients are not getting in their everyday lives is fraught with trouble for you as the practitioner and potentially harmful to your clients. It is better to set limits early than to establish a pattern of behavior and then have to change it. Setting limits after an established pattern of behavior, which by your inaction you have condoned, puts you and your client at risk. A vulnerable client can feel rejected in these circumstances, which can disrupt the therapeutic alliance.

A skillful therapist can reframe actions as well as thoughts or words. If approached by a client to engage in a form of touch such as a hug that you may feel is inappropriate, you should recognize the need behind the action but redirect it: "You have really worked very hard in our work together, and I am really pleased at what you have achieved. Great job!" (as you extend your hand for a congratulatory two-handed handshake). A two-handed handshake conveys a deeper level of caring without crossing the line into an area of touch that may be too intimate or easily misconstrued.

Therapist Self-Disclosure

New and even experienced practitioners often feel a certain level of discomfort around this issue:

- How much of myself do I reveal?
- What if a client asks me a personal question? How do I respond?
- Can I reveal too much? Will that interfere with the therapeutic process?
- What if I reveal too little? Will this affect the client's view of me as a real person? Will this affect the therapeutic process?
- What if I have negative feelings toward a client or dislike how we are interacting?

Irving D. Yalom (2003), MD, in his book, *The Gift of Therapy: An Open Letter to a New Generation of Therapists and Their Patients*, categorizes three types of therapist self-disclosure, with his recommendations for each:

- The mechanism of therapy—Full disclosure
- Revealing here-and-now feelings—Use discretion
- Revealing the therapist's personal life—Use caution

Let's look at each in more detail.

Therapist self-disclosure is not a single entity but a cluster of behaviors, some of which invariably facilitate therapy and some of which are problematic and potentially counterproductive.
—Irving D. Yalom, The Gift of Therapy (2003)

The Mechanism of Therapy   One of Yalom's (2003) initial goals in working with clients is to establish an authentic relationship with them. The first opportunity to do this involves the practitioner's full disclosure of the therapy process and the rationale for treatment. General information is contained in the practitioner's informed consent and disclosure form. Other information can be exchanged only in a direct dialogue: What are the therapist expectations of the client? Does the therapist expect the client to read suggested material, try out certain behaviors between sessions, or engage in other homework? What does the client expect of the therapist? Unfortunately, many practitioners never establish these ground rules at the outset; then both practitioner and client silently struggle to figure out each other's intentions. Bad habits create ineffective sessions and have a negative effect on progress.

Most clients come to the first session with a fair amount of anxiety and discomfort. Setting the proper guidelines for therapy can help put clients at ease. It also helps the practitioner set the ground rules for confidentiality and client participation. In the mechanism of therapy, Yalom (2003) suggests full disclosure.

Revealing Here-and-Now Feelings   Yalom (2003) believes that the establishment of this authentic relationship with the client involves the practitioner disclosing feelings about the client in the therapy session. This should not be done, however, without the consideration of this important question: Is this in the best interest of the client? The relationship between a therapist and his or her client is very intimate. The difficulties that a client has in his or her relationships with others are often played out in the relationship established with the practitioner. If a client is distant, confrontational, rude, or fearful with others, he or she will often be the same with the practitioner. Yalom believes that if a practitioner is observing and feeling these things, he or she should reveal this to the client in order to work through these issues. The practitioner is not able to directly observe the client interacting with others. The only relationship practitioners can observe is the one between themselves and their client. If practitioners express the difficulties they are having together, the client can be helped in other relationships where the same interactions may be occurring.

TIP
The art of revealing your own feelings is an accomplished skill. Balance your desire to express with the needs of the client.

Revealing the Therapist's Personal Life   How much or how little personal information to share with clients can be difficult to determine, and each practitioner needs to determine his or her level of comfort. At times, giving a brief example of how you solved a problem similar to what the client is facing can be appropriate. For example, sharing some of the difficulties you had as a new stepparent and how you approached building a relationship with your stepchildren can be a way of sharing some personal experience that can potentially benefit your client. Sharing personal information can also help establish rapport. At some point during the therapy process, most clients want to know a little more about you. Do you have children? What ages are they? What do you like to do for fun? They want to know about your "humanness." It can be an important part of rapport building and create a sense of connectedness.

The spectrum of ease in sharing information among therapists varies: some believe that it should not occur at all; others believe in sharing quite a bit. Pope, Tabachnick, and Keith-Spiegel (1987) found that 32% of the psychologists they surveyed use self-disclosure as a therapy technique fairly to very often; 2% stated that it was unethical to do so; and 17% stated that it was ethical only under rare circumstances. One's level of self-disclosure is a personal decision.

Be wary of revealing too much personal information as it could lead to switching roles with your client. When this occurs in excess, the client is put in the role of the therapist, taking care of the emotional needs of his or her "client" (the therapist). If this occurs, clients may alter their behavior by withholding information they perceive to be distressing, thus altering the therapeutic process and your effectiveness as a practitioner. One way to avoid sharing information inappropriately is to ask yourself before you disclose, "How will this information serve my client?" Once the threshold of sharing too much personal information is crossed, it is very difficult to go back. When this occurs, there is increased risk of causing harm to the therapeutic relationship.

Consider an example of role switching:

Sheila had been in therapy with Tracy for about 8 weeks, working on her depression symptoms. A recent estrangement from a good friend had left her doubting her own judgment and self-worth. One week, as Tracy brought

Sheila into her office, Sheila noticed that Tracy looked as though she had been crying. When she asked Tracy if she was all right, Tracy began to weep and acknowledged that her husband had just left her. Sheila spent the rest of the session comforting Tracy and did not discuss her own needs. Tracy apologized and said she would not impinge on Sheila's therapy time again. At following sessions, Sheila was reluctant to talk about her own grief about her lost friendship, fearing it would remind Tracy of her marital problems. The therapy becomes less and less useful for her.

As we have seen, there is quite a variation in the frequency of therapist disclosure. Why do therapists disclose? Does disclosure serve a specific purpose? Hill and Knox (2002, p. 259) gathered information from a variety of studies and summarized the reasons given by therapists on why they disclose personal information to their clients:

- To give information
- To resolve their own needs
- To increase personal similarity between themselves and their clients
- To model appropriate behavior
- To foster the therapeutic alliance
- To validate or normalize client experiences
- To offer alternative ways for the client to think and act
- Because clients wanted it

Clients believed that therapists disclosed information for the following purposes:

- To normalize their experience
- To reassure them
- To help them make constructive changes

After reviewing the literature, Hill and Knox (2002, p. 263) made seven recommendations for therapists regarding self-disclosure:

1. **"Therapists should generally disclose infrequently."** The more disclosure occurs, the less effective it may be. Used

sparingly it can be an effective tool. Overused it can be irritating to the client, less effective, and even inappropriate or unethical.

2. **"The most appropriate topic for self-disclosure involves professional background whereas the least appropriate topics include sexual practices and beliefs."** Disclosing professional background, what Yalom (2003) refers to as the mechanism of therapy, is appropriate and can build trust and clarity. Research indicates that therapists who disclose intimate material are viewed more unfavorably than those revealing nonintimate information.

3. **"Therapists should generally use disclosures to validate reality, normalize, model, strengthen the alliance or offer alternative ways to act or think."** Disclosure in these cases can be helpful to the therapy process and add to the development of the therapeutic relationship.

4. **"Therapists should generally avoid using disclosures that are for their own needs, remove the focus from the client, interfere with the flow of the session, burden or confuse the client, are intrusive, blur the boundaries between client and therapist, overstimulate the client, or contaminate the transference."** Disclosure used for these purposes can have a destructive effect on the process and the therapeutic relationship. When practitioners use disclosure to address their own unresolved issues, they are in danger of role switching, which can cause harm to the relationship and process of therapy.

5. **"Therapist self-disclosure might be particularly effective when it is in response to similar client self-disclosure."** In this case, self-disclosure may reassure the client and establish that his or her behavior is within the realm of normalcy.

6. **"Therapists should observe carefully how clients respond to their disclosures, ask the clients about their reactions, and use that information to conceptualize their clients and decide how to intervene next."** Be aware of the effects of your disclosure: Does the client react positively? How does it affect the therapy relationship? What effect does it have on the client's view of you?

7. **"It may be especially important for therapists to disclose with some clients more than others."** Some clients may need a certain level of therapist disclosure to build trust, whereas

other clients may be annoyed that you are talking about yourself and taking up their time. Each client may need to be treated with his or her own unique level of therapist disclosure. Be aware of cultural differences as well.

Bartering

There are no clear ground rules for this practice, although the APA (2003) does allow bartering (Section 6, paragraph 5: Barter with Clients/Patients), with the following guidelines: "Psychologists may barter only if (1) it is not clinically contraindicated, and (2) the resulting arrangement is not exploitative."

The problem is knowing what is considered clinically contraindicated or exploitive. Often the exploitive nature of the situation is not obvious until it is too late. One of the easiest ways to get into an ethical dilemma is to trade services with your client. This kind of situation can start easily enough: Your client really needs therapy, and you are doing good work together. She cannot afford to pay you, though. You hate to end treatment prematurely just because she cannot pay. She is a fabulous cook and offers to bring you dinner once a week in exchange for sessions. Or you "hire" her to help with billing or cleaning or yard work. Soon you realize that you are dependent on her help, that she is resenting the arrangement, or that it is not working out for you. Now you are not only a therapist, but also a supervisor and employer who may need to "fire" your "employee" because the arrangement is not working out. How can your "employee," whom you just fired because the arrangement was not working out, return to a trusting and therapeutic relationship with you? While the client's needs may pluck your altruistic heartstrings, the potential of doing damage to the psyche of your client by exploitation is quite high. You can avoid a situation like this by sticking with cash payment. You can offer sessions spaced further apart or a reduced rate, or suggest that she return to treatment when her finances allow; or you can refer her to community agencies that may be appropriate for treatment or financial assistance.

T. C. Portman, PhD (personal communication, November 29, 2007), differentiates between goods, which are used in lieu of money, and services, which are used for payment. Bartering for goods is more acceptable because it does not involve the same kind of dual relationship that bartering for services does. However, there are still potential pitfalls and a risk of exploiting your client. For example, it would not be unreasonable in a rural area for a practitioner to accept bales of hay in lieu of payment as long as the hay is valued at the going market rate and not discounted by the client because of your therapeutic relationship. Some practitioners accept artwork from clients; however, this can be problematic as it can be very difficult to establish a value for artwork. Generally, if it creates a dual relationship or there is a discount involved, do not do it. It may be exploitive and cause damage to the therapeutic relationship, which is not usually evident until it is too late.

Multiple Relationships

Multiple relationships can sneak up on you. An acquaintance from your church discovers that you are a psychotherapist and asks if you could see him for therapy. Your accountant asks if you could "take a look at" her troubled teenager. To provide competent and ethical services to your clients, you must have a single role: their psychotherapist. Any time you are asked to provide services to a person you know in other settings you have an obligation to explain the inappropriateness of initiating treatment. Make an effort to recommend a few other therapists, and quietly withdraw. Of course, as discussed earlier, you also have a responsibility not to encourage or allow existing clients to add a different role to your therapeutic relationship. This can be particularly difficult, and sometimes impossible to avoid, if you are practicing in a small community. In cases where a dual relationship cannot be avoided, the American Counseling Association's (1995, Section A.6, Dual Relationships) Code of Ethics and Standards of Practice has some guidelines: "When a dual relationship cannot be avoided, counselors take appropriate professional precautions such as informed consent, consultation, supervision and documentation to ensure that judgment is not impaired and no exploitation occurs."

The most common types of multiple relationships occur in social, business, financial, supervisory, political, administrative, or legal contacts. The harm occurs when the relationships obscure the practitioner's sense of objectivity. The relationship outside of therapy can adversely influence the therapist's decision making. For instance, if you are treating the daughter of your accountant, you may be reluctant to inform the parent of the destructive influence of her behavior on her child's mental health if you are dependent on her professional expertise.

Multiple relationships may also increase the risk of harm to clients. Counselors have a lot of influence with their clients. If the therapist has another relationship with the client outside of therapy, that power differential can be potentially exploitive. Consider the following example:

Mary is a third-grade teacher in a small town. Her student, Robert, tells her his mother is a psychotherapist. Intrigued, Mary talks with Robert's mother, Sandy, and finds her easy to talk to about the challenges of parenting and teaching. Mary realizes that she is feeling burned out about teaching and wants to see Sandy as a therapy client. Sandy is somewhat concerned, but because they live in a small town and Mary has few other options for therapy, she agrees to see her. Things go well until Robert stops turning in his homework and becomes increasingly aggressive with other students. Mary would like to talk with Sandy about Robert's problems, but Sandy is both the parent of her student and her personal therapist. She does not want Sandy to become angry with her for bringing up Robert's problems; she fears that Sandy might discontinue the therapy. Sandy's power differential over Mary keeps Mary from competently doing her job as a teacher.

Down- or Up-Coding of Diagnoses

Any time you wish to bill a third party for psychotherapy services, you will be asked to provide an accurate diagnosis, using the coding system in the most current *Diagnostic and Statistical Manual of Mental Disorders* (*DSM*). We have seen both up-coding and down-coding of diagnoses. Therapists are sometimes tempted to down-code (report a less serious or stigmatizing diagnosis) to avoid labeling the client. For example, you may be treating a well-respected businessman who is experiencing psychotic symptoms, and you may be reluctant to provide a diagnosis reflecting this for fear the diagnosis will somehow stigmatize your client and affect his standing in the community. Some practitioners do not believe in the diagnostic/coding model and choose not to use the

DSM at all if they can help it. If they do use it, it is for billing purposes only and does not inform their case conceptualization or treatment plan.

There is also the opposite situation, in which practitioners up-code (report a more serious diagnosis) rather than provide an accurate diagnosis. A practitioner may be treating a client who is one of the "worried well," with no true diagnosis at all, but the client and practitioner want insurance to pay for the treatment anyway. The therapist records an Adjustment Disorder or Dysthymia instead of a diagnosis of a V-code, which may not be reimbursable. (See Chapter 5 for more on working with insurance companies.)

Brandt Caudill Jr., Esq., is a defense attorney who represents psychologists, psychiatrists, social workers, and other mental health professionals in malpractice actions, licensing board hearings, and similar legal matters. He has some advice for practitioners who are involved in either up-coding or down-coding of diagnoses:

> The general rule is that the diagnosis for treatment and diagnosis for insurance should be the same. The law does not recognize or permit the therapist to have one diagnosis for treatment purposes and one diagnosis for billing or insurance purposes. In fact, the existence of two such diagnoses offers an opposing attorney a great opportunity to impugn the therapist's credibility. A patient should only be diagnosed with the accurate diagnosis. (Caudill, n.d., www.kspope.com/ethics/malpractice.php)

Your diagnosis must be accurate to be legal. A client who does not have a diagnosis that meets the payer's definition of medical necessity should be informed that he or she will need to pay privately for any treatment desired. Up-coding to gain authorization and payment for treatment is dishonest and unethical, and ultimately adds to health care costs for everyone. Down-coding can likewise have serious consequences: If your medical records indicate a less serious diagnosis and an adverse event occurs, you could be accused of malpractice for not recognizing and treating the more serious disorder.

Practicing Outside Your Scope of Practice

Practitioners should always strive to treat their clients within the scope of their practice. When practitioners go outside of their scope of practice, they put their client and themselves at risk.

Once again, defense attorney Brandt Caudill Jr., Esq. (n.d.) gives the following example:

> An example of this is in a case from New Hampshire, Hungerford v. Jones 722 'A. 2d 478 (1998), where one of the allegations was that a social worker, who had limited experience in treating patients with repressed memories, led a patient to believe that she had been sexually abused by her father, when she had not. A key point in the decision of the Supreme Court in New Hampshire allowing the father to sue his daughter's therapist was that the therapist's only training in the area of repressed memories was one lecture on memory retrieval techniques that she attended at a weekend symposium. The therapist should not use any techniques without being thoroughly trained and experienced in them. It is probably below the standard of care per se to use a technique after only being trained in it one time. It is not uncommon with some treatment approaches such as EMDR or Bioenergetics, for therapists to attempt to begin using the techniques before completing the entire training. As a practical matter, initiating the use of the technique without completing the training can lead to potential liability and/or licensing board actions. (www.kspope.com/ethics/malpractice.php)

Client Rights

The Right to Refuse Services

Clients always have the right to refuse services. Your obligation is to make an assessment, recommend a course of treatment, and provide the services you are recommending. If your client disagrees with your assessment or your treatment recommendations, you may agree to a short period of negotiation to gather more information about your client and allow your client to gather more information about the treatment you are recommending. Or you could recommend another therapist who may be a better match. Do not spend too much effort trying to persuade a client that your treatment is the best one, and do not compromise your treatment plan too much in an effort to engage the client in therapy. You may find that clients who initially reject your treatment recommendations come back later with a more open mind.

Termination of Services

Under what conditions may a practitioner terminate therapy with a client? The APA's (2003, Section 10.10) Ethical Principles and Code of Conduct specify guidelines for terminating therapy:

Psychologists terminate therapy when it becomes reasonably clear that the client/patient no longer needs the service, is not likely to benefit, or is being harmed by continued service.

Psychologists may terminate therapy when threatened or otherwise endangered by the client/patient or another person with whom the client/patient has a relationship.

Except where precluded by the actions of clients/patients or third-party payers, prior to termination psychologists provide pretermination counseling and suggest alternative service providers as appropriate.

Terminating Services for Lack of Payment

What about practitioners who are in private practice in a fee-for-service setting? Can they ethically terminate services with a client who does not pay his or her bill?

The NASW (1999b, section 1.16c) Code of Ethics gives this guideline regarding payment issues:

Social workers in fee-for-service settings may terminate services to clients who are not paying an overdue balance if the financial contractual arrangements have been made clear to the client, if the client does not pose an imminent danger to self or others and if the clinical and other consequences of the current nonpayment have been addressed and discussed with the client.

A "Vacation from Therapy"

In some situations, you may choose to give your client a "vacation from therapy" (Linehan, 1993a). If so, explain your reasons clearly, and let her know what she needs to do to return to therapy: "We aren't making much progress in therapy because you have been 30 to 45 minutes late for each of the past four sessions. I think we should take a break for now, and when your schedule allows you to be on time for sessions, we can consider starting again." In some cases you may want to give your client a "field project": a time to practice the skills and behaviors he has learned in therapy without regular appointments. If you are having difficulty with a client termination, consult with a colleague.

Terminating psychotherapy can be challenging. You can prevent most ethically dangerous situations by being clear at the beginning that your work together will have a definite beginning, middle, and end (see Chapters 9, 10, and 11 for more on the stages of a therapy episode). Negotiate the length of expected treatment at the outset. You should also be explicit about your business practices: what you charge, how you deal with insurance billing, policies on your availability outside of sessions, and confidentiality. If you need to terminate therapy for unexpected reasons, let your client know your reasons prior to termination and provide some assistance in finding another therapist.

Access to Records

Ethical problems can arise over access to your records. You have an obligation to prevent anyone from accessing your records of treatment without the client's expressed permission. Let each client know what circumstances may legally compel you to report information or warn others. Each state has laws about this, so become familiar with your state's requirements. You may be required to report suspected child or vulnerable adult abuse or imminent threat of suicide or homicide.

Clients may request that you release their record of treatment to an agency (e.g., for disability claims) or to a lawyer (e.g., for use in divorce, custody, or other legal actions), to another practitioner, or directly to the client. Always have a current, signed release of information when you have been asked to release any records. Have a frank discussion with your client about the pros and cons of this action. Consult your state laws about clients' rights to their own records. In some cases, it is advisable for the client to read the record in the presence of the therapist. This is especially important if, in the therapist's judgment, the record contains information that may be clinically confusing or there is a possibility of a traumatic reaction to the material contained in the records.

If you believe that the release will cause harm to your client, but the client is insisting on it, the NASW (1999a, Section 1.08a) Code of Ethics has some guidelines:

> Social workers should provide clients with reasonable access to records concerning the clients. Social workers who are concerned that clients' access to their records could cause serious misunderstanding or harm to the client should provide assistance in interpreting the records and consultation with the client regarding the records. Social workers should limit clients' access to their records, or portions of their records, only in exceptional circumstances when there is compelling evidence that such access would cause serious harm to the client. Both clients' requests and the rationale for withholding some or all of the record should be documented in clients' files.

Another problematic ethical situation can occur if your client asks you not to keep any records at all of your treatment. Clients may fear that their records could end up in the wrong hands. It is understandable that some clients may not feel comfortable having you keep a record; however, that record is also there to protect you as a practitioner. (See Chapter 3 for more on record keeping.) At a minimum, the record should contain a written consent to treatment, basic identifying information, an evaluation and treatment plan, and a chronological record of each contact. Without a record, you could become vulnerable to any number of legal risks: your client could sue you for malpractice, or your client's family could sue you after an unexpected death or other adverse event. You could also be caught without a defense if the client reports you to a licensing board for an ethical violation. Explain to your client exactly what you put in your chart, and why. (See Chapter 4 for more on documentation.) In some circumstances, it may be helpful to show the client the chart notes at the end of each session, or even to give clients a copy, especially if your notes include helpful information and homework assignments. If the client is still not comfortable with your record-keeping needs, you may need to examine whether you can treat the client under those circumstances.

Research

If you are involved in any sort of research involving your clients, you must follow established research protocols. Informed consent is essential. If at any point you feel your client may be harmed by any aspect of the research, your client's well-being must be your first priority. Be aware of any power differentials; for example, if your client is getting free treatment while in the research project, and cannot afford treatment otherwise, he may be vulnerable to subtle coercion. Always get expert consultation on research design and any ethical issues involved.

Grievance Procedures

As part of your consent to treatment agreement, include a discussion of grievance procedures. Encourage clients to talk with you right away if they have any concerns about your treatment or ethics. Do your best to resolve the disagreement amicably. It may stem from a misunderstanding, a lack of agreement on the diagnosis and treatment plan, billing problems, or boundary issues. You may need to agree to refer your client to another provider; if so, be gracious about it.

Complaints to Your Licensing Board

Be aware that clients may also make a formal complaint to your state licensing board. If this happens, be prepared to answer the complaint (a complete, up-to-date client record should help with this process). You may want to consider retaining an attorney knowledgeable in professional ethics to assist you, as your license and livelihood may be on the line. If your client's care is being paid for by her insurance company, she may also complain about you to them. Be prepared to explain your side in the disagreement and to negotiate a fair resolution. If there is a pattern of repeated complaints, your contract with the insurance company may be at risk.

Even with ethical guidelines, an infinite variety of situational combinations can be left open to interpretation. If you have the unfortunate experience of being investigated by your state licensing board, your actions will be closely scrutinized. Those judging your actions have the benefit of hindsight without knowledge of the nuances of the particular situation. So what is one to do?

Stephen Feldman (2001, p. 113), a licensed psychologist and lawyer who consults widely on ethical issues, makes the following recommendation in his book *How to Stay Out of Trouble with Everyone: A Handbook of Law and Ethics for the Mental Health Professional*:

> Whenever you need to make a decision in one of these vague or uncovered ethical areas, your safest course is to have a policy in place, describe the incident in your chart notes, and include a clinical reason for what you did that is consistent with your policy. As with clinical judgment, your confidence in your ethical judgment grows with time, education, experience and consultation with thoughtful colleagues.

Summing Up

We hope you can see that a strong foundation in ethics is necessary for practice. Awareness of ethical issues is extremely important to ensure the safety of the client, to preserve the practitioner's reputation, and to decrease the practitioner's financial and legal liability risk. It is during the loneliness and ambiguity of everyday practice that your ethical decision-making skills will be put to the test. Although it is impossible to provide answers to every ethical dilemma, we hope that you will now, at least, ask the right questions.

=**EXERCISES**=

1. Under what conditions would you feel compelled to file an ethics complaint against a colleague?
2. Examine your practice and identify a real or potential ethical dilemma. What should you do? Why? What will you do? Why? Discuss your dilemma and possible solutions with a colleague.
3. Consider the following situations:
   - A client looks up your phone number, calls you on the weekend, and asks if you can get together for coffee.
   - A child client gives you a drawing she's done.
   - A client gives you expensive tickets to a concert.
   - A client can't pay for sessions once his insurance runs out; he offers to fix your car in trade for sessions.
   - A client wants to sit next to you and put her head on your shoulder during sessions, saying "My last therapist said it was good for me."
   - A client reveals that a previous therapist has begun calling him and suggesting they go out on dates.
   - A client has begun stalking you, and you decide to end therapy with her.
   - A client has a severe psychotic disorder and wants you to treat him without medications.
   - A client asks you for a copy of your chart notes to use in her harassment lawsuit against her employer.

   In each of these situations, decide what behaviors would be ethical, and what you would do under these circumstances:

(*Continued*)

- What action would you choose and why?
- What are the ramifications of less than ethical behavior in each of these scenarios?
- How would unethical behaviors affect the client? How will this affect the therapist?

4. A common practice is to avoid labeling a client with a personality disorder. Inaccurate recording of diagnosis is unethical and can put the practitioner at a greater liability risk. Consider the following case:

A female therapist was treating a man who had a history of childhood trauma. He also met criteria for Borderline Personality Disorder, but the practitioner did not want to label this client and chose not to record this diagnosis. Since the personality disorder diagnosis was not foremost in her mind, it did not influence her thinking regarding the treatment plan or her approach. Unfortunately, she also engaged in healing rituals with him outside of her office, initially at his encouragement. His spouse became suspicious of this type of activity and complained to the insurance company that was paying for the treatment from the contracted practitioner. When the practitioner stopped the practice that she had been willingly participating in, the client became very angry with her. Through a series of events, he felt traumatized by the practitioner's actions. He and his spouse planned to sue the practitioner for malpractice.

Analyze this situation. What are the ethical issues involved in this case? What practitioner behaviors put her at a greater legal liability risk?

5. Under what circumstances would you reveal the following information about yourself to a client? Why?

- That you have a cat
- That you are married and have five children
- That you live in a certain neighborhood

(Continued)

- That you attend a specific church
- Your favorite restaurant
- Your philosophy of psychotherapy
- That you are feeling angry about a personal matter
- That you are feeling angry about something the client has said in session
- That you have a particular disease
- That you are involved in a malpractice lawsuit brought by a former client

Resources

Bernstein, B. E., & Hartsell, T. L. (2000). *The portable ethicist for mental health professionals: An A-Z guide to responsible practice*. New York: Wiley.

Feldman, S. (2001). *How to stay out of trouble with everyone: A handbook of law and ethics for the mental health professional*. Seattle, WA: Still River Foundation Press.

The primary ethical codes in the psychology profession are the following:

The American Association of Marriage and Family Therapists' AAMFT Code of Ethics
www.aamft.org/resources/LRMPlan/Ethics/ethicscode2001.asp

The American Counseling Association's Codes of Ethics and Standards of Practice
www.counseling.org/Resources/CodeOfEthics/TP/Home/CT2.aspx

The American Psychological Association's Ethical Principles of Psychologists and Code of Conduct
www2.apa.org/ethics/code2002.doc

The National Association of Social Workers' Code of Ethics
www.socialworkers.org/pubs/code/code.asp

3

Legal Issues

What You Will Learn
- How the *Tarasoff* case impacts the client's right to confidentiality
- The importance of understanding and responding to "duty to warn" situations
- How "duty to report" statutes affect confidentiality rights
- The challenges of confidentiality when working with a minor
- How the law affects record keeping and retention
- The function of professional licensing boards
- How to apply the four elements of malpractice
- The difference between supervision and consultation
- How to respond if you receive a subpoena

The nightmare of every practitioner is having to appear before the licensing board or going to court regarding a malpractice suit. Being aware of your responsibility under the law is the first step in minimizing your risk. This chapter reviews the major legal issues affecting a practitioner as well as case examples to illustrate how you can stay out of trouble.

Confidentiality

Confidentiality is sacred in the field of psychotherapy. The business of psychological counseling could not exist without it. Clients attending a session need to feel comfortable expressing their innermost thoughts and emotions. They expect that the information revealed is private and will not be shared with others. This is critical to the integrity of psychological treatment. Practitioners should treat all information disclosed within the therapeutic relationship as confidential. This applies to audio, video, and computer files as well as written and verbal information.

TIP

The Health Insurance Portability and Accountability Act of 1996 (HIPAA; U.S. Department of Health and Human Services, 2003) established privacy rules for the use and disclosure of health care information. This legislation limits the circumstances in which an individual's health care information can be used by health care practitioners, hospitals, and other "covered entities." It also defines the operational guidelines for the allowable disclosure of information for treatment, payment, research, care coordination, and quality improvement activities. The reader is referred to the resource section for further details.

There are, however, two exceptions to the confidentiality rule: "duty to warn" and "duty to report." Consider duty to warn from a historical perspective.

Tarasoff v. Regents of the University of California

Prior to 1976, a therapist was *not* under obligation to notify an individual if, in the course of therapy, a client made a credible threat of physical harm to that individual and there was serious danger of violence to that individual. The therapist's duty was to the client, not to any other party. The Supreme Court of California's ruling in *Tarasoff v. Regents of the University of California* (1976) changed that. The following is a description of the case by Learning Point Associates from the Pathways to School Improvement web site:[*]

> The legal precedent of this concept was set in the case of *Tarasoff v. Regents of the University of California* (1976). In this case, according to Keith-Spiegel and Koocher (1985), a University of California student named Prosenjit Poddar was seeing a psychologist at the university's student health center because a young woman named Tatiana Tarasoff had spurned his affections. The psychologist, reasoning that Poddar was dangerous because of his pathological attachment to Tarasoff and because he intended to purchase a gun, notified the police both verbally and in writing. The police questioned Poddar and found him to be rational; they made Poddar promise to stay away from Tarasoff. Two months later, however, Poddar killed Tarasoff. When Tarasoff's parents attempted to sue the University of California, health center staff members, and the police, the courts dismissed the case.

Keith-Spiegel and Koocher (1985, p. 62) describe what happened next:

> The Tarasoff family appealed to the Supreme Court of California, asserting that the defendants had a duty to warn Ms. Tarasoff or her family of the danger and that they should have persisted to ensure [Poddar's] confinement. In a 1974 ruling, the court held that the therapists indeed did have a duty to warn Ms. Tarasoff. When the defendants and several amici curiae [literally, "friends of the court," or entities who file a brief with the court even though they are not parties to the suit] petitioned for a rehearing, the court took the unusual step of granting one. In their second ruling (Tarasoff, 1976), the court released the police from liability without explanation and more broadly formulated the duty of therapists, imposing a duty to use reasonable care to protect third parties against dangers posed by patients.

McWhinney, Haskins-Herkenham, and Hare (1992, p. 3) note the effects of this case:

> The case of Tarasoff v. Regents of the University of California (1976) imposed an affirmative duty on therapists to warn a potential victim of intended harm by the client, stating that the right to confidentiality ends when the public peril begins. This legal decision sets an affirmative duty precedent in cases of harm to others that is generally accepted within the social work profession.

---

[*]*Duty to Warn* by Learning Point Associates, 1998, Pathways to School Improvement web site. Retrieved June 23, 2006, from http:ncrel.org/sdrs/areas/issues/envrnmnt/css/cs3lk1.htm, which is part of the publication *Critical Issue: Addressing Confidentiality Concerns in School-Linked Integrated Service Efforts,* http: ncrel.org/sdrs/areas/issues/envrnmnt/css/cs300.htm. Reprinted with permission.

According to Davis and Ritchie (1993, p. 27), this case indicates that "notifying police is not sufficient action to protect the counselor from a lawsuit if the client's threat is carried out."

Initially there was concern that this ruling would keep potentially violent individuals from seeking treatment, but this does not appear to be the case. Subsequently, other states adopted the same or similar statutes. While there are many similarities between states, there are some variations.

TIP

To determine your responsibilities as a mental health practitioner under the law, you should check regulations in your own state.

Duty to Warn

It is not unusual for mental health practitioners to deal with individuals who are angry and who express these feelings in session. Sometimes the anger is generalized and a means of discharging pent-up and powerful emotions. Other times it is very specific and even directed at a particular individual. What is your duty under these circumstances?

For sake of illustration, the Revised Code of Washington (RCW) statute 71.05.120 states:

> [Practitioners have a] duty to warn or to take reasonable precautions to provide protection from violent behavior where the patient has communicated an actual threat of physical violence against a reasonably identifiable victim or victims. The duty to warn or to take reasonable precautions to provide protection from violent behavior is discharged if reasonable efforts are made to communicate the threat to the victim or victims and to law enforcement personnel.

The following three conditions need to be present in order for you to break the statute regarding confidentiality and reveal the content of your session to someone without the client's expressed written consent:

1. There needs to be an actual threat.
2. The client must threaten to use physical violence.
3. There needs to be a reasonably identifiable victim.

The real world is always a little less clear. Consider the following scenario.

A 35-year-old male is in counseling for anger management after having a verbal outburst at his place of employment. His employer has sent him to counseling because they are concerned about his behavior. Up to this point there have not been any actual incidents of physical violence, but others around him are feeling increasingly threatened. He feels he is being treated unfairly by the company. He reports a "personality clash" with his supervisor. He is becoming increasingly frustrated with his situation, resulting in increased physical agitation both on the job and whenever he starts to talk about his situation. Five minutes before the session ends he states that he will punch his boss in the face the next time he sees him.

The session ends. What do you do? Is this an actual threat, or just a way to verbalize his frustration? There certainly is an identifiable victim and a threat of a very specific act of physical violence. However, what if this is just a means of processing frustration and a verbal indication of what the client would *like to do* but not what he *intends to do*. What if you do reveal this information to his boss and the police, and the client loses his job? He then sues you for breach of confidentiality, stating that he never intended to actually commit this act of violence and that you as the practitioner failed to assess his intentions. It can be very difficult to predict what may happen and what an individual's true intentions actually are.

Stephen R. Feldman (2001, p. 23), a psychologist, lawyer, and the author of *How to Stay Out of Trouble with Everyone: A Handbook of Law and Ethics for the Mental Health Professional*, has some wise advice about how a practitioner should handle these situations:

> The statute [RCW 71.05.120 (2)] does not require us to be mind readers or seers. We need to ask if the threat is actual. Then we'll know. Whenever I have a client make a dangerous threat, I tell them that if they are serious I am going to have to pick up the phone and report it. I ask them to tell me if they are planning to actually do what they said, or are they just expressing their anger and frustration in the form of a figure of speech. So far they have all backed off the reality of the threat, and have done so convincingly. In fact, they have felt relieved that I heard and understood their frustration, anger and feelings of powerlessness for what they are. Usually those sessions proceed very well from that point on. The client feels better understood (and I feel quite relieved). We can move forward to some useful work addressing those feelings.

It is helpful to explore with clients what they actually mean by their statements to determine the true level of threat. These statements should be taken seriously, but one should not jump to the conclusion that the client actually intends to carry it out without sufficient investigation.

Let's take the scenario with the angry client a step further. You ask the client if he actually intends to punch his boss and he says, "You bet I do. He deserves it after the way he has treated me. I don't care if I lose my job, somebody needs to teach him a lesson." If, after several attempts to understand his intentions, you believe that he will carry out his threat of physical harm to his boss, under the statute you must call the police *and* warn his boss. Breaching confidentiality is a serious matter, but in this case, the law states that preventing physical harm to another, identifiable person trumps the client's right to privacy. If, after a thorough investigation, it becomes clear that the client is expressing his anger and frustration with his boss and does not intend to carry out that threat, then there is no duty to report.

Clinical and legal issues can be complicated; therefore, consulting with a trusted and knowledgeable colleague can help one understand the many facets of the situation clearly as well as identify possible courses of action. Whatever the decision you make, it is advisable to make sure you chart the client's behavior, your interpretation of the threat level, and the rationale for your actions or inaction. If, at a later date, your actions or inaction are called into question, your chart notes are your record of the interaction. (See Chapter 4 for more on documentation.)

Duty to Report

What should a practitioner do if abuse of someone is revealed during the session? Most states have a "duty to report" regulation stipulating that a practitioner has the obligation to report this to the proper authorities. If a practitioner has reason to believe that a person has been harmed or abused by another, it is the practitioner's responsibility by law to report it. Once reported, it is the responsibility of the investigatory agency, such as Child Protective Services or Adult Protective Services, to determine the validity of the accusations. Note that the duty to report covers abuse or neglect not only of a child but also of a dependent or vulnerable adult.

Once again, for sake of illustration, the RCW statute 26.44.030, 1(a) regarding the duty to report states: "When any practitioner, . . . [the statute lists a number of practitioner types] has reasonable cause to believe that a child has suffered abuse or neglect, he or she shall report such incident, or cause a report to be made, to the proper law enforcement agency."

Once a practitioner has knowledge of an incident of abuse, he or she must report it no later than 48 hours "after there is reasonable cause to believe that the child has suffered abuse or neglect. The report must include the identity of the accused if known" (RCW statute 26.44.030). The practitioner's responsibility is further outlined in RCW 26.44.040:

An immediate oral report must be made by telephone or otherwise to the proper law enforcement agency or the department of social and health services and, upon request, must be followed by a report in writing. Such reports must contain the following information, if known:

(1) The name, address, and age of the child;
(2) The name and address of the child's parents, stepparents, guardians, or other persons having custody of the child;
(3) The nature and extent of the alleged injury or injuries;
(4) The nature and extent of the alleged neglect;
(5) The nature and extent of the alleged sexual abuse;
(6) Any evidence of previous injuries, including their nature and extent; and

(7) Any other information that may be helpful in establishing the cause of the child's death, injury, or injuries and the identity of the alleged perpetrator or perpetrators.

Confidentiality and Working with a Minor

Confidentiality issues are more complicated when working with minors. Who is considered a minor? Please check your state regulations, as there are some variations from state to state. We will use the Washington Administrative Code (WAC, 2003) as a reference. In this case, WAC 246-924-363(4) outlines the limited confidentiality rules for minors. A minor is considered anyone under the age of 13. A practitioner who works with minors is under the obligation to inform the client that his or her right of confidentiality is limited. This means that the client's parents can have interactions with the practitioner that disclose confidential information without a release of information from their child. It also means that parents have access to the records just as if they were the client. It is important to clarify these guidelines with both the parents and the minor prior to treatment. For the minor client, confidentiality is of a limited nature. The parents have the right to full access. However, the WAC also states that practitioners should act in the child's best interest. They have the ability to use discretion in deciding what information to release to the parents as outlined in WAC 246-924-363(4):

> (4) Legally dependent clients. At the beginning of a professional relationship, to the extent that the client can understand, the psychologist shall inform a client who is under the age of thirteen or who has a legal guardian of the limit the law imposes on the right of confidentiality with respect to his/her communications with the psychologist. For clients between the age of thirteen and eighteen, the psychologist shall clarify any limits to confidentiality between the minor and legal guardians at the outset of services. The psychologist will act in the minor's best interests in deciding whether to disclose confidential information to the legal guardians without the minor's consent.

Misunderstanding the rules of confidentiality can create situations that compromise the clinical integrity of the treatment. For example, you may lose the trust of a minor client if you reveal to the parents some behavior that he or she is engaging in. On the other hand, you may be pressured by the parents to reveal unnecessary information to them, and they may become upset with you for not doing so. Establishing these rules before treatment protects everyone. It creates a clinical balance between the minor's need for confidentiality and the parents' need to know relevant information that involves their child. It is a good idea to have an additional Consent to Treat a Minor form in conjunction with the practitioner's disclosure form.

What about clients over the age of 13 but still under the age of 18? The Washington statute RCW 71.34.530 (formerly 71.34.030) states that a client age 13 or older can engage in treatment with a mental health counselor without the parents' consent. These minors have full rights to confidentiality, just as if they were adults. The practitioner can do family sessions with the parents, but the practitioner cannot reveal information from the individual sessions without the expressed written consent of the minor client.

Record Keeping

We have regularly performed chart audits and have seen firsthand that record keeping varies considerably from one practitioner to the next. Some have well-documented notes on preprinted forms that capture required information; others jot a few cryptic notes on a yellow legal pad. A small number of private practice practitioners occasionally do not write notes on a face-to-face encounter with a client. (See Chapter 4 for more on the importance of documentation.)

It is important to read the statutes of your state regarding paperwork requirements of record keeping for mental health practitioners. We refer to the Washington Administrative Code 246-809-035 regarding record keeping and retention:

(1) The licensed counselor providing professional services to a client or providing services billed to a third-party payor, shall document services, except as provided in subsection (2) of this section. The documentation includes:
   (a) Client name;
   (b) The fee arrangement and record of payments;
   (c) Dates counseling was received;
   (d) Disclosure form, signed by licensed counselor and client;
   (e) The presenting problem(s), purpose or diagnosis;
   (f) Notation and results of formal consults, including information obtained from other persons or agencies through a release of information;
   (g) Progress notes sufficient to support responsible clinical practice for the type of theoretical orientation/therapy the licensed counselor uses.

Client Request Not to Keep Records

A client may request that you do not keep progress notes. Perhaps the client is a prominent member of the community or had a negative experience with a past practitioner regarding a breach of confidentiality. The client may want to take extra precautions. The Washington Administrative Code 246-809-035 defines record keeping under these circumstances under subsection (2):

> (2) If a client requests that no treatment records be kept, and the licensed counselor agrees to the request, the request must be in writing and the counselor must retain only the following documentation:
> (a) Client name;
> (b) Fee arrangement and record of payments;
> (c) Dates counseling was received;
> (d) Disclosure form, signed by licensed counselor and client;
> (e) Written request that no records be kept.
> (3) The licensed counselor may not agree to the request if maintaining records is required by other state or federal law.

Agreeing to refrain from taking notes can potentially increase the risk for the practitioner. The practitioner needs to consider the ramifications of such an action. What if the client later alleges practitioner misconduct regarding treatment? What if the client commits suicide, and your records are requested via court order? What if such events occur years later and you do not have a mental recall of the details of the case? In all of these cases, though you have followed the law as written you may open yourself to legal liability. If an extraordinary event occurs and you do not have any notes to indicate your thinking at the time, you will be unable to substantiate your actions. Caution is highly recommended when you receive a request to refrain from keeping notes. If you feel uncomfortable with such a request from a client, you may consider referring him or her to another practitioner.

Challenge for the Practitioner

What if a client requests that records not be kept and wants the treatment paid for by a third-party insurer? It is recommended that the practitioner check with the insurer for information regarding their policies in this matter.

Some plans may allow a certain number of sessions per year without requiring a medical necessity justification. However, you still need to enter a *DSM* diagnosis when you bill the insurer. Health plans that require a medical necessity justification will likely not pay for treatment that is not clinically documented. The client is free to enter into a private pay arrangement with the practitioner as long as the agreement is made in writing regarding waiver of the keeping of records. Paying privately assures that no information leaves the practitioner's office without the client's expressed written consent.

Record Retention

How long should records be kept? The usual time period varies from 5 to 8 years from the last visit. In some cases, it can also vary by discipline, with psychologists needing to retain records longer than therapists with a master's degree. In the case of minors, the retention period begins when the minor reaches 21 years of age. Some practitioners never destroy their records; in case of a complaint, licensing board inquiry, or legal suit, they want a complete record on every client and believe that this is the best form of protection. Please check your state regulations to determine your retention responsibility. It can vary dramatically; for example, New York requires a record retention period of 6 years, whereas the state of Massachusetts requires 30 years (GSC Home Study Courses, 2006, pp. 6–7).

These records also need to be maintained safely, with properly limited access, usually in a locked cabinet. A licensed counselor must also make provisions for retaining or transferring records in the event of going out of business, death, or incapacitation. These provisions may be made in the practitioner's will, in an office policy, or by ensuring that another licensed counselor is available to review records with a client if the original counselor cannot.

Dealing with Licensing Boards

A mental health practitioner is more likely to have a client make a complaint to the licensing board than to be sued for malpractice. Suing for malpractice takes a lot of time, effort, and money.

One needs to retain a lawyer and gather evidence to make a case; however, a disgruntled client need only write a letter to the licensing board to open an investigation. (See Chapter 2 for more on client rights.)

Licensing boards have two main functions:

1. To protect the public from unqualified practitioners
2. To protect the profession in the eyes of the public

Licensing boards establish professional requirements and grant licenses to qualified individuals. They set the standard for the minimum qualifications for practitioners. Practitioners must submit proof of education from an accredited school. By setting particular standards, such as attaining a certain acceptable degree and fulfilling a certain number of supervised hours, licensing boards also protect the profession. In most states, psychologists must pass a written and an oral board exam. Only a licensed psychologist can use that title. People who work in the psychology field but do not have a PhD in psychology cannot call themselves psychologists. In this way, the public is protected from being treated by an unqualified practitioner, and the profession's reputation is protected by not having unqualified practitioners in their ranks.

However, there is often confusion among the public regarding the terms used by certain occupations. For instance, those who have received a Master of Social Work degree can apply for a state license as a licensed clinical social worker. However, bachelor's-level practitioners who work in the state department of social services are often referred to as social workers even though they do not have this advanced training.

Licensing boards receive complaints from the public and therapists regarding the behavior of licensed practitioners. They are responsible for fully investigating complaints and determining if there is any merit to them. Licensing boards are usually made up of peer professionals who are actively practicing in the field and are aware of the standards of care and the ethical issues that may be relevant in a particular case. As with all human organizations, however, they can vary in their interpretation of standards and the severity of the sanctions they impose. As they giveth, so can they taketh away! If a practitioner is suspected of professional misconduct, an investigation occurs that can lead to sanctions, including the ultimate sanction: the revocation of license. Exposure to training in ethical principles may decrease your risk of going before the licensing board.

Knowing the areas of the most frequent complaints can help keep you out of trouble (Pope & Vasquez, 1998). Data from psychology licensing boards over a 14-year period show that the most frequent disciplinary actions involved violations in the following areas, in descending order of frequency:

- Dual relationships (sexual and/or nonsexual)
- Unprofessional or negligent practice
- Fraud
- Conviction of crimes
- Inadequate or improper supervision
- Impairment
- Confidentiality
- Records and documentation
- Using false information in applying for a license

Challenge for the Practitioner

Can a licensing board impose sanctions if a civil malpractice case is not filed or is dismissed? Yes. A practitioner can be sanctioned even if there was no legal damage to the client. The licensing board is primarily focused on the behavior of the practitioner as it relates to the standard of care of the profession. Licensing boards often use the APA and/or the NASW ethical standards as a guideline. Sanctions can be imposed even though there is no complaint by a client or damage sustained.

Licensing boards thoroughly investigate complaints and have the power to request chart notes and computer records (including e-mail) and to interview people relevant to the case. This process can take months, sometimes over a year. Practitioners can have their own legal representation, and negotiations often occur as to the type and severity of sanctions imposed. Typical sanctions are:

- Mandatory ethical training, particularly related to violation of boundaries with clients
- A monetary fine that can range into the thousands of dollars
- Regular supervision by a peer professional
- Limitation of practice, such as not being allowed to treat the opposite sex or a particular age group
- Temporary suspension of licensure until certain conditions are met
- Full revocation of license

What Is Malpractice?

Pope and Vasquez (1998) analyzed data over a 15-year period and found that malpractice claims against psychologists fell into the following categories (with the most frequent listed first):

- Sexual violations
- Incompetence in developing or implementing a treatment plan
- Loss from evaluation [This would indicate a situation where a person is evaluated and loses a job due to the diagnosis or prognosis]
- Breach of confidentiality or privacy
- Improper diagnosis
- Other (a mysterious category of individual claims not falling into any other category)
- Suicide
- Defamation (e.g., slander or libel)
- Countersuit for fee collection
- Violation of civil rights
- Loss of child custody or visitation
- Failure to supervise properly
- Improper death of patient or third party
- Violation of legal regulations
- Licensing or peer review issues
- Breach of contract

What constitutes malpractice, or "bad practice"? For a malpractice suit to be brought into a court of law, a civil wrong must have been committed that is made up of the following four elements (S. Feldman, 2001, pp. 8–9):

1. *Duty:* This occurs when a client is taken into your practice. There is a professional expectation that the client will be treated with the skill and

2. *Breach:* Failure to meet the standard of a reasonable and prudent practitioner. A breach may occur because of something the practitioner did or neglected to do. This is usually determined by peer review of your actions.
3. *Proximate cause:* A sequence of unbroken events where the practitioner's actions were the direct cause of the client's damage and not the natural progression of the original problem.
4. *Damage:* The actual damage sustained by the client as a result of the practitioner's actions. Expert witnesses are called in to examine the client and testify as to the current mental status of the client and how this relates to the practitioner's actions.

> expertise of a reasonably prudent practitioner who is treating the client under the same or similar circumstances. If you enter into an agreement to take on a client, you have this duty.

The first two elements, duty and breach, are fairly self-explanatory. For there to be proximate cause, the negative outcome needs to occur as a direct result of the therapist's action or inaction, without any other confounding variables. There also needs to be some identifiable damage, such as loss of life, loss of occupation, emotional distress, or physical injury.

TIP

Many liability insurance companies for mental health practitioners offer additional legal defense fee coverage (usually up to $5,000.00) for a nominal fee. This coverage can be used to hire an attorney if you are sued or to represent you before the licensing board. Should your license and livelihood be at stake, this could prove to be a very wise investment.

The following is a real-life scenario experienced by a colleague of the authors.

A psychologist who works in a multidisciplinary clinic does a Minnesota Multiphasic Personality Inventory (MMPI) on all clients who come in to be treated. He does not administer the full version but does an empirically validated shorter version. A client sues one of the other practitioners in the clinic for inappropriate sexual behavior.

The psychologist who did the testing is brought in to testify regarding the results of the client's MMPI, which showed a propensity toward delusional thinking and possible psychotic episodes. The client loses the inappropriate sexual behavior case. The client then blames the psychologist who did the testing for this loss, and sues him for the loss of the first case on the grounds that the psychologist provided incorrect treatment (the short version of the MMPI), which was a breach of the standard of care. The client states that the damage was financial loss and emotional distress.

Let's examine each element:

1. *Duty:* The psychologist has the duty to be properly trained and have the knowledge to accurately administer, score, and interpret the test.
2. *Breach:* The client's attorney argued that the standard of care was breached with the improper administration of the test. The defense brought in witnesses to testify that the psychologist's actions were within what other psychologists would do in the same situation.
3. *Proximate cause:* There was other testimony besides the psychologist's that occurred in the first case. The loss of the first case could not be attributed solely to the psychologist's actions.
4. *Damage:* In this case, damage did occur in the form of financial loss as a result of losing the first case and the emotional distress caused by the court process. However, the cause of the damage could not be tied directly to the psychologist's actions.

As you can see, not all of the four elements of malpractice were proved in this case. In fact, the court dismissed the client's case and ordered the client to pay all court costs.

The Difference between Supervision and Consultation

The terms "supervision" and "consultation" are sometimes used interchangeably, but they have very different meanings and degrees of legal liability (S. Feldman, 2001). When mental health practitioners seek the guidance and professional opinion of other mental health professionals, they are consulting. The treating practitioner directs the treatment of the client and has the full liability for his or her own therapeutic actions. The practitioner who is being consulted acts as educator and advisor and gives his or her professional opinion on the case in response to the consulting practitioner's presentation. This consultant is providing information only and does not have any responsibility for the treatment. The usual practice is that only the clinical information is presented and the identity of the client is protected. Practitioners who are consulted do not have any liability in this situation, and the consulting practitioner decides what information is relevant to the client's care. (See Chapter 5 for more on developing peer consultation.)

A practitioner who directly supervises another practitioner who treats the client has the same liability as the treating practitioner. The supervisor is usually someone with more experience in the field. The supervisee is often a trainee or a beginning practitioner who does not have the same depth of understanding or breadth of experience. A supervisor is responsible for the clinical decisions of the supervised practitioners.

Receiving a Subpoena

Most practitioners will never receive a subpoena in their professional careers. The likelihood is greater, however, if you work in forensic psychology or with children or child custody issues. If you do receive a subpoena, don't panic! If you have kept adequate records you should not have anything to worry about. (See Chapter 4 for more on record keeping.)

As a mental health practitioner, the type of subpoena you are most likely to receive is one for a deposition. The purpose of a deposition is to discover information that may be relevant to the upcoming trial. This type of subpoena does have a mandatory 2-week prior notice period, based on the date you are required to appear. This time period allows the client to seek a protective order from the court. The purpose of the protective order is for the client to request that your records be protected under the claim of privilege by filing a motion to quash. If you receive a subpoena it is advisable to notify your client so that he or she can file the motion to protect the information in your records. This is the client's responsibility, not yours.

Bernstein and Hartsell (2005, p. 88), authors of *The Portable Guide to Testifying in Court for Mental Health Professionals: An A–Z Guide to Being an Effective Witness,* offer these guidelines for mental health practitioners who receive a subpoena:

- Attorneys seeking disclosure of health information should not be trusted to provide you with accurate information about *your* duties and obligations.
- Seek *competent* legal advice when confronted with a subpoena before responding.
- Without a protective order or order quashing the subpoena, you must appear in court, but do not disclose confidential information or produce records until the judge orders you to do so.
- Securing competent legal advice is crucial to ethically and legally responding to a subpoena.
- When confronted with a court order, comply fully but consistently with the order. Be careful not to disclose information not called for by the protective order.

Summing Up

Being involved in legal proceedings can be nerve-racking for the average practitioner, particularly if it is a new experience. You want to make sure that you fully understand the procedures and what is required of you. Most practitioners want to do the right thing but aren't always sure what that is under the circumstances. When in doubt, consult an attorney or a trusted colleague who has been through the process before.

EXERCISES

1. Under what circumstances is a practitioner obligated by law to warn another person about information that is disclosed in a counseling session? Who should the practitioner contact?
2. Under what circumstances does a practitioner have a duty to report? Who needs to be contacted?

(Continued)

3. Consider the following scenario:

   A therapist sees a client who expresses suicidal ideation. The client states that he is thinking about killing himself and has a specific plan. This client has repeatedly expressed suicidal ideation in previous sessions but has never made an attempt. The therapist believes this is a situation much like many others in the past. She does not consult with anyone, nor does she do a formal risk assessment. The client leaves the session feeling very despondent. He goes home, and a few hours after the session commits suicide.

   Have the four elements of malpractice been met? How?
   What could the therapist have done differently?

Resources

Bernstein, B. E., & Hartsell, T. L. (2004). *The portable lawyer for mental health professionals: An A–Z guide to protecting your clients, your practice, and yourself* (2nd ed.). Hoboken, NJ: Wiley.

Bernstein, B. E., & Hartsell, T. L. (2005). *The portable guide to testifying in court for mental health professionals: An A–Z guide to being an effective witness.* Hoboken, NJ: Wiley.

Learning Point Associates. (1998). Pathways to School Improvement web site, *Duty to Warn.* Retrieved June 23, 2006, from http:ncrel .org/sdrs/areas/issues/envrnmnt/css/cs3lk1.htm which is part of the publication: Critical Issue: Addressing Confidentiality Concerns in School-Linked Integrated Service efforts, http:ncrel.org/sdrs/areas/ issues/envrnmnt/css/cs300.htm. Reprinted with permission.

A summary of the HIPAA privacy rule by the U.S. Dept of Health and Human Services can be viewed at www.hhs.gov/ocr/privacysum mary.pdf.

The National Association of Social Workers web site (www.social workers.org) contains a wealth of information on legal issues, including practical tools such as the HIPPA compliance tool kit. Some of this information can be accessed only by NASW members.

4

The Importance of Documentation: Using Client Charts to Keep Care Focused

What You Will Learn
- Why others may see your charts
- Why documentation is essential to a successful therapy practice
- The uses of a pretreatment telephone contact form
- How to develop and use a disclosure/provider-client agreement
- The release of information form
- The client history form
- The essential elements of an intake form
- Using a mental status exam and symptom checklists
- The essential elements of a treatment planning form
- Why clear, organized, and complete progress note forms are important
- The termination summary form

In this chapter we outline the most important parts of a client file. Each part of the file serves a specific purpose. The vast majority of the notes that you keep in your treatment records will never be seen by anyone but you. However, each record has the potential to be seen by a variety of other people for clinical and legal reasons. Therefore, each chart should be viewed as such, not just as your personal notes. One never knows when a chart will be requested by another practitioner, the court system, or the licensing board, so it pays to set up a method that not only works as a reminder for you, the therapist, but can also act as a clinical and legal record.

Who Will See Your Charts?

A number of people may potentially see your charts:

- Clients who ask to see their own records.
- Other mental health practitioners (psychologists, social workers, mental health counselors, and psychiatrists).
- Other health care practitioners, such as primary care physicians.
- Representatives of the legal system, such as lawyers and judges. Clients or lawyers may request or subpoena your records in child custody cases or in an investigation of a crime. (See Chapter 3 for more on legal issues related to record keeping.)
- Executors of the client's will. An executor of a client's will has the right to request client records. The executor has the right to release the records to other family members. Family members may be particularly interested in the chart notes in the case of a suicide or other adverse event.
- Insurance companies. Insurance companies may request a chart review and audit based on medical necessity.
- Licensing boards. Boards investigating a complaint of merit may request copies of charts. (See Chapter 3 for more on working with licensing boards.)
- Government officials. Officials gathering information on clients to determine qualification for certain government programs, such as social security disability, have the right to see clients' charts.

TIP

Myth or fact? Mental health practitioners may keep a separate set of personal notes about a case, which is not part of the "official" chart and is not subject to disclosure in the case of a subpoena.

(Continued)

> **FACT**
>
> False! A subpoena requires the submission of all information obtained about the case. Anything related to the case—written documentation, letters from the client, pictures, drawings, or treatment information from a previous practitioner—are considered part of the official chart and subject to disclosure (S. Feldman, 2001, p. 61).

Before the Client Arrives: Getting Your Files Ready

One of the most important things you can do as you begin your psychotherapy practice is to create a documentation process. The forms you create or select will have a strong and lasting impact on your success. Having clear, comprehensive, and cohesive charts for each client will focus your care at each step of the therapy process. Clear and thorough documentation will help you to:

- Establish sound business practices.
- Focus your care to be effective and efficient.
- Establish the best treatment plan for each client.
- Document your clients' progress.
- Evaluate your success.
- Problem-solve when therapy isn't working.

It is often helpful to assemble complete charts (all the forms needed for each client) to have on hand. This will help you avoid hunting for forms just before (or even during) your sessions.

The Clinical Documentation Sourcebook: The Complete Paperwork Resource for Your Mental Health Practice by Donald E. Wiger (2005) provides a wealth of ideas for new practitioners. It includes a CD-ROM of forms for you to adapt and use for your own practice and examples of well-reasoned documentation. If you would like to create your own forms, this chapter provides guidance regarding essential documentation elements.

Pretreatment Telephone Contact Form

This form collects basic information, including the potential client's name, contact information, referral source, presenting problem, and payment source. You can also use this form to begin to plan treatment. Is this a client you can help? Is this a client who is motivated? What about payment issues? Also include scheduling information (e.g., "Can only schedule for after 5 PM on Tuesdays and Thursdays").

Sample Form
Pretreatment Telephone Contact Form

Client name: _____
Phone: _____ OK to leave detailed message? ☐
Referred by: _____
Presenting problem:

_____

_____

Scheduling preferences: _____
Payment source: _____
Private pay: _____ Sliding scale: _____
Insurance company: _____ Policy number: _____
Mental health benefit: _____
Other information: _____
Appointment scheduled: _____
Or referred to: _____

Disclosure/Provider-Client Agreement

The disclosure agreement is a prepared statement of important information for your client. It should include a brief narrative about yourself, your licensure, and your approach to treatment. Include payment policies, your fees for different kinds of sessions or services, cancellation and no-show fees, and how you work with insurance and other third-party payers. Also include grievance procedures. State law may mandate giving information to your client about how to contact the licensing board regarding filing a complaint. This information should be given to the client in the first session. Ask the client to sign the disclosure form at the first session as an acknowledgment of understanding and informed consent to treatment, as well as an agreement to comply with payment policies. (See Chapter 5 for more on payment policies.) Keep the original for your records and give the client a copy.

Sample Form
Disclosure/Provider-Client Agreement

My education, training, and licensure:

My philosophy of mental health treatment:

My fees:

No-show/late cancellation fees:

My payment policy:

Grievance procedure:

Disclosure policy:

I have read and agree to the above policies.

Client Signature: _____ Date: _____

Release of Information

A signed release of information (ROI) form gives you permission to disclose or receive records and consult with previous or current providers. It may also give you permission to share certain information with family members, employers, or legal and social service providers. Be sure to check with your own state requirements for confidentiality of records and the scope and limit of ROIs. An ROI should include, at minimum:

- Client's name, birth date, or other identifying information
- To whom information may be released
- From whom you may seek information
- Specific information that may be released
- Date of effect (beginning and end date)
- Client's signature and date
- Your signature and date

It is often helpful to give a copy of the signed ROI to the client; keep the original in the chart. To get records from another provider, you may need to fax or mail a copy of the ROI to that provider.

History Form

Use this form at or before your first session. If time permits, mail it to clients before their first session and ask them to complete it and bring it to the first session. Alternatively, you can ask your clients to come 15 to 20 minutes early to their first appointment to complete it. This form should include the following:

- Identifying information, contact information, family information, and who to contact in case of emergency
- Developmental history, educational/vocational history, and psychotherapy history
- Current providers (i.e., primary care physician, medical specialists, or alternative medicine providers)
- Current medications (psychiatric and otherwise), and who is prescribing them
- Health history and information about current or past use of drugs, alcohol, tobacco, and caffeine

Ask if there are firearms in the home or otherwise accessible. Finally, ask clients about their expectations of therapy. Take time to briefly review this information at the beginning of your first session, and review more thoroughly after the session.

Sample Form
Client History Form

Please fill this form out to the best of your ability and bring it to your first session.

Name: _____ Phone number: _____

Address: _____

Emergency contact: _____

I was referred by: _____

Primary care provider: _____

My reason for seeking psychotherapy now:

_____

_____

What was your childhood like?

What is your educational history?

What is your vocational history?

Who is in your current family?

Have you participated in mental health treatment in the past?

If so, with whom?

What was the outcome?

Are you seeing any other mental health or medical providers currently?

(Continued)

Who?

For what conditions?

Are your currently on any medications (for mental health or medical conditions)?

What medications?

Who is prescribing them?

Is there any other health history you'd like to mention?

Do you use alcohol?

How much?

How often?

Do you have any concerns about your use?

Do you abuse any drugs or medications?

How often?

Do you have any concerns about your use?

Do you use caffeine?

How often?

How much?

Do you have any concerns about your use?

Do you use tobacco?

How often?

Have you tried to quit?

Are there firearms or other weapons in your home?

What are your goals for therapy?

What would you like to accomplish in our work together?

Is there anything else you'd like me to know before we begin?

Intake Form

In your first session with a client, you should accomplish two things simultaneously. You will want to establish rapport—a sense of compassionate concern for the client and his or her problems and hopefulness about his or her ability for recovery. You will also want to get a clear picture of what brings the client to therapy, the client's perception of the presenting problem, what the client has already tried, and how the client thinks you can help. To do this seamlessly, you must have a comprehensive yet uncomplicated intake form. Spend a few minutes making a genuine connection with your client. Let clients know that for your work with them to have the greatest chance of success, you need them to help you understand the presenting problem and possible causes. (See Chapter 9 for more on conducting a structured interview.)

The intake form should include the following, completed by the therapist:

- The client's statement of the problem
- The client's statement of his or her goals
- The client's statement of what he or she believes causes the problem
- A complete mental status exam
- A symptom checklist
- An initial diagnostic impression (*DSM:* Axis I–V)
- A case formulation and initial treatment plan

After the first session, review the intake carefully and add any notes that you did not write down during the session. Your diagnosis, case formulation, and treatment plan may change somewhat over the first few sessions, but writing down your initial impressions can help treatment to begin with a clear focus.

Sample Form
Intake Form

Client name: _____ Date of intake: _____

Client's statement of the problem:

Client's statement of goals of treatment:

Client's view of the causes of the problem:

Mental status exam:

    Appearance:

    Body movement:

    Speech:

    Affect:

    Mood:

    Perception:

    Thought content:

    Judgment:

    Insight:

    Other:

Symptoms:

    Mood:

(Continued)

Anxiety:

Somatic (sleep, eating, pain):

Interpersonal:

Cognitive:

Diagnostic impression:

Axis I:

Axis II:

Axis III:

Axis IV:

Axis V:

Case formulation:

Initial treatment plan:

Signature: _____ Date: _____

Mental Status Exam

A mental status exam is your written observations about the client's presentation. It should be a part of your initial intake and should be briefly included in your progress notes for each session. For thoroughness, a written checklist is best, though narrative may be added as needed to clarify your observations.

Symptom Checklist

A symptom checklist can help quickly summarize the client's symptoms. It may give you an indication of initial Axis I–V diagnoses using *DSM* criteria. Include biological, emotional, and behavioral symptoms of major diagnostic categories. For example, include physical signs of depression, such as excessive sleeping, insomnia, early awakening, appetite increase or decrease, slow speech or movements, and other somatic complaints. Emotional and behavioral symptoms may include anxiety, panic attacks, excessive counting, difficulty concentrating, hyperverbal speech, impulsivity, or auditory hallucinations.

Treatment Plan

Treatment plans contain identifying information, *DSM* Axis I–V diagnoses, time frame, and a signature with a date. Each treatment plan includes three essential elements: problems, goals, and objectives. A formal treatment plan provides specific direction to your psychotherapy sessions. It should be informed by your evaluation and assessment, client goals, and your clinical recommendations. It will allow you to assess progress in therapy, make alterations in treatment when indicated, and know when treatment is complete. It will also help to justify the expense of psychotherapy to your client and to any third-party payers. It is often helpful to give a copy to the client so that he or she fully understands the plan and is invested in the outcome.

The *problem statement* is a combination of the client's statement of the problem ("I can't focus at work and I'm not getting things done") and your clinical assessment of the problem ("ADHD [Attention-Deficit/Hyperactivity Disorder] symptoms of lack of concentration and follow-through are interfering with vocational functioning").

The *goal statement* is what the client would like to change; it is the answer to the question "If you woke up tomorrow and everything was fixed, what would you be doing?" It is the outcome you and your client will both be working toward, for example: "I will be able to focus at work at least 80% of the time and will complete my projects within the time frame expected." Ideally, you will establish a goal that is measurable. This helps to keep expectations realistic for both you and your client and helps you to notice natural end-points in your treatment.

The *objectives* are the specific steps that you and your client plan to accomplish to move from the problem behavior to the goal behavior. These, too, should be specific and measurable, for example:

Therapist will review ADHD symptom checklist with client to clarify diagnosis.

Client will discuss medication options with primary care or psychiatric provider and make a decision on whether to initiate medication trial.

Therapist will teach at least 5 strategies for improving concentration and follow-through.

Client will practice at least 3 of these strategies per week and record practice attempts on daily practice diary.

Your treatment plan will be a work in progress. You may achieve certain goals quickly and then move on to more advanced goals, or you may need to revise goals and objectives in response to slower-than-expected progress. New situations may arise with new problems and goals for the client. In any case, be sure to notice and celebrate when goals and objectives are met and to acknowledge when treatment is over. (See Chapter 9 for more on treatment planning.)

TIP

Review your treatment plan before each session. It will guide your interactions and help you to stay focused on the issues that brought your client to therapy. It is your best defense against meandering, "how was your week?" therapy!

Sample Form
Treatment Plan

Client name: _____ Date: _____
Diagnosis:

Axis I:

Axis II:

Axis III:

Axis IV:

Axis V:

Problem 1:

Goal 1:

Objective 1:

Problem 2:

Goal 2:

Objective 2:

Problem 3:

Goal 3:

Objective 3:

Therapist signature: _____ Date: _____

Client signature: _____ Date: _____

Progress Notes

The days of jotting down impressions on a yellow pad during and after a session are long gone. Progress notes are an integral part of your treatment and documentation. They will help you establish goals and objectives for each session, document your client's mental status and response to treatment, and document the interventions you make within the session. Effective progress notes will help you start the next session with a clear plan of action and help you know when treatment should end. Finally, progress notes can help you explain and defend your treatment if an adverse event occurs.

Progress notes should include the following:

- Client's full name
- Date (including year), time, place, and duration of session
- Any other persons present
- Brief mental status exam
- Current diagnosis and any diagnosis changes
- Current functional status (Global Assessment of Functioning [GAF]; ability to function at home, work, or school)
- Subjective observations: what the client says about himself or herself (e.g., "I'm feeling much better"; "I had an argument with my roommate")
- Objective observations: what you notice about the client (e.g., "Pressured speech and frequently jumping out of seat during session")
- Interventions: what you did to encourage changes in the client's understanding and behavior
- Response to treatment (e.g., "Client agreed to work on communication homework and appeared focused on improving relationship with family")
- Plan for next session or termination
- Therapist's signature (legible) and date (including year)

A clear, well-thought-out, and frequently used form will help you document all necessary information in a minimum of time. Checklists can be used in some parts of the note, but it is advisable to include a narrative section as well. Be willing to share your progress note form and contents with your client when asked and explain why these notes are important in focusing treatment.

Sample Form
Progress Note

Client name: _____ Date of session: _____
Any other persons present: _____
Mental status:

Current diagnosis:

    Diagnosis changes:

    GAF:

Current functional status:

    Home:

    Work/school:

    Interpersonal:

    Somatic/medical:

Subjective observations:

Objective observations:

Interventions:

Response to treatment:

Plan for next session or termination:

Signature: _____ Date: _____

Clinical Considerations

Should charting occur during the session or after? This can be a matter of personal style and preference; however, charting after a session may be a significant issue when you start to see client after client in succession. Under these circumstances, it is easy to fall behind in paperwork and forget details of the session. Some practitioners spend time catching up on paperwork on the weekends. Some practitioners do not like to take notes during the session. They want to maintain eye contact and give their full attention to the client. They believe that focusing on charting rather than the client is disruptive. Other practitioners believe that therapeutic continuity is important and want to capture the important elements of the session. Every practitioner needs to find a method that works with his or her own style of interaction.

We believe in a balanced approach. Explain to the client that, at times, you will be taking notes during the session to record the important elements of the session. This can be done in a way that still maintains rapport and eye contact. Most clients seem to be comfortable with this method and are very impressed that at the next appointment 3 weeks later, you have a detailed recollection of the previous session. This can provide continuity from session to session and gives the client a sense of confidence in your abilities because of your attention to detail. What good is it to give client homework and then not follow up on it the next session? Those moments are some of the most important moments of therapeutic progress and are the foundations for change. If you are waiting for the weekend to chart your last 15 clients, chances are you will miss this level of detail. Find your own style and do what works for you, but also be aware of how the simple act of charting may affect the client's outcome. Spend a moment to review the previous session's notes prior to entering the next session.

Your notes may eventually be seen by the client, other medical or legal professionals (with a release of information), licensing boards (in the event of an ethical complaint against you), or representatives of an insurance company paying for the treatment. It is imperative to have a legible, complete record of your work.

Termination Summary

Every episode of therapy has a natural end-point. Therapy should neither fade away nor continue indefinitely. Your interventions and the client's response during sessions will help you recognize when termination is appropriate. Certain clients need a few sessions to attain their goals and end therapy. You may agree at the outset that you will work together to solve problems quickly. Be sure to acknowledge the end of the treatment episode with the client. (See Chapter 11 for more on ending treatment.)

Other clients may have more complex treatment needs, and treatment may be ongoing over a series of treatment episodes. At the end of an episode of treatment, review the goals and objectives you have worked on to completion. Recommendations for further work can be helpful in the summary should the client return later. Giving your clients a copy of your treatment summary may help them to appreciate their progress. Knowledge of a plan for the future can help with relapse prevention as well. (See Chapter 11 for ideas on setting up a relapse prevention plan.)

Your treatment summary should include presenting problems, goals, objectives, and whether objectives were completed. It should include the start and end date of therapy, the client's diagnosis, and the GAF score at the start and end of treatment. It should also include your recommendations for follow-up (e.g., "Continue using daily lists and scheduling to keep on track at work"; "Return for follow-up if mood swings increase"). Include your signature and date.

TIP

A good termination summary that outlines the presenting problem, the client's accomplishments, some of the client's struggles, and what would be helpful to work on in the future can be very helpful should the client return after an extended absence.

Sample Form
Termination Summary

Client name: _____

Date of first session: _____ Date of last session: _____

Diagnosis: At start of treatment   At termination

    Axis I:

    Axis II:

    Axis III:

    Axis IV:

    Axis V:

Presenting problems:

Goals:

Interventions:

Outcomes:

Recommendations for follow-up:

Signature: _____ Date: _____

Summing Up

Proper chart documentation is necessary for record keeping purposes, and it serves an important role in organizing the therapist's thoughts and plans for treatment and keeping the work with the client focused. It also serves an important liability role so that in the case of an adverse event, your actions and rationale for the type of treatment you chose are well documented. Develop the forms you need and assemble a complete documentation system early in your psychotherapy career.

EXERCISES

1. What forms do you have in a complete chart? Why do you use each one? Are there forms in this chapter that you do not use? Share your chart forms with a colleague and discuss the pros and cons of each.
2. Look at your charts from the viewpoint of another practitioner looking at them for the first time.
   - Is everything adequately documented?
   - Could another practitioner understand what you are doing with this client and why you are doing it, just by reading the chart?
   - Does your progress note reflect your assessment and plan for the client, or is it just a brief record of what happened to the client this week?
3. What resources have you found useful in developing forms? Books? Software? Other therapists? Designing them yourself? How often do you revise forms?
4. Design and explain a complete treatment note format, using information from this chapter.
5. Do you like to chart during sessions or afterward? Why?
6. Look at your personal style of record keeping and examine how you can balance gathering information, maintaining rapport, and recording the information in an efficient fashion.

Resources

Wiger, D. E. (1998). *The psychotherapy documentation primer.* New York: Wiley.

Wiger, D. E. (2005). *The clinical documentation sourcebook: The complete paperwork resource for your mental health practice* (3rd ed.). Hoboken, NJ: Wiley.

5

Establishing Your Practice

What You Will Learn
- How to create a unique professional identity
- How to develop and market clinical specialties
- How to develop your fee schedule
- How to provide value to clients who pay for therapy out of pocket
- How to respond to missed appointments
- The importance of peer consultation
- How to generate referrals from physicians, educational presentations, advertising, and your web site
- How health care costs and insurance work
- The three components of medical necessity
- How to demonstrate medical necessity to an insurer
- Tips for doing effective utilization review with insurers
- Definitions of health insurance terms
- How health insurance companies calculate reimbursement rates
- How to manage your time effectively
- The four elements of a professional office space
- Trends on the horizon
- The use of technology in professional practice

A psychotherapy practice is a business. Whether you open a private practice, join a group practice, or work for an agency or institution, you will need to use your skills to generate value to the purchasers of your services. Ideally, the purchasers of your services are satisfied and tell others about the good work you do.

Other practitioners will be competing with you for clients and fees. It is important to create a unique professional identity that accurately communicates exactly what you offer to clients.

Creating a Professional Identity

Review your responses to the exercises in Chapter 1. What is your unique practice style? What value do you offer your clients? Are you a recognized expert in any particular area? Do you provide a treatment or have an area of expertise that no one else has in your location? If so, these may be the building blocks to creating your professional identity and a way to distinguish yourself from the crowd. Spend time researching other practitioners in your community (or the community in which you wish to practice). What do they offer? How do they package their services to appeal to potential clients? What areas of practice might meet an unfulfilled need?

Your professional identity includes these factors:

- Your discipline and licensure
- Specific service modalities you provide (individual, group, family, etc.)
- Your expertise in specific therapies you provide (cognitive-behavioral therapy, eye movement desensitization and reprocessing, solution-focused therapy, etc.) and the diagnoses you treat (eating disorders, chronic pain, depression, etc.)
- Your connection to the community (memberships and active participation in community organizations, religious or spiritual groups, schools, etc.)
- Your connection to purchasers of services (clients, insurance plans, agencies, etc.)
- Your professional connection to other health care practitioners: family practice physicians, psychiatrists, and other psychotherapists
- The image you project with your business cards and stationery
- Your web site

Your professional identity is communicated to others through your office, your business cards, your brochures, your advertising—anything that tells potential clients and purchasers about you and your services. In this chapter, we discuss how these elements will help you to build your practice.

Developing Specialties

As you develop your practice, you may find yourself especially drawn to specific treatment methods. If you choose to develop specialties, be sure to get adequate training before trying a new technique with a client. For example, just reading a book about eye movement desensitization and reprocessing (EMDR) is not going to give you the skills needed to use this method. Specific training programs of various levels are required to develop expertise.

Hypnosis is another specialty that requires advanced training. It can be helpful for a number of client problems. Other body-centered methods, such as thought-field therapy and graduated exposure, are best used after thorough training. Mindfulness-based psychotherapies are becoming more popular, and training is becoming more widely available. Dialectical behavior therapy (Linehan, 1993a, 1993b) can be useful after thorough training and ongoing case consultations.

One of our colleagues (T. C. Portman, personal communication, November 29, 2007) has the following recommendations when applying any specific therapeutic technique.

- *Do not use any technique that you cannot consciously connect to an approach.* For instance, EMDR is an approach to working with clients who have experienced trauma. A technique used without being connected to an approach is an empty technique, and there is a danger that it may be used inappropriately.
- *Have a rationale for why it should help.* For example, EMDR pairs cognitive and psychophysiological awareness with the traumatic image and stimulates the processing of the trauma so it can be resolved.
- *Be able to believe in the theory supporting the rationale.* The symptoms of hyperarousal and nightmares are the mind/body's ineffective attempts to resolve the stuck trauma. The eye movements in EMDR activate the processing of the trauma that has been stuck and brings it to its processing conclusion. By doing so, the connection between the image, emotions, and physiological reaction to the trauma is changed and symptoms are reduced.

- *Understand the overarching philosophy behind the theory.* The philosophy behind EMDR is that there is plasticity in the brain and that change is possible using this specific technique.

Understanding the rationale, theory, and philosophy behind a technique guides your actions so that you use the technique in appropriate situations.

Once you have adequate training and a source for advanced supervision when needed, think about how to package your specialty to clients and to insurance companies and other potential payers. You may want to create a one-page summary of your experience, training, and certifications, as well as your rationale for whom it may help, how it is initiated, and the treatment's potential benefits. Avoid making a specialty a "one size fits all" proposition; no one treatment is likely to be the best therapy for every client who walks through your door. How you package yourself to insurers can make a difference. Insurers may not need to add another general practitioner to their panel. If you can demonstrate that you can help them with some of their high-cost client diagnoses, such as eating disorders, chronic pain, or personality disorders, you can make yourself more attractive in a competitive market and increase the likelihood of being admitted to their panel.

Depending on the specialty, consider developing handouts and homework sheets to use with clients. This will help to extend the therapy into your clients' daily lives. Having handouts readily available can make it much easier to educate your clients about the therapy's benefits. (See Chapter 16 for more on developing specialties.)

What Will You Charge?

Your fees will depend on several factors. Understanding how much your competitors (other psychotherapists) charge for similar services can give you a rough estimate of what you can charge. In addition, look at your level of experience in the field and in the community. If you are just starting your practice, you will most likely charge less than those already established in the community. If you provide a service that no one else provides, you may be able to charge more than the prevailing rates. Be aware that psychotherapy rates may vary depending on regional differences, rural versus city practices, insurance reimbursements, and publicly funded services available.

Your fee schedule should include charges for any of the following services you provide:

- Initial evaluation
- Individual psychotherapy
- Family or couples psychotherapy
- Group psychotherapy
- No-show and late cancellation fees
- Nonclinical documentation fees (e.g., preparing letters or filling out forms for schools, employers, or court proceedings)
- Consultation fees (e.g., presenting educational programs, providing testimony in court, or providing extensive education or support for families of clients)

Your fees should be spelled out clearly to potential clients, in writing, before services begin, usually in your consent for treatment form. You may choose to offer a sliding fee scale based on client or family resources for low-income clients, or you may offer a discount for those paying you directly at the time of service. Some practitioners also provide a certain percentage of low-cost or pro bono work as a way of giving back to the community and providing access to services that some populations may not have.

When Your Client Pays Out of Pocket: Providing Value

Insurance payment for services can reduce the client's motivation to participate fully in treatment planning or to get value out of each session (more about this later in the chapter). This is not true, however, for clients who pay you out of pocket. These clients want value for their money. They may comparison-shop for psychotherapy services, as one might shop around for a good lawyer or doctor. They may rely on word-of-mouth reputation, hourly rates, and treatment methods. They are more likely to demand a thorough but efficient evaluation, clear treatment planning, and favorable outcomes from therapy; they will not want to waste their money on needlessly long, expensive, and ineffective treatment.

You can provide value to clients by demonstrating that you can provide cost-effective treatment. Be sure to involve your client in treatment planning, and give a realistic estimate of the amount of time and money a particular course of treatment is likely to take. (See Chapter 9 for more on discussing treatment plans with clients.) Be sure to review your treatment plan and the client's progress before each session, and review progress with your client frequently. After each session, your client should be able to walk out the door with a new insight or skill and have a tangible sense of where he or she is in relation to the plan that you have developed. After the session, review progress toward completion of the treatment plan and begin to plan the next session. Clients who achieve resolution of their presenting problems in an efficient way are likely to recommend you to other potential clients.

What about Missed Appointments?

Every therapist must struggle with the issue of missed or late-cancelled appointments. If a client misses an appointment, you have lost the fees you would have earned with this client or another who might have been scheduled. Time is a finite resource. Ask other local practitioners how they handle no-shows and late cancellations. You may want to charge a flat fee for any missed appointment, or you might decide to make exceptions for truly unavoidable situations (e.g., having to take a sick child to the doctor).

Some practitioners allow one excusable absence per episode of treatment. When missing sessions becomes habitual, it is not only a matter of finances but can also involve other therapeutic issues, such as compliance, lack of motivation or commitment, or even the avoidance of facing difficult material. Many clients are reluctant to confront a practitioner if something in their treatment is not going well. They often cancel, miss appointments, or just seem to fade away with no closure for the practitioner or the client. It can be helpful to find out why a client is missing appointments. You may uncover a "therapeutic hump" or barrier that the client is having that prevents him or her from making clinical progress. This can be a pattern for certain clients: Every time they start to make progress, they stop therapy. Discussions about missed appointments may turn out to be an important clinical moment. You will never know if you do not ask!

Developing Peer Consultation

As you establish your practice and develop a professional identity, it will be important to develop consistent and reliable peer consultation. The knowledge necessary to practice in the mental health field is both broad and deep and can take a lifetime to accumulate. Getting insights and intervention recommendations from other practitioners is not only helpful, it is often necessary. Other practitioners will see things that you do not. Consultation with other knowledgeable practitioners makes you a better therapist. If you are working in an agency or a group practice, this kind of consultation may be built into the system. It is helpful to get to know professionals of various disciplines to establish informal mutual consultation relationships. Use every opportunity for consultation to test and improve your clinical insight and expertise.

If you are starting out in private practice, it can be difficult to establish helpful peer consultation. New practitioners often pay an experienced provider to meet with them weekly or monthly to review cases and discuss personal issues that arise in the course of a clinical practice. You may also want to talk with other providers in your community about beginning or joining an established peer consultation group. These groups typically have three to eight therapists who meet on a regular basis. Such groups establish their own norms and processes for consulting. Each provider may have the opportunity to present one or more cases and solicit feedback from the group. Peer groups may also form around particular treatment methods to further their members' education and consult on challenges in applying the treatment.

Informal peer consultation arrangements are also frequent. If you know a few fellow therapists, ask them if you can consult with them occasionally about tough cases, and offer to be available to them as well. These consultations are especially useful for checking out your response to client emergencies.

In all these settings, client confidentiality must be maintained. Client names should not be used, and all members of the consultation group or dyad must agree to keep client information confidential. Even client situations should not be discussed outside the peer consultation format, as they may inadvertently lead to client identification.

Generating Referrals

If you want your practice to become financially successful, you will need to think carefully about how to generate referrals. How will your potential clients learn about you? If you are on insurance panels, you may get referrals from them. If you have an opportunity to get to know the referring staff at these insurance plans, do so. It will be easier for them to refer a client to you if they know a bit about your personal style, as well as your professional credentials.

Getting Referrals from Physicians

Many psychotherapists establish relationships with local primary care physicians and psychiatrists. Physicians often want to refer patients for psychotherapy, and many troubled clients go to their primary care provider first. This is often a good plan, as the physician can rule in or out medical causes for the problem and establish any medical treatment needed. (See Chapter 15 for more on medical causes of psychological symptoms.) Physicians will be more likely to refer patients to you if:

- They have met you in person.
- They know about your credentials, specialties, and insurance panels.
- They have had positive experiences in consulting with you.
- They hear positive things about you from their colleagues.
- They have your business cards or brochures on hand.
- You are accessible and coordinate treatment with them.

Take part in any networking opportunities you may have to meet and get to know local physicians. Community groups, lectures, faith communities, and community health activities can all be points of contact. Without being pushy, introduce yourself, your credentials, your specialties, and the fact that you are looking for new clients. Always have business cards on hand, and offer to meet with your contacts or consult with them if it seems appropriate. Keep a list of physicians you have met and cultivated.

When you get a referral, a brief note of thanks to the physician will be helpful in maintaining the relationship.

Getting Referrals from Educational Presentations

Another potential referral source is through giving educational presentations to community groups. Work up a few topics on which you can give a short presentation; develop handouts and perhaps even a PowerPoint presentation you can use. Offer to give a short, informational program to any appropriate groups you know. You can do this with:

- Rotary or other service clubs
- YMCA/YWCA groups
- Churches
- Health clubs
- Community food cooperative groups
- School or parent groups
- Professional organizations

Choose topics that relate somewhat to your practice, but do not make your practice the focal point. You can have brochures or business cards available after the presentation; some of the participants are likely to pick one up and call you to schedule an appointment.

An informative newsletter that you send out periodically to your mailing list of professional contacts, potential clients, and referral sources can be a powerful way to build your practice. According to Laurie Cope Grand (2002, p. 4), author of *The Therapist's Newsletter Kit*, a newsletter enables you to:

- Reach out to new potential clients and referral sources
- Stay in touch with current and past clients
- Bring back past clients
- Educate people about your area of specialization
- Provide added value to your counseling services
- Showcase your knowledge
- Highlight your skills
- Enhance your credibility
- Stimulate referrals

- Inform readers of facts they may not have known
- Keep you in the front of people's minds
- Publicize your practice to the media
- Network with community businesses and organizations
- Tie in with information on your web site

Cope Grand's (2002b) book comes with a CD-ROM of sample newsletters that you can easily personalize and send out. It also offers plenty of ideas for how you might create your own content for your newsletters. Your newsletter can also be part of your educational presentation materials, providing an ongoing reminder for participants of your practice and expertise.

Getting Referrals from Advertising

One other common practice-building activity is advertising. Look at whether and how other psychotherapists in your community advertise. A prominent advertisement in the local phone book can be a good investment. You can put your business card or brochure on community bulletin boards. Or you can buy small, tasteful ads in local newspapers or magazines.

Practitioners in the mental health field often avoid the concept of marketing. There is a sense that marketing is acceptable for a product but not for mental health counseling. Some practitioners believe that one should not need to promote oneself, and that to do so is actually contraindicated for a legitimate practitioner.

Linda L. Lawless (1997, pp. 76–77), MA, author of *How to Build and Market Your Mental Health Practice*, lists five common myths about marketing a mental health practice:

> *Myth 1*: There is one magic marketing solution.
> Most people not involved in marketing mistakenly award it some magic or rainmaker mythology. The truth is that there is no one answer to marketing. Answers vary from person to person and region to region. The only magic is good planning and perseverance.
>
> *Myth 2*: I don't need to get involved in marketing since my practice is currently full.
> It is easy to feel complacent and safe when things are going well. It's generally when things take a turn for the worse that people wake up. Denial in the mental health profession is rampant. Many believe that their reputation or degree will always keep them successful. In a time of rapid change and ever-increasing competition, patient loyalty and many letters after your name will not ensure future success.

Myth 3: Marketing requires a compromise of one's ethics and integrity.

Marketing is the act of educating others about what you do. Simply telling your neighbor what you do is marketing. When you are proud of your work, you enjoy telling others about it. If your marketing is authentic and honest, you will not compromise your ethics.

Myth 4: I only need to market when I start something new or when my practice caseload gets low.

Marketing needs to be a way of life. If it is a one-shot effort, there will be a one-shot response. To avoid wide swings in referrals, marketing must be done often. Referrals you have today may be bought up or leave the marketplace. Good marketing, like the cultivation of a garden, needs to be done regularly to maintain peak productivity.

Myth 5: Word-of-mouth marketing about my expertise and training will assure success.

You can be the best therapist in the world, but if no one knows about you except the few people you have served, your professional future is insecure. With more people looking to their health insurance to pay for mental illness, there are fewer out-of-pocket resources. Successful practitioners must continue to explore and develop market resources beyond word of mouth.

How to Build and Market Your Mental Health Practice (Lawless, 1997) contains a wealth of practical, detailed information and worksheets to help you develop an effective marketing plan.

Getting Referrals through Your Web Site

In this technological age, it is almost a necessity to have a web site. It can be a good opportunity for potential clients to read your biography, see a photograph of you, and get an idea about how you practice. As a practitioner, you are selling your time, but there is only so much time in a day. A web site works for you 24 hours a day and is a way of communicating with prospective clients. Having a web site gives you a certain amount of credibility. Many people now use the Internet rather than conventional printed media. Having an electronic newsletter that goes out to interested individuals and organizations can keep your name prominent and help to establish your professional identity. (See the resource section for ideas on developing a newsletter.)

Working with Insurance Companies

Health insurance is a major source for psychotherapy reimbursement. Some therapists are able to thrive in an all-private-pay practice, but most need to work with insurance companies for a large portion of their income. It is popular in some circles to criticize and bemoan the insurance industry (while happily accepting insurance payments), but it is worth your time to learn and understand how health care insurance works. We hear negative comments from practitioners about managed care, but like it or not, it is probably here to stay. For many employers, the concern is that unmanaged coverage leads to treatment driven by practitioner preferences for vague and unmeasurable goals (Schwartz & Weiner, 2003). We have found that the most reasonable course is a check-and-balance system that takes into account the client's expressed need and the practitioner's proposed treatment plan. Both need to conform to the coverage limits and meet the criteria of medical necessity.

A good relationship with health insurance companies can increase your income by providing a steady flow of referrals.

Understanding Health Care Costs and Insurance

Health care is a major expense in society, and one that is increasing each year. As a psychotherapist, you are a health care provider. If you diagnose disorders and provide treatment for these disorders, you are participating in the health care industry. However, some practitioners see themselves as independent and not a part of this system; these therapists should probably rely on an all-cash practice. As the cost of health care increases, everyone has a stake in keeping costs down while keeping quality of care high. Most employers are requiring higher contributions from employees for the cost of health insurance. If you have seen the cost of your own health insurance rise each year, you know all too well that we must find more efficient ways to manage health care costs.

Health insurance is provided in three major categories:

- Government programs (such as Medicare, Medicaid, and similar programs)—funded by the taxes we all pay.
- For-profit insurance companies—funded through premiums paid by purchasers. Most of this money is paid out for medical services, but some is paid to stockholders.
- Not-for-profit insurance companies—funded through premiums paid by purchasers. Most of this money is paid out for medical services, but any extra is reinvested into the company in the form of more staff, buildings, or equipment.

The purpose of health care insurance is similar to the purpose of auto insurance. You pay your auto insurance premium every month. Most of the time, you get nothing back from the company. However, if you do have an auto accident, your insurance will pay out money to cover your losses, often much more than you have paid in premiums. If everyone had an expensive accident every year, the cost of the insurance would become too high for anyone to purchase. Insurance is predicated on the fact that most people will pay in more than they get out. In cases where there is a catastrophic event, those insured are protected from severe losses.

Health care insurance companies can stay solvent only if they are able to keep costs lower than income. Because health care costs vary based on many factors, the risk involved is significant. Health care insurers are stewards of the premiums that each member pays. They have a fiduciary responsibility to members to use these dollars carefully to keep the cost of insurance from rising too quickly.

Most health care insurance in the United States (at this time) is purchased by employers for the benefit of their employees. When a company purchases health insurance, it enters into a contract with the insurance provider. This contract states how much money the company will pay the insurer and what benefits will be paid out for health care expenses. These benefits are spelled out in detail in the contract, and the insurer has a responsibility to pay out only these benefits. For example, if the contract specifies that the insurer will pay for inpatient treatment in a hospital, but not on a luxury yacht, the insurer will not cover treatment on a yacht. Paying for services that are not specified in the contract would be a breach of the contract and would ultimately increase the cost of the insurance beyond what the employer can pay. Employers pay a large amount of the employee's premium. When employees use a lot of health care services, the company's rates go up the following year. In the interest of keeping costs down, many companies have a focus on wellness and prevention. The focus on medical necessity came about as a result of employer concerns about rising health care costs.

What Is Medical Necessity?

Health insurance pays for only "medically necessary" treatment of medical conditions. Health insurance contracts generally have a technical definition of medical necessity in their texts; these may differ between companies. In general, though, medical necessity involves:

- A medical disorder (either diagnosed or suspected) that impairs functioning (health, social, vocational, or school)
- A recognized treatment (not experimental) that has a likelihood of reducing symptoms or improving functioning

If you are planning to seek reimbursement from health insurance for your clients' behavioral health care, you will invariably run into this concept. Health plans will reimburse practitioners only for treatment that they consider medically necessary. In physical medicine there are usually specific physiological markers such as blood tests or scans to substantiate a diagnosis. In the mental health field the diagnosis is often more subjective and relies on the practitioner's skill in gathering clinical information and formulating a diagnosis. The formulation of what the problem is and how to treat it can be influenced greatly by the practitioner's orientation and point of view. (See "A Trip to the Therapist's Couch" in Chapter 1.) Sometimes the presence of a mental health benefit can influence the diagnosis and treatment plan.

Determining medical necessity for mental health care involves three components.

Establishing the Presence of a Mental Illness

To meet medical necessity, the client needs to be diagnosed with an Axis I diagnosis as described in the current edition of the *DSM*. Life circumstance problems (known as V-codes) would not qualify. In addition, some insurers have other exclusions, such as diagnoses in the Paraphilia section of the *DSM*. A client can be in a certain level of distress, need counseling, but not have a diagnosable problem. As an example, let's look at someone who is generally functioning well but is under a lot of stress at work. There are no serious vegetative signs. This client wants some help with decision making and determining a career path. A care manager would likely not see this situation as medically necessary. This is a life circumstance problem (V-code) and not a mental illness. Therefore, it would not be covered under the behavioral health benefit.

Treatment Conforms to Established General Principles

Treatment should be performed by a licensed mental health prac-titioner and delivered in a face-to-face session. At this point in time, health insurance does not cover telephone or Internet counseling. Treatment should also follow the ethical standards of the major mental health professional organizations. Methods used would be generally accepted as legitimate approaches and would not be considered experimental.

The Level of Treatment Intensity Should Match the Severity of Illness

For example, a practitioner requests to see a client diagnosed with an Adjustment Disorder every week for the next 2 years. A case manager reviewing this request would seriously question the necessity of such an intense level of treatment for this type of dis-order. He or she would not consider that frequency of treatment medically necessary and would suggest instead an 8- to 12-session treatment episode, with a review upon conclusion of those ses-sions. (See Chapter 9 for more on treatment planning.)

Many practitioners have a difficult time understanding the concept of medical necessity. They think that if a client has a therapeutic need, it must be medically necessary to treat it. This may not be the case, however, in the eyes of managed care and insurance coverage. Managed care and the concept of medical necessity came about because of rising behavioral health care costs and employers (who are paying a great deal of those health care costs) asking what they are paying for. As a result, insurers established medical necessity to determine the different shades of need as a way to cover some and exclude others. Many practition-ers see this as a way of undertreating clients to save money, while employers are concerned that without specific medical necessity criteria practitioner preferences can lead to overtreatment based on vague and unmeasurable goals (Schwartz & Weiner, 2003). This invariably sets up some level of conflict. It is the clinician's or utilization reviewer's job to establish some sense of balance based on the coverage criteria.

Sabin and Daniels (1994) describe three models for thinking about medical necessity that are good examples of the various shades of client need. Each model creates a different view of what should be covered and why. Most practitioners' thinking about why their treatment should be covered falls into one of these three categories.

The welfare model sees psychological distress as the primary reason for insurance coverage. In this view, the presence of distress alone, no matter what the etiology, justifies the treatment even if it is not the result of a mental illness. If suffering occurs because of people's circumstances and they are not able to overcome it, they should be able to access health insurance for help.

The capability model shares much of the philosophy of the welfare model but uses *DSM* criteria for diagnosing a mental disorder, although in a very broad way, to justify coverage. It does not require that the symptom be a result of a mental disorder, but it must cause "impairment in one or more areas of functioning" (Sabin & Daniels, 1994, pp. 10–11). In this view, health care coverage should be used to help those with some diminished capability, no matter what the cause. For example, in this model, a person who is very shy and having trouble interacting with others should be able to use his or her health care coverage for this problem even though shyness is not considered an illness.

Health care coverage uses what Sabin and Daniels (1994) calls the *normal function model*, which states that "healthcare coverage should be restricted to disadvantages caused by disease and disability unless society explicitly decides to use it to mitigate other forms of disadvantage as well" (Sabin & Daniels, 1994, p. 10). This model makes distinctions between treating a mental illness and enhancing human capabilities, such as treating the shy person for social interaction difficulties. The focus of this model is to restore and maintain function due to a diagnosable mental health problem.

According to Schwartz and Weiner (2003), behavioral health care clinicians and care managers view the purpose of psychological treatment in an insurance environment with the following in mind:

- To remove impediments to usual coping activities
- To help individuals get unstuck so that they can resume the process of development and growth

Clinical and utilization reviewers often function in an educational capacity to help practitioners manage care well. This is done by encouraging changes in practitioner practice patterns and offering clinical consultation in the early stages of treatment or at critical junctures. Knowledge of these parameters can help the private practice therapist understand the ground rules so that the experience is a better one for all.

Demonstrating Medical Necessity

When you are working with an insurance plan that pays for mental health treatment, it is important that you demonstrate that medical necessity criteria have been met. The more clearly and concisely you communicate this, the easier it will be to get authorization and payment.

Joseph, a psychotherapist, gets a phone call from a potential client, Steve. Steve says he is feeling depressed, his wife is angry with him all the time, and he has racing thoughts that keep him from getting to sleep at night. Joseph needs to call Steve's health insurance company to get preauthorization for services. He calls, and after giving identifying information, he says, "Steve has symptoms of dysthymia, major depression, or possibly Bipolar Disorder (*DSM* 300.4, 296.2, or 296.80). These symptoms are causing decreased functioning in terms of health (sleep Impairment) and socially (relationship with wife). I'd like to do an evaluation to determine the most appropriate diagnosis and to determine a treatment plan. The treatment plan will most likely include an evaluation by a physician for consideration of medications, behavioral changes (sleep hygiene, increased exercise, improved communication with his wife), and cognitive interventions (identify thoughts that may be contributing to Steve's symptoms and generate more effective thinking patterns). The goal will be to reduce symptoms of depression, conflict with his wife, and sleep impairment, and to improve his functioning in terms of health and social relationships."

Joseph is authorized for four sessions with Steve. After the third session, he sends in the following written request for more sessions:

- *Diagnosis:* Major Depressive Disorder, single episode, moderate (296.22)

- *Symptoms:* depressed mood, insomnia, fatigue, difficulty concentrating, and anhedonia
- *GAF:* 56
- *Problem:* depressed mood (as evidenced by Beck Depression Inventory score)
- *Goal:* improve mood (as evidenced by improvement in Beck Depression Inventory score)
- *Intervention:* identify thought patterns that contribute to depressed mood, teach cognitive-behavioral skills for replacing these with more effective thought patterns, and teach improved communication skills.
- *Problem:* insomnia, fatigue, difficulty concentrating
- *Goal:* improve sleep, energy, and concentration
- *Intervention:* encourage medication compliance, introduce behavioral strategies for improved sleep, encourage regular exercise
- *Plan:* individual psychotherapy for eight more sessions; consider adding marital therapy when depression symptoms stabilize.

The insurance plan reviewer authorizes eight more sessions, for a total of 12, and reminds Joseph that marital therapy is not a covered service under Steve's plan.

Completing a thorough evaluation and treatment plan at the start of treatment can ease the process of requesting more sessions. This therapist was able to identify the components of medical necessity and communicate them clearly and concisely to the insurance company. He was also able to communicate his treatment plan clearly to his client and to provide effective, efficient psychotherapy.

How to Do Utilization Review with Insurance Companies

The previous example demonstrates the basics of utilization review, which occurs whenever you request authorization for services. By approaching the insurance plan representative with a straightforward assessment, treatment plan, and realistic request, you will be able to develop mutually respectful relationships with those who can authorize payment for care. A good reputation with care managers will help you help your clients get the care they need. Even though you may have disagreements with them at times, it is important to establish mutual respect by developing a shared rapport based on the clinical issue at hand. If you demonstrate competence and focused treatment, you will be more likely to get your requests for further sessions approved.

Tips for Doing Effective Utilization Review

- Know the medical necessity criteria and coverage limitations of the health insurance plan. Do not ask for things that you know are not covered.
- Understand that care managers cannot create a benefit that does not exist (e.g., more sessions than are specified in the insurance contract, coverage for an excluded diagnosis, coverage for experimental treatments).
- Understand that care managers want to authorize coverage; your job is to provide the information that can justify it.
- Provide the proper documentation requested within the time frame allotted.
- Provide documentation in an easily readable format (typed or very neat handwriting, large enough font). Care managers may read hundreds of requests a month; a document that is hard to read is less likely to be favorably received.
- Provide accurate diagnoses and GAF scores, and be prepared to explain them clearly.
- Provide a treatment plan that logically relates to the diagnosis and specific symptoms and functional impairments. There should also be a likelihood that this plan is achievable.
- Be open to feedback and suggestions from care managers; they want you to be successful with your clients, and may have a perspective that will help you be more effective.

A Few of the Most Common Problems with Reauthorization Requests

- Elements of the report are not consistent. There are lists of debilitating symptoms, yet the functional impairments are very mild and the GAF score indicates a high level of functioning.
- The treatment plan does not match the diagnosis.

- Symptoms seem to be worsening over time, rather than improving.
- Each request is exactly the same as the previous ones, with no indication of either progress or a change in treatment strategy to improve outcome.
- There is too little (or occasionally too much) detail in the treatment plan.
- The treatment interventions are not specific (e.g., "cognitive-behavior therapy" rather than "Identify and modify cognitions that contribute to hopelessness").

Definition of Health Insurance Terms

Appeal: The procedure for appealing a coverage decision is included with a denied referral in case the member or provider believes that it was denied incorrectly. Either party has the right to send in a written request with evidence documenting why he or she believes the service should be covered. The appeal is usually reviewed by a psychologist or psychiatrist within the same organization. If the client or practitioner still feels that the service should not be denied, he or she can often make an appeal to the next level, an independent assessment outside the health plan. There is a specific window of opportunity to do this, usually up to 90 days. After this time the denial stands and the parties lose their right to appeal. This process may be subject to state and federal laws.

Benefit: The benefit is the number of outpatient therapy sessions or days in the psychiatric hospital that a member has access to as a result of paying a monthly premium.

Care Manager or Case Manager: This is a clinician whose responsibility is to work with the contracted providers. Care managers can authorize or deny service, do utilization review, and provide care coordination.

Claim: When practitioners bill an insurance company for services they have rendered to a health plan member, they are said to submit a claim. A claim involves the date of service, the type of service, a diagnosis, the amount billed, and all of the pertinent demographic data of the practitioner. A claim can be paid, suspended, or denied. If a claim is paid, the health plan will send the practitioner a check for the services rendered minus any copays or coinsurance. Claim suspension is usually the result of inaccuracy in the paperwork related to the claim; the claim will be held in processing until the problem is resolved. A denied claim is not paid, and the practitioner and client receive an "Explanation of Benefits" explaining why. Most claims are now submitted electronically, which can speed up the payment process.

Coinsurance: The amount, expressed in a percentage, that a health plan will cover for a particular service is the coinsurance. For example, 80% coinsurance means that the health plan pays that amount and the client pays the remaining 20% of charges.

Copay: The amount that a client pays a practitioner for the client's portion of the session is the copay. For example, a practitioner is contracted with the health plan to provide counseling services at $80 per hour. The client has a $20 copay, so he pays the practitioner that amount at the time of service and the health plan pays the practitioner the remaining $60. The type of plan the employer buys for employees determines the amount of the copay. The greater the cost borne by the employee, the less costly the insurance plan is likely to be in the form of monthly premiums.

Contracted provider: This refers to a practitioner who has a written contract with the health plan to provide a specific service, such as mental health counseling.

Covered service: This is the type of service that a health plan will reimburse a practitioner for providing. It can be diagnostically specific, such as covering counseling for depression but not for V-codes; or it can be modality specific, such as not covering marital therapy. It involves the type of service, such as paying for inpatient psychiatric care but not for long-term residential treatment.

Deductible: The deductible is the charge that a client needs to incur before health insurance starts to pay. For example, a member has a $250 deductible. This means that she has to incur $250 of direct costs before the health plan starts to pay.

Explanation of benefits: An EOB is a document sent by the health plan to both practitioners and members upon submission of a claim explaining the type of service and what was paid.

Premium: The premium is the amount a member of the health plan (or his or her employer) pays every month to remain active with the health plan. Paying this amount allows members to access their benefits.

Referral or authorization: Most managed care plans require that members get a referral prior to using the service. The referral authorizes a specific number of counseling sessions for a specific length of time. Sessions done outside this time period or more than the authorized number of sessions will be denied.

Utilization review: To request for more outpatient therapy sessions beyond the originally contracted number, practitioners must undergo a utilization review process. The written request usually includes a 5-Axis diagnosis, the presenting problem and symptomatology, a specific proposed treatment plan, and a specific number of sessions requested. This is reviewed by the health plan care or case manager or utilization review staff.

How Health Insurance Companies Calculate Reimbursement Rates

Prior to 1992, health care practitioner insurance payments were based on the "usual and customary fees." This can vary quite a bit throughout the country. The federal government, through the Medicare program, set up a payment system called the Resource-Based Relative Value Scale (RBRVS) to set some national standards. However, the cost of doing business is different in a large city compared to a sparsely populated rural area. The system needed to take regional variations into account as well as the resources needed to provide the service. The value is based on the actual service performed, the cost of providing the service, and the cost of professional liability insurance. Originally, RBRVS was used for physician services, but is now widely used for behavioral health practitioners as well.

How the Resource-Based Relative Value Scale Works

There is a formula for the three components of RBRVS (actual service performed, the cost of providing the service, and the cost of professional liability insurance) that results in a Relative Value Unit (RVU) associated with each current procedural terminology (CPT) code. Some typical behavioral health CPT codes are:

- 90801: Psychiatric diagnostic interview examination
- 90806: Individual psychotherapy, insight-oriented, behavior modifying and/or supportive, in an office or outpatient facility, approximately 45 to 50 minutes face to face with the patient

- 90847: Family psychotherapy (conjoint psychotherapy) with the patient present

Each of these CPT codes is put through the formula and assigned an RVU (based on 2007 values), such as:

- 90801: 3.79
- 90806: 2.35
- 90847: 2.81

The RVU for a 90801 is greater than the RVU for a 90806 because an intake session involves seeing the client and writing up a report, which takes more time. There is also a different skill set involved in doing a diagnostic evaluation compared to a standard 50-minute psychotherapy session. A 90806 usually involves a single client. Couples counseling or family therapy involves two or more people. This is more complex than individual therapy and requires a different set of skills, so the RVU is higher. Increased value usually translates into a higher reimbursement rate. Another element of the reimbursement formula is what is called a conversion factor. A conversion factor is a dollar amount, used to calculate the rate of reimbursement.

$$RVU \times conversion\ factor = rate\ of\ reimbursement$$

Imagine that you are a psychologist who is contracted with an insurer to provide counseling sessions at a conversion factor of $38.50. Let us see what the reimbursement rate is for each of these CPT codes:

$$90801: 3.79 \times \$38.50 = \$145.92$$
$$90806: 2.35 \times \$38.50 = \$90.48$$
$$90847: 2.81 \times \$38.50 = \$108.18$$

Working with decimal points creates some odd reimbursement rates down to the penny. If you are contracted with an insurer at the rates just listed and you bill $90 for a 90806, the insurer will pay you $90 (minus the copay), not $90.48. If you bill $100 for the session, the insurer will pay you the contracted rate of $90.48 (minus the copay). The rate of $90.48 is the maximum that the insurer will pay.

What about Copays?

Continue with the same example. The client has a $20 copay. He pays the practitioner that amount at the time of service, and the health plan pays the practitioner the remaining amount, in this case $70.48.

What If This Client Has a Deductible?

This same client has a $250 deductible that he has not fulfilled yet. You have seen him for an intake ($145.92) and four psychotherapy sessions ($90.48 each), and you bill the insurer for each service. Your standard rate for an intake is $150 and for a psychotherapy session is $100.

Practitioner bills:	$550.00
Insurer's maximum allowable:	$507.84
Deductible:	−250.00
Amount paid to practitioner by the insurer:	$257.84

The client pays you the amount of his deductible ($250), so ultimately you receive the full $507.84 for the service of providing the evaluation and four psychotherapy sessions.

What Happens in Subsequent Sessions?

Now that your client has fulfilled his deductible, the normal copay will apply. The insurer will reimburse the contracted rate for a 90806 ($90.48), minus the copay of $20, resulting in a payment to the practitioner of $70.48.

Why Do Insurers Use This System?

Every year some CPT codes are eliminated and new ones created; RVUs change every year as well. By contrast, the conversion factor is a fixed variable. Conversion factors are usually determined by the insurance plan based on its budgetary concerns and an evaluation of the current rate trends in the marketplace. By using a conversion factor rather than a fixed rate per CPT code, insurers can easily adapt to changes in CPT codes and RVUs without having to change a practitioner's contract every time that happens.

Time Management

A private therapy practice is rarely a 9-to-5 job. As an independent businessperson, you have control over how many clients you will see in your practice. Some psychotherapists prefer a part-time schedule; others work more than a 40-hour week. Some discipline is required, especially when you are starting your practice.

Your time will be divided into several activities.

Office Setup and Maintenance

You will need to rent, furnish, and maintain your office space, including a waiting room. If you are joining an established group practice, this may already be done, but you will be responsible for personalizing your space.

Marketing

You will need to develop a marketing strategy, establish relationships with possible referral sources, advertise, and network. This is especially important with a new practice, but will continue to take some time and effort even after your practice is well established. Keeping informed about changes in the profession and local trends, adjusting to changes in referral sources, and revising your advertising strategies are all necessary, or you may see your business drop off unexpectedly.

Therapy Sessions

This should take up the bulk of each day. You may need to adjust your preferred schedule to be available when your clients are. Many clients prefer afternoon and early evening appointments. Think carefully about how much time you will need between sessions. Many therapists schedule 50-minute sessions on the hour, leaving 10 minutes between sessions (if your sessions end on time). Be sure to allow yourself time to eat meals, stay hydrated, go to the bathroom, and walk around a bit between sessions. If you are hungry, thirsty, or have stiff muscles, you will not be able to focus on your client's needs. Consider leaving more time between sessions (e.g., schedule two client sessions in a row, then a half-hour break) to stay fresh for your clients. Also consider the time involved in taking and making emergency phone calls during your day.

Phone Calls to and from Clients and Other Professionals

We live in an age of cell phones, voice mail, and e-mail, yet getting in touch with busy clients may be difficult. You may need to respond to phone calls from potential clients, current clients with a crisis or with a request to reschedule, former clients who wish to return to service, psychiatrists or primary care providers, other therapists, community service organizations, and utilization reviewers. Many therapists schedule phone calls for certain times of the day (e.g., 11:30 to noon and 4:30 to 5:00). However, you may need to make or receive urgent calls at other times, so try to maintain some flexibility in your scheduling.

Documentation

You will need time to set up charts, review intake information, write up evaluations and treatment plans, and write chart notes for each session. It is very difficult to remember the nuances of six to eight therapy sessions if you leave all of your charting to the end of the day. Think about how you want to schedule charting; you may need to try several ways until you find one that works best for you. Be wary of spending too much or too little time on documentation. Remember that your documentation is your first line of defense against any legal or licensing challenges. (See Chapter 4 for more about documentation.)

Billing and Financial Record Keeping

Develop a method for tracking client billing information, sessions authorized, sessions completed, charges, write-offs, and payments. This enables you to get paid for your time, and also prevents misunderstandings and conflicts with clients over money. Make sure you and your clients both know and agree on how much they are being charged for each service you provide and how charges will be paid. This information should be acknowledged by you and your client on your "Consent for Treatment" form (keep a copy!). If possible, use electronic billing; some computer programs are available that combine record keeping with claims generation. Decide how often you will send in claims to insurers. Batching them monthly may be easier but will delay payment and affect your cash flow. Check your insurance payment remittances carefully and be sure they are correctly credited to each client account. Many practitioners hire a billing company to send in claims; if you do this, be sure that you have clear communication channels with the company.

In general, when dealing with insurers, don't send in a claim unless the service has been authorized. Get the referral first, then bill. This cuts down on reprocessing time for both you and the insurer. Create a system for accepting cash payments from your clients, both for copays and for unreimbursed services. Be prepared to give a complete receipt for any money accepted (with the date, client's name, amount, and your name and credentials). Have a secure place in your office to keep payments, and deposit them promptly. Be sure to develop a system for tracking all of your business income and expenses for tax purposes. If needed, hire an accountant to help you set up systems, and be sure you understand tax regulations in your state.

Professional Development

Set aside some time each week for professional development. Although you will not be paid for this time, it will result in keeping your practice up to date and your motivation high. Attend trainings in your field, take classes, get peer consultation, and read relevant journals. Allow time for personal reflection about your mission and your career.

Your Physical Space

The first impression that you make with a client is often provided by your office and waiting room. It is important for your office to reflect:

- Professionalism
- Comfort
- Confidentiality

- Your personal clinical style
- Furniture proximity
- Face validity

Let us look at each of these elements.

Professionalism

Your office should reflect professionalism. Are your degrees and credentials posted? Are the office and waiting area clean and neat? Do you have appropriate books displayed? Do you have business cards, brochures, and other documents available? In general, you should not have advertisements for products for sale in your office.

Comfort

Your office should provide comfort to your clients. Are there comfortable places to sit (in both waiting area and office)? Is the lighting comfortable? Avoid too-bright fluorescent lights and lighting that is too dim. Whenever possible, provide natural lighting. Do you have pleasant, calming artwork in your spaces? Do you have a few general-interest magazines available in your waiting room? It often helps to have quiet music playing.

Confidentiality

Your office should demonstrate that confidentiality of client information is respected. All client information should be in locked cabinets. Do not have detailed, confidential conversations with clients in the waiting areas and doorways. Do not have conversations with or about clients in the presence of other clients. Pay attention to sound-proofing; if clients sitting in your waiting room can hear every word said in your office, they are not going to be comfortable talking with you there about their own confidential material. Be aware of whether you can hear people in adjacent offices; if you can hear them, they can hear you!

Your Clinical Style

Your office should reflect your personal clinical style. Books and artwork convey your interests and style. If you use humor in your therapy, humorous artwork is appropriate. If your therapeutic style involves an appreciation of nature, artwork and plants may be an appropriate reflection of this in your office. On the other hand, personal interests outside the venue of your work may be inappropriate to display, such as personal religious or spiritual orientation, hobbies, or non-therapy-related organizations. Even if you love dogs, a large photo of your favorite pet in the waiting room may be disturbing to a new client who is fearful of dogs.

If you have overt religious symbols and reading material in your office, clients may feel that you cannot be helpful to them if they do not share your beliefs.

Furniture Proximity

Where do you put your chair in relation to where the client is sitting? Is it too far away to make a connection? Is it so close that it invades the client's personal space? Are you sitting behind a desk so that there is a physical barrier between you and the client? The general rule is to arrange your furniture so that the client has easy access to the door. These are all issues worth considering when setting up your office so that you create an environment that is most conducive to a comfortable, therapeutic exchange.

Face Validity

Does your office communicate that you can deliver what you say you can? For instance, if you are involved in performance enhancement and coaching high-powered executives and salespersons who want to double their income or sales, your office should not be run down and in need of repair.

Trends on the Horizon

The behavioral health field, like all other aspects of the health care system, is in a constant state of evolution. How the average practitioner practiced 20 years ago is very different from how people practice today. So what is on the horizon? What are some of the trends? How can you position your practice to survive and even thrive?

Integration of the Latest Brain Research

Research is exploring the frontiers of the mind and expanding our knowledge of how the brain works. As this continues to occur, research-based psychotherapy interventions targeting specific brain processes will occur. The increase in the practice of neuro-feedback is an example. Interventions are becoming increasingly targeted on treating attentional issues, hyperactivity, substance abuse, anxiety (including Posttraumatic Stress Disorder), depression, Obsessive-Compulsive Disorder, learning disabilities, cognitive impairment, and anger. Look to brain research to provide "talk therapy" practitioners new ways of interacting with their clients to increase clients' ability to process information and improve positive outcomes.

Insurance Trends

A clear trend in health insurance is for the recipient of health care services to bear more of the cost of the service. Why is this happening? Historically, most health care premium costs have been borne by the employer. It is estimated that health care costs raise the price of each General Motors car by $1,500 (Froetschel, 2007). It is becoming increasingly difficult for large businesses to compete in overseas and domestic markets because of the costs of health care. One of the solutions is to have the individual user of health care services pay a higher share of the costs. This is happening in several ways.

Increased Deductible Costs
Many health plans are now selling individuals and employers high deductible plans. Deductibles of $1,500, $2,500, and even $5,000 are not uncommon. These plans are less expensive for the employer to purchase, and subsequently more affordable for the employee on a monthly basis. However, there may be more out-of-pocket expenses for the frequent users of health care services. Under this type of plan, the employee pays the amount of the deductible first, before the insurer starts to pay.

Self-Funded Plans
Employers pay the actual costs of their employees' health care rather than the costs of the average person in their insured pool.

Employers gamble that their costs will be less than the average. More large companies are becoming self-funded and adding wellness programs with an emphasis on smoking cessation, stress and weight management, and leading a healthy lifestyle. Their rationale is that if they improve the health of the employee, costs will come down.

Higher Copays and Coinsurance

The amount that an individual pays for a service or a prescription is higher. In an attempt to control costs, health insurance companies are designing products so that the patient bears more of the up-front costs of the service. For example, instead of a $10 copay for a service such as a counseling session, the copay is $30. This higher cost to patients makes them evaluate whether the service is really necessary and is something that they are willing to pay the higher amount for. Subsequently, this also means that, besides the patient paying more, the health insurance company is paying the provider less.

Health Care Savings Accounts

Rather than pay for a higher level of coverage, an employer may put a certain amount of money in a health care savings account (HSA). Employees can spend that money as they wish to pay for medical expenses. The intention is that an HSA can pay for services that come under the deductible. For instance, your client has a $1,000 deductible and wants to have 10 sessions of psychotherapy with you at $100 per session. If the client has not satisfied the deductible, insurance will not cover your services. The client, however, has $1,500 in an HSA, so the $1,000 for the counseling sessions can be paid for out of this account.

TIP

One common misconception is that coverage is determined by the health plan arbitrarily. In reality, the employer who purchases the plan decides on the coverage limits it obtains for its employees. The health plan carries out the contract that the employer purchases.

The result for the behavioral health practitioner is that more of the up-front costs for therapy will be paid for by the client before the insurance payment kicks in. At $100 per session out-of-pocket expenses, it does not take long for the average person to wonder if he or she can continue to pay at that rate. At the risk of becoming repetitive, this is one of the reasons we have stressed the importance of focused treatment. As more of the costs are borne by clients, clients will be more selective in using their health care dollars. They want to get more value for their money. Creating a reputation for getting clients the results they seek within a reasonable time frame will create an image of you as a valuable practitioner to both clients and third-party payers. (See Chapter 10 for more on setting up time frames.)

Mental Health Parity

Another trend that is occurring both nationally and on a statewide basis is mental health parity. Mental health benefits have been more restrictive than benefits for medical problems. For instance, many plans cover 10 or 12 days in a psychiatric hospital, whereas no day limit occurs if you are hospitalized for a medical illness. Likewise, there may be limits on the number of outpatient therapy sessions available to see a behavioral health practitioner, whereas these same limits do not exist for physical problems. Mental health parity means that mental health treatment would be "on par" with medical treatment. Just as there is no limit on the number of days a patient can spend in the hospital for a kidney ailment, under parity there would not be a limit on the number of days in a psychiatric hospital for a mental illness. Most coverage for behavioral health problems is limited to a certain number of outpatient sessions per year. Under mental health parity, that restriction is also lifted. The outpatient benefit essentially becomes unlimited, contingent on meeting medical necessity criteria.

Mental health parity laws exist in a handful of states, and others are trying to enact this type of legislation. Parity has been discussed for years in Congress, and it is likely that it will be signed into law on a national level in the near future.

It is important to remember that the same issue of medical necessity will apply under mental health parity—in some cases, even more so. Reviewers managing behavioral health utilization will likely look for more justification of a diagnosis and a comprehensive, focused treatment plan. Clients who have a chronic mental illness will benefit by increased, consistent coverage throughout the year. Practitioners who want to see clients with an Adjustment Disorder for a great length of time will find it more difficult to justify the medical necessity of doing so.

The Use of Technology

Technology is increasingly affecting all our lives, and the behavioral health field is no exception. Some of the following are being used on a limited basis and will become more commonplace in the years to come:

- Practitioners will have greater access to business information through the Internet. Some health plans share a single port of entry into a web-based portal, where practitioners can log on to check members' eligibility, the status of a claim, and the amount of a copay.
- Direct electronic billing will greatly reduce the amount of turn-around time for reimbursements.
- Greater sharing of clinical information in the form of electronic record keeping is available.
- Communication and distribution of reauthorization requests with health insurance utilization reviewers is available through secure servers via the Internet.

Distance or Internet Counseling

Another use of technology affecting behavioral health is distance counseling through the Internet. Practitioners who are comfortable with this type of practice can potentially expand their practice beyond their geographic location and face-to-face sessions. Clients who are in rural areas and do not have access to a wide variety of practitioners may benefit by this type of treatment. Clients with Agoraphobia who are unable to leave their house can have contact with practitioners that they would never be able to without this technology. Some clients may even prefer the anonymity of this type of treatment. Liability, coverage, and practice issues for distance counseling have yet to be resolved. Although still in its infancy, distance counseling will likely evolve and develop as a niche practice. Look for more standardization of this type of prac- tice in the future.

Video Counseling

Many isolated rural communities do not have the depth and breadth of practitioners available in urban areas. What happens if there is not a mental health practitioner for hundreds of miles? Telemedicine, the use of video technology, can link isolated areas to practitioners in urban areas via a video hookup. Technology is increasingly sophisticated so that clear, life-size images are now available that simulate sitting directly across from the client. Phil Hirsch, PhD (personal communication, August 22, 2007), reports that initially clients are reluctant to engage in this type of treatment. Once they do, however, there is no difference in client satisfaction between face-to-face and video sessions. It is likely that insurance will eventually cover these types of sessions under specific criteria.

Summing Up

In this chapter we have discussed the many elements you must consider as you set up a successful psychotherapy practice. Setting up a fee schedule, advertising your services, and working with insurance companies all take time and effort. For most of us, they are not the fun part of being a therapist, but are essential to build- ing a sustainable practice. Attention you pay to these elements both at the beginning of your practice and throughout your career will help you to become the psychotherapist you want to be.

EXERCISES

1. Write a sample fee scale, including your policy for missed appointments.
2. For each of the following case scenarios, write a concise, clear request to a managed care insurer for additional sessions (you may invent details):

(Continued)

- You have seen Betty for the first three authorized sessions. She reports having severe headaches that interfere with her ability to work and socialize with friends, and her primary care physician has recommended counseling to address emotional issues that may be contributing to the headaches.

- George has called requesting an initial session for problems he's been having with anxiety, including a need to count and check many things in his daily life.

- Jill has been in therapy with you for about 3 years. She has chronic suicidal ideation and a history of self-harm and feels so "damaged" that she cannot work or attend school consistently.

- You have seen Brian for 10 authorized sessions. He has been inconsistent in attending sessions and seems unwilling to do anything different in his life to alleviate his depressed mood and lack of motivation. He is also quite disorganized and has difficulty completing tasks.

3. Create a marketing brochure that describes you and your approach to psychotherapy.
4. Do you have a professional web site? Why or why not? What would you include in a web site?
5. Do you prefer to see clients who pay with insurance or those who pay privately? Why? Do you notice any difference in motivation between these two types of clients?
6. Do you have a peer consultation group? Do you have informal peer consultation resources?
7. Have you offered any educational presentations in your community? What topics could you offer? What groups might be interested?
8. Create an ideal weekly schedule, including elements discussed in this chapter.

(Continued)

9. Define the following insurance/managed care terms in your own words:
   - Appeal
   - Benefit
   - Care manager or case manager
   - Coinsurance
   - Copay
   - Contracted provider
   - Covered service
   - Deductible
   - Explanation of benefits
   - Premium
   - Referral or authorization
   - Utilization review
10. Describe your own ideal office space.
11. What do you think the effects of mental health parity would have or have had on your practice style? Why?

Resources

Cope Grand, L. (2002a). *The therapist's advertising and marketing kit.* Hoboken, NJ: Wiley.

Cope Grand, L. (2002b). *The therapist's newsletter kit.* Hoboken, NJ: Wiley.

Lawless, L. L. (1997). *How to build and market your mental health practice.* New York: Wiley.

Lawless, L. L., & Wright, G. J. (2000). *How to get referrals: The mental health professional's guide to strategic marketing.* New York: Wiley.

Stout, C. E., & Cope Grand, L. (2005). Getting started in private practice: The complete guide to building your mental health practice. Hoboken, NJ: Wiley.

There are a variety of practice-building consultants who work with practitioners to create their ideal private practice:

Joe Bavonese, PhD, and Melhim Restum, PhD, offer their own successful practice-building techniques on their web site, www.uncommon-practices.com. They consult on creating and improving a web site and Internet marketing and have a comprehensive practice-building training program. They offer lots of free articles and reports and even a free practice analysis and teleconference. You can contact them at (800) 940-0185.

Lynn Grodzki, LCSW, MCC, is a psychotherapist and professionally certified business coach from Silver Spring, MD. She is the author of *Building Your Ideal Private Practice: A Guide for Therapists and Other Healing Professionals* (2000), and *12 Months to Your Ideal Private Practice: A Workbook* (2000). She can be contacted through her web site, www.privatepracticesuccess.com. She also offers a free newsletter, Private Practice Success.

Linda Lawless, MA, LMHC, LMFT, is the author of *How to Build and Market Your Mental Health Practice* and *How to Get Referrals* and the founder of the Professional Practice Institute: www.professionalpracticeinstitute.com.

Psychotherapy Finances offers business resources for behavioral health providers. They are available at www.psyfin.com.

SECTION II

WORKING WITH CLIENTS

6

The Therapeutic Relationship

What You Will Learn
- How to establish rapport with your clients
- Carl Rogers's three necessary components of change
- The elements of the therapeutic relationship for which there is evidence of effectiveness
- How to build a therapeutic alliance with your clients
- How to communicate empathy
- How to develop goal consensus and collaboration with clients
- Client financial pressures
- How to give feedback to clients and elicit their feedback about the therapy process
- How to repair alliance ruptures
- The three common behavioral expressions of countertransference
- Why it is the quality (not quantity) of relational interpretations that matters to clients
- The four matching variables that help to enhance the therapeutic relationship

Few styles and methods of psychotherapy can be of use to clients unless a strong therapeutic relationship is formed. Despite all of the different approaches and philosophies, the one thing that the different types of psychotherapy share is the relationship between therapist and client. The components of this relationship often happen naturally: We go into this field because we have a knack for building relationships. However, there are specific components of the therapeutic relationship that need to be present in order to improve therapy outcome. In this chapter, we explore several aspects of the psychotherapeutic relationship, focusing on the work of Carl Rogers and John Norcross. We realize that for some readers this is very basic, while others may not have had this emphasis in their training.

What Makes the Counseling Relationship Different?

The counseling relationship is different from any other relationship (T. C. Portman, personal communication, November 29, 2007) because it is:

- A paid relationship
- Detached from other legal, family, friend, or business involvement
- Unidirectional, with the focus on the client
- Goal-directed for the betterment of the client
- Unbiased, nonjudgmental, nonevaluative
- Autonomy-promoting versus dependency-promoting
- Unbalanced, with the therapist having the power
- Dissolvable

All of these factors promote a comparatively safe relationship and environment for a person to explore important personal and emotional material and to experiment with new ways of viewing himself or herself and new ways of behaving. It is important for the practitioner to protect these relationship components as a working contract, whether explicitly stated or not.

Establishing Rapport

One of the first things any psychotherapist must do when meeting a client for the first time is build rapport. Clients come to therapy expecting to be understood. They want to develop a relationship built on mutual understanding. A harmony of purpose and a willingness to be creative together in identifying and resolving painful experiences are the building blocks of an effective therapeutic relationship.

As therapists, we develop this rapport through an attitude of openness and exploration. In Zen terms, we approach each client with "beginner's mind." We put aside any preconceptions of the client and focus our attention on seeing and hearing the human being in front of us. We are genuinely curious about who the client is, what she cares about, how she perceives the world and her place in it. We look for both commonalities with and differences from the client. We communicate our open and accepting curiosity with body language, relaxed eye contact, and gently probing questions. We may choose to mirror the client's pace to provide a sense of safety.

As part of building rapport, therapists must also pay attention to their internal reactions to the client. A therapist may notice liking or disliking the client, pulling toward or away from the client, understanding the client or feeling confused. These feelings often reflect how others in the client's life react to him, or they may reflect the therapist's own preoccupations or prejudices. These reactions, while not the focus of therapy, certainly shape the therapeutic experience and need to be observed, noted, and reflected upon during or after the session.

At a point during the therapeutic process, these reactions may be shared with the client. As a therapist, you may feel noticeably uncomfortable in the first session, and it becomes clear that this is not a good therapist-client match. If so, letting the client know this—without blaming or judging—and suggesting another therapist can be the kindest and most ethical course of action. In addition, sharing your positive reactions with the client may be useful in building rapport.

It is often appropriate at different stages of a psychotherapeutic relationship to ask clients how the relationship is going. At times, a therapist may feel that it is going quite well, but the client is not satisfied with the relationship or the content of sessions. Or the opposite may be true: The therapist feels that rapport is weak, but the client feels understood and accepted. Relationship repair can be an important part of therapy, as it may help a client learn how to repair her own personal relationships. It can also help the client remain in therapy until progress is made.

Carl Rogers and the Therapeutic Relationship

It was Carl Rogers who first emphasized the importance of the therapeutic relationship in psychological healing. Rogers believed that unconditional positive regard, congruence, and empathy were necessary components of change. (See Chapter 1 for more on Carl Rogers.)

Positive Regard

Positive regard involves treating clients warmly, with a sense that they are worthy and capable people (even if they do not feel that way about themselves). It is unconditional in that it does not depend on the client's behavior. The focus is on seeing the client as a person rather than a cluster of behaviors. Rogers's contention is that all people have a need for love, affection, and respect from others. Many people, however, do not grow up in an environment that nurtures these qualities; they develop dysfunctional patterns of behavior to survive in a dysfunctional environment. It is important, then, to accept clients as they are in a nonjudgmental way.

TIP

Accepting clients as they are is an important component of positive regard. The foundation of acceptance and respect allows clients the freedom to express themselves.

This is not always a straightforward task. Some clients are easy to like; others are not. If you are working with a client toward whom you have difficulty showing positive regard, observe your feelings and responses. Is the client being unacceptably disrespectful or unnecessarily angry toward you? Is the client passively waiting for you to "fix" him? Does the client have some annoying personal habits? Does the client remind you of someone in your personal life? Identify whether the characteristics you dislike are under your client's control. If they are, it may be useful to share your response with the client.

 Robert went to see Ruth for therapy. He was generally unhappy with his life. He felt hopeless and friendless: "They've all given up on me." At first, he seemed open to possible solutions to his depression, but after every suggestion from Ruth, he would say, "That won't work. I've tried it before. What a dumb idea!" Ruth found herself dreading sessions with Robert, though he reported that the sessions were helpful as they allowed him to vent his unhappiness. Finally, Ruth expressed her difficulty with the barriers he was setting up and how it made her feel: "I want to help you feel better about yourself and your life. I like feeling helpful to my clients, but I do not feel I am being helpful to you at all. When you tell me that my recommendations for you are never going to work, I feel hopeless. I wonder if some of your friends have felt the same way." Robert was taken aback, but nodded sadly. "That's what they all say. They don't feel good around me. But I don't know what I can do differently—it's just they way I am." Ruth asked Robert if he'd be willing to try something different in therapy sessions as a way to improve his friendship skills. He reluctantly agreed, and they worked out a practice plan: When Ruth would make suggestions, he would say, "That's an interesting idea. Let's talk about how that might work." Though it felt strange to say at first, Robert found that he started feeling more hopeful. Ruth found that she was liking Robert more and stopped dreading sessions with him. Eventually Robert started using similar phrases when interacting with potential friends and developed new relationships that were pleasant for him.

If the characteristics you dislike are not under the client's control (e.g., she reminds you of your fifth-grade teacher), you will need to try to change your perception of the client's characteristics. Exchanges such as the one between Robert and Ruth can remove therapeutic barriers that, if left unresolved, will ultimately interfere with therapeutic progress or even lead to premature termination.

Congruence

Another of Rogers's components necessary for change is congruence, which involves the therapist interacting with the client in a real, genuine, and open manner, such as in the example of Ruth and Robert. Norcross (2004) states that congruence is higher when the following elements are present:

Therapist Displays	Client Displays
Self-confidence	High levels of self-exploration
Positive mood	
Increased involvement and activity	
Responsiveness	
Smoothness of speaking exchanges	

We will discuss more of Norcross's research on the role of congruence in effective psychotherapy later in this chapter.

Empathy

Empathy involves understanding the client's viewpoint as if it were your own. The therapist should be sensitive and accurate in the interpretation of the client's feelings. Therapists who follow a Rogerian approach believe that people have the internal resources needed to achieve personal growth, and that a genuine, caring therapeutic relationship is a necessary component for client development and self-actualization.

We discuss the importance of empathy in the psychotherapeutic relationship as it relates to Norcross's research later in this chapter.

John Norcross and the Division 29 Task Force

In 1999, the psychologist and researcher John Norcross organized a task force to investigate the role of empirically supported therapy relationships in treatment effectiveness. Known as the Division 29 Task Force, its charge was to answer two fundamental questions:

1. What works in general in the therapy relationship?
2. What works best for particular clients?

The task force reviewed the literature and categorized the various elements of the therapy relationship as demonstratively effective, promising and probably effective, or insufficient research to judge.

What Works in Therapy?

The Division 29 Task Force reviewed the large body of scientific literature regarding psychotherapy and identified which aspects of the therapeutic relationship had empirical evidence to support its use. There was evidence to show that the following are effective:

- Therapeutic alliance
- Empathy
- Goal consensus
- Feedback

These aspects of the therapeutic relationship were promising and probably effective:

- Positive regard
- Congruence and genuineness
- Repair of alliance ruptures
- Discrete use of self-disclosure
- Management of countertransference
- Quality of relational interpretations

Therapeutic Alliance

The therapeutic alliance refers to the sense that both the therapist and the client are on the same team, with the same goals. Its ingredients include rapport, empathy, and positive regard, as well as clear communication and agreement about the nature of therapy and the specific goals of each person. It also includes an agreement on the type of tasks needed to achieve those goals. These goals will differ based on the characteristics of the client and therapist, the style or philosophy of therapy, and the needs that each brings to the relationship.

It is important to develop a clear understanding of your own philosophy of therapy. (See Chapter 1 for more on developing your philosophy of therapy.) If you see yourself as a very directive, behaviorally based therapist, it will be difficult for you to develop a strong therapeutic alliance with a client who comes to you with existential concerns and a general goal of better self-understanding. Likewise, if you see yourself as a client-directed, insight-focused therapist, it may be difficult for you to establish an alliance with a client who wants quick solutions to a pressing problem.

Problems with the therapeutic alliance are often detectable in the first few sessions, as you complete your evaluation and develop your mutual treatment plan. It is best to address these problems directly. It is reasonable to communicate early in treatment that you may have a different therapy style than what the client is looking for. If the gap between expectations is small, you may be able to negotiate a compromise.

Stan comes to his first therapy appointment with Edward ready to look for solutions to problems in his marriage. He is not feeling as close to his wife as he'd like to, and he realizes that it may be related to his heavy work schedule, which leaves little time for family. As Edward completes his evaluation and begins to work with Stan on a treatment plan, he begins to recognize that there is a slight disconnect between them about the purpose of therapy. "Stan, I'm noticing that you are looking for some pretty quick solutions to the problems in your marriage. I want to let you know that although I think we can come up with some answers fairly quickly, I see some other, deeper issues that might make it difficult for you to follow through with anything we plan. I'm wondering if we can include both solution-focused work and some deeper work to help you become more aware of your own emotions, goals, and values. Do you think that you could agree with a plan that includes both aspects?"

At times, however, the gap is much larger. You might do both your client and yourself a favor by pointing out (without judgment, of course) that a therapist with a different philosophy of care might be a better match. Ignoring the differences in expectations can be detrimental to the client and frustrating for the therapist. At best, little progress will be made, and both the client and the therapist will feel that therapy has not been successful.

Once the therapeutic alliance has been formed, it can become a concern again if errors or misunderstandings occur. Repairing the alliance can be an important part of the therapy process. Remain observant of your own experience of the therapy relationship, and check in with your client from time to time about how he or she feels therapy is progressing. Clarify misunderstandings (yours and your client's), apologize when you have made a mistake, and point out when your client's behavior is negatively impacting your therapeutic alliance. Repairing the therapeutic relationship can be a model for repairing other important relationships in the client's life. Unresolved rifts between therapist and client can damage the therapeutic alliance. Consult with a trusted colleague if this occurs, and try to determine what contributed to the communication breakdown. Consider the following example of relationship repair.

Jennifer had been in therapy with Paul on and off for several years. She had been depressed when she first started therapy, but had made steady progress through a combination of cognitive-behavioral and supportive interventions. One week, Jennifer came to the session excited about a new job opportunity in another city. Rather than recognizing and validating Jennifer's happiness about the new opportunity, Paul began to focus on some of Jennifer's old cognitive errors about her self-worth being dependent on her ability to be successful in her career. Crestfallen, Jennifer grew silent. Paul felt confused and asked Jennifer how she was feeling. Jennifer replied that she felt disappointed that Paul could not simply be happy for her. Paul acknowledged his mistake in failing to validate Jennifer's positive emotions. He then began to repair the relationship by asking supportive questions about the new job opportunity and sharing in her excitement.

Empathy

The Division 29 Task Force, in its meta-analysis of 47 studies, found that there was a positive causal link between empathy and positive therapy outcome. Empathy is a component of any positive relationship, but in the context of a therapy experience it can help facilitate the client's emotional exploration. This freedom to explore can help define the experience as personally meaningful to the client and help facilitate healing.

Empathy is the ability to understand another person's emotions, thoughts, and experiences from that person's point of view. We all want to know that others understand us, not just intellectually but on an emotional level. We want to "make sense" to the people around us. Communicating that we make sense to others is similar to what Linehan (1993a) calls "validation." (See Chapter 13 for more on Linehan's work.) It is one thing to feel empathy for another, but it is another thing to communicate this effectively to the person. So there are two necessary components to empathy: the therapist's sensitivity and ability to understand the internal experience of the client and the skill to communicate this to the client in a meaningful way.

How does a psychotherapist communicate empathy to clients? First, the therapist must notice his or her own empathy response—so practicing self-awareness while in session is crucial. Next, the therapist decides if an empathy response would be helpful or harmful to the client at that moment. Most often it is helpful, but there are times in sessions when it would only distract from the work at hand. Finally, the therapist communicates empathy through body language (smiling, nodding, or leaning slightly forward), eye contact (appropriate to the client's cultural mores), and words. Words alone may not communicate the whole experience of empathy. Consider the following example.

Sarah comes to see Margaret for therapy about her extended grief over the deaths of her parents in a boating accident. They talked for some time about the details of their deaths and Sarah's emotional reaction at the time and currently. Margaret, sitting up straight, unsmiling, and making firm eye contact, says, "I think I know how you feel. The loss of both parents at the same time can be devastating." Sarah experiences this comment not as empathetic, but as cold and clinical.

Be aware of using your whole being to express empathy. Does your voice tone match your intention? Does your body posture match the meaning of your words? Make sure that all of these components are in alignment. Notice how you express empathy with your friends and family. Notice how others show empathy toward you, and your own response to it.

Goal Consensus and Collaboration

The therapy relationship implies a contract between two parties. Each party, the therapist and the client, has certain responsibilities to create a productive, satisfying experience. Initially there needs to be mutual recognition of the problem. Once that occurs, both need to agree not only on the goals of therapy but the means to get there. The therapist's responsibility is to design a treatment plan that can be effective in helping the client change. The client's responsibility is to let the therapist know if the plan feels comfortable and attainable and to follow through on the recommendations. The most well-considered plan will not be effective if the client is not agreeable to its implementation. (See Chapter 9 for more on treatment planning.)

This type of collaboration and mutual engagement has been shown to increase the number of clients who return to therapy after the initial session (Tryon, 1985). Practitioners who have a higher percentage of returning clients after the first session are also more likely to see them for more than 10 sessions (Tryon & Tryon, 1986).

TIP

Some practitioners are very good at developing unconditional positive regard. They develop a warm, supportive relationship with their client but do not go beyond that. They assume they are collaborating by being in the same room together. The collaborative nature of the therapist-client relationship is not explicitly stated. The therapist makes the mistaken assumption that collaboration is occurring automatically without any feedback from the client. When the therapist neglects the collaborative nature of the relationship, it is usually by not fully sharing the therapy responsibilities with the client.

One indication of client participation is, of course, what happens in session. But what happens outside of session is at least as and probably even more important. Giving the client homework can be a way of extending the therapy hour. One study indicated that it is not necessarily the quantity of homework assigned but the quality (Schmidt & Woolaway-Bickel, 2000). Consider the following example.

Kaylee was deeply depressed when she began therapy with Simon. She agreed to work with her primary care provider on medication strategies, to increase the amount of time she exercised, and to begin to normalize her sleep patterns. However, she continued to report feeling depressed despite some evidence that she was doing better. Simon asked Kaylee to keep a daily record of her mood and behaviors, measuring sadness, sleep, exercise, and medication compliance. After several weeks of this, both Kaylee and Simon noticed that Kaylee was skipping her medication and oversleeping about every 3 days, and the following day her sadness was elevated. This gave Kaylee the motivation she needed to become more consistent with her medication and sleep cycle, and she soon saw more consistent improvement in her mood.

Understanding Client Financial Pressures

It is important to recognize the role that finances play in the therapeutic process. It can either provide the means to continue therapy or it can cause pressure that may interfere with continuity. When the client's therapy is covered by insurance, it is important to acknowledge at the first or second session what the client's health insurance benefit is, how many sessions have been initially approved by the health insurance company, and how the therapist sees the treatment unfolding within those parameters. Likewise, in a private-pay situation, it is helpful to estimate the length of treatment so the client can prepare financially. Practitioners typically concentrate on the clinical plan and often neglect to discuss a financial plan that feels comfortable to the client. Often, an appropriate clinical plan is overridden by a client who cannot sustain the financial expense. When this occurs, therapy is terminated prematurely with little notice. (See Chapter 5 for more on discussing the cost of therapy with clients.)

Feedback

Feedback is an important component of the therapy relationship. There are several different types of feedback. For example, practitioners give feedback to their clients regarding behavior as it relates to their presenting problems. It is also important to give clients positive feedback when they have faced and overcome difficult challenges or done homework assignments. This type of feedback can anchor the client's new behavior so that it will be internalized and repeated in the future. Therapist feedback is particularly helpful in the early stages of the relationship. Once that relationship is established, even negative or corrective feedback can be effective and accepted by the client if it relates to the therapy goal.

> "I notice that every time you try to attempt to change your behavior you tend to make it harder for yourself by picking a difficult time to do it so that it doesn't work out very well."

Negative feedback may be more acceptable to the client if it is sandwiched between statements of positive feedback.

> "I can see that you are really making an effort to change, but I notice that every time you try to attempt to change your behavior you make it harder for yourself by picking a difficult time to do it so that it doesn't work out very well. Your determination to overcome this is very admirable. The good news is that we can work with that. Let's look at some ways to increase your chances of success."

Clients give practitioners important feedback about the helpfulness of the treatment plan, as well as how the therapeutic relationship is going. It is important for the practitioner to check in with the client on how things are going with questions such as the following:

- Are we on the right track?
- Are you getting what you need?

- How are we working together? Do we need to change anything?
- Are your goals still relevant?
- How about the pace? Are we going too fast? Too slowly?

Some clients may not feel confident enough to give their therapist negative verbal feedback. Watch for subtle postural changes or signs of visceral discomfort and gently inquire how they are feeling. Frequent and productive inquiry about how the process is going and getting feedback from the client can go a long way in avoiding therapeutic ruptures. Validation can help legitimize clients' feelings and give them "permission" to disclose them.

Positive Regard, Congruence, and Genuineness

Norcross (2004) found that positive regard, congruence, and genuineness were probably effective. We have discussed these aspects of the therapeutic relationship in the beginning of this chapter, while looking at Carl Rogers's insights.

Repair of Alliance Ruptures

A rupture occurs when there is a disruption in the therapeutic alliance. Because the therapeutic alliance is one of the most important aspects of the therapeutic relationship, a break can have devastating effects. Practitioners are human, too, and sometimes misunderstand client's intentions, assign an inappropriate task, or say something that offends the client. It is important to recognize these moments, apologize if appropriate, and change the task, goal, or direction of the treatment to minimize the disruption. A positive therapy outcome can be dependent on how the practitioner handles these situations.

Disruptions are usually related to different understandings of the goals or the tasks needed to achieve those goals. For example, if a client comes into treatment with the goal of investigating why she behaves in a certain way, she may want to spend a lot of time exploring her history with the intention of gaining insight. If the practitioner is focused on symptom relief and neglects the history, the client will feel she is not getting the kind of care and attention she needs. Another example is a client who comes into therapy with the notion that the practitioner will be directive and give him advice about what to do. If the practitioner has a nondirective style and looks to the client to define the direction, there will be a disconnect leading to dissatisfaction for both parties. In cases like these, either the therapeutic alliance is never formed or it breaks down over time. (See Chapter 7 for more on developing collaboration with clients.)

Managing Countertransference

The management of countertransference is challenging because it often involves unconscious triggers and defense mechanisms that can bring up strong feelings in the therapist. According to Gelso and Hayes (2002), the therapist's internal conflict is usually manifested in several different types of behaviors:

- Withdrawal
- Overinvolvement
- Underinvolvement or avoidance of the client's material

These behaviors may occur as a result of exposure to client material related to a specific situation or may be part of the therapist's personality structure. Consider how each of the following therapist behaviors could play out in a specific situation.

- **Withdrawal:** Carl's wife passed away 6 years ago. One of his existing clients who came to see him about a different issue is now caretaking his wife, who was recently diagnosed with a terminal illness. Carl finds that as his client's wife's illness progresses, strong feelings of grief are overcoming him. In his off hours, he finds himself withdrawing socially. During sessions he has a hard time remembering what they have discussed in previous sessions, and his level of active involvement lessens. He finds himself fatigued and unable to provide the kind of support his client needs.

- **Overinvolvement:** Alice grew up in a family where her parents were often absent. They rarely attended her school and extracurricular activities. This negative childhood experience was actually a motivating factor in her choosing the counseling profession. Because

Countertransference: *The totality of feelings experienced by a professional toward the patient (client) whether conscious or unconscious whether prompted by the client's dynamics or by issues or events in the clinician's own life*
—Katz (2007)

she knew how it felt to be unsupported, she wanted to provide support to others. She vowed that she would always support her clients, and she sometimes does so when it is not warranted. She is often so supportive that she neglects challenging and encouraging her clients to change. Although her clients feel very comfortable talking with her, they usually do not make much progress. Is she being overly supportive as a way to compensate for her lack of support as a youth?

- **Underinvolvement:** Jayne was experiencing a great deal of stress at home, and it was beginning to affect her effectiveness as a therapist. She was taking care of her elderly parents, engaging in serious conflicts with her two adolescent sons, and having daily headaches. When she met her new client, Malcolm, an 82-year-old widower with depression and conflicts with his adult sons, she tried to develop empathy and rapport with him. However, Jayne soon found herself zoning out during sessions. The client's problems were triggering some of her own struggles with the same issues, and she found she could not develop an active and effective treatment plan with him. Her lack of involvement was soon evident to Malcolm, and he simply stopped coming to sessions.

These are examples in which the internal processes of the therapist have made the leap into overt behavior and are interfering with the therapeutic process. If these therapist perceptions remain internal and are not acted on, they can provide valuable insights into the therapist's own issues and be valuable assets toward understanding the inner world of the client. This understanding can often help in working more effectively with the client. It is important to identify and examine these feelings and reactions and get some consultation if they are interfering with the therapy process or your ability to be fully present. Renee Katz (2006), PhD, MSW, FT, author and co-editor of *When Professionals Weep: Emotional and Countertransference Responses in End-of-Life Care*, examines countertransference issues related to end-of-life care, but the principles are applicable to any therapeutic interaction. The reader is referred to her book for detailed guidelines that can help a practitioner dealing with countertransference issues and to Chapter 10 of this book, which goes into this topic in more depth.

Quality of Relational Interpretations

Sharing insights and pointing out behavior patterns that the client may not be aware of can increase the client's view of the therapist as a competent participant in the therapeutic process. Therapist interpretations of the client's behavior, possible motivations, and the impact of the client's behavior on others can increase the client's insight. The research literature indicates that therapist interpretations are perceived by clients as making connections, going beyond what the client has overtly recognized, and pointing out themes or patterns in the client's behavior (Norcross, 2004). This can be overdone, however. High rates of interpretation don't necessarily lead to positive outcomes. The quality of the interpretation is what matters, not the quantity. The most important aspect of an intervention is to focus on the main interpersonal themes with which the client is struggling.

What Works Best for Particular Clients?

The Division 29 Task Force also asked the following question: What works best for particular clients? They found four matching variables that helped to enhance the therapeutic relationship (Norcross, 2007):

1. *Client preferences:* Not everyone has a strong preference, but when they do it usually involves the characteristics of the therapist and his or her interactive style.
    *   *Tepid/warm:* How does the practitioner interact with the client? Is the therapist warm and inviting or more neutral?
    *   *Passive/active:* This refers to the ratio of listening to talking. Some clients like to do most of the talking and want the therapist to listen and occasionally lend an insight; others want to hear a lot more of what the therapist is thinking.
    *   *Formal/informal:* Some clients prefer a more casual atmosphere; others want a very businesslike environment.

- *Therapist gender and ethnicity:* This is important to about 15% of the client population who have a very strong preference. The remainder want a practitioner who is competent and has the expertise to help with their problems regardless of their gender and ethnicity.

2. *Real-time client feedback:* Regular feedback with the client in session can address any changes needed in the treatment methods, the quality of the therapeutic relationship, and the overall client satisfaction regarding progress and goal attainment.

3. *Stages of change:* It is important that the therapist's interventions match the client's stage of change.

4. *The degree of directiveness* of the therapist is related to the resistance level of the client. Cooperative clients may welcome a great deal of direction on the part of the therapist. However, strong therapist direction can be contraindicated with resistive clients, as it may increase the client's resistance even more.

We are often involved in making referrals for complex cases and find that attention to client preferences can enhance the likelihood of a strong therapeutic alliance, leading to a positive therapy outcome. Mismatches between the client's expectations and the particular style of the practitioner often lead to a dissatisfying experience and termination after a few sessions.

Summing Up

This chapter has focused on a number of therapist characteristics that contribute to a positive and effective relationship with clients. It may be useful to review each of these components with a clinical supervisor or colleague to identify your own areas of strength and weakness.

=EXERCISES=

1. How do you know when you have established good rapport with a client? What would you do if you did not feel you had good rapport with a client by the third or fourth session?

(Continued)

2. Which elements of the therapeutic alliance are important to you? How would you know if a rupture in the alliance has occurred? How would you respond? Why?

3. How do you express empathy with a client? Practice demonstrating empathy nonverbally. Practice demonstrating it verbally. Can you express empathy even when you don't feel it?

4. What percentage of your clients return after their first session? Why do you think they return or don't return? When they don't return, what's your response?

5. Have you experienced a situation in which a client did not continue therapy due to financial concerns? Do you discuss the likely length and cost of therapy in the first few sessions? Is it useful and ethical to alter your treatment plan to better match your client's financial capabilities?

6. How often do you request feedback from your clients about how therapy is going? When you do, what do you say? When you don't, why not? What do you do with the feedback when given? Do clients ever offer feedback to you even when you don't ask for it?

7. Have you experienced countertransference when working with a client? How did you handle it? What was the client's response?

7

How Will You Interact
with the Client?

What You Will Learn
- How to use OARS to motivate clients
- How to elicit "change talk" in your clients
- Understanding client satisfaction and how to respond to client complaints
- How to create a sense of hope
- How to accurately elicit the client's concerns and develop collaboration
- Insight versus behavior change: the quest for "why"
- How to set realistic treatment expectations

Practitioner interactions can affect the quality of care, the outcome, and clients' overall satisfaction with the therapy experience. From the first moment of contact to the conclusion of therapy, there are literally hundreds of interaction opportunities. There is research to indicate that certain characteristics of therapists are associated with successful treatment. Counselors working in the same setting and offering the same treatment approaches show dramatic differences in rates of client dropout and successful outcome (Miller & Rollnick, 2002, p. 6). In this chapter, we explore several tools for effective therapist-client interactions.

Motivational Interviewing

A simple, helpful, and powerful guide to interacting with clients, known as OARS, comes from Motivational Interviewing (Miller & Rollnick, 2002, pp. 65–76). The acronym OARS stands for:

Open-ended questions
Affirmations
Reflective listening
Summaries

Open-Ended Questions

Open-ended questions are those that cannot be answered by a simple yes or no. Questions such as "You mentioned that you have been under a lot of stress lately. Can you tell me more about that?" give the client the opportunity to supply details about the problem.

Affirmations

Affirmations can be used to recognize client strengths or give a compliment. Because many clients come to therapy with a sense of personal failure, it is important to point out their hidden strengths. "You said that you weren't anxious this whole week. That is quite an accomplishment! How did you manage to do that?" (combining both an affirmation and an open-ended question!). Affirmations can be rapport builders and help to instill hope and confidence that change is possible. However, they need to be sincere and not overused.

Reflective Listening

Reflective listening is a cornerstone of therapeutic work. The most powerful way to interact with a client is to truly listen. However, be cautious about reflecting back to the client verbatim. If done repeatedly, the client is likely to become frustrated and sense a lack of forward motion. Instead, pair your reflective listening with a statement such as "You have not been able to find a job. That must be incredibly frustrating for you and a real blow to your confidence." If the therapist is accurate, it often increases the intensity of the session, which can lead to deeper work.

Summary Statements

Summary statements serve several purposes: they reinforce what the client has been saying; their accuracy demonstrates that you have been listening; and they give the client the opportunity to hear what has been said from a different perspective. According to Miller and Rollnick (2002, pp. 74–76), there are three types of summary statements:

1. *Collecting summaries* are used in the early, exploratory phase of treatment. They are short ("What else?") and help the client maintain some momentum in the description of the issues. Be careful not to use them too frequently or they may interrupt the client's natural process.
2. *Linking summaries* connect the client's present statements with something he or she has said previously. The purpose is to encourage reflection on the relationship between the two. The focus of linking summaries is often on client ambivalence. Consider the following example.

   It sounds like you are feeling two conflicting things. Last week you said that you really wanted to stop using food as an emotional crutch. You realize the effect on your health and how your weight limits your activities. However, this week you are expressing that you are not sure that you have the willpower to resist temptation. You want to change, but at the same time you have some thoughts that you might not be able to.

3. *Transitional summaries* are used when you want to change focus. They summarize the information that the client has disclosed and combine this with how the client is feeling. It is often used at the end of the first session to bring all of the pieces of information together. Miller and Rollnick (2002, p. 75) recommend introducing a transitional summary that explains what will follow, such as in the next example.

To listen fully means to pay close attention to what is being said beneath the words. You listen not only to the "music," but to the essence of the person speaking. You listen not only for what someone knows, but for what he or she is. Ears operate at the speed of sound, which is far slower than the speed of light the eyes take in. Generative listening is the art of developing deeper silences in yourself, so you can slow your mind's hearing to your ears' natural speed, and hear beneath the words to their meaning.
—Peter Senge

"I would like to try to pull together what you have said so far, so we can see where we are and where we are going. Let me know if I miss anything important that we have covered. You came in because . . ." (Miller & Rollnick, 2002, p. 75).

Transitional summaries are also useful when moving from an exploratory to a collaborative treatment planning phase. According to Miller and Rollnick (2002), they are a good way to end the first session or start the second.

Eliciting Change Talk

The focus of motivational interviewing is eliciting "change talk." Miller and Rollnick (2002) explain that motivational interviewing is directive. The practitioner gently guides the client toward eliciting change talk and pays less attention to nonchange talk. While the OARS method helps to move the session along by getting more information, affirming client strengths, and summarizing what has been disclosed, focusing on change talk helps to resolve ambivalence. Helping the client resolve this ambivalence in a nonconfrontational way is a hallmark of motivational interviewing. The therapist takes on the role of facilitating the client's change talk. Miller and Rollnick (pp. 77–78) state that change talk falls into the following categories:

- *Recognizing the disadvantages of the status quo:* "I guess this really isn't working too well is it?" "It seems like things just keep getting worse."
- *Recognizing the advantages of change:* "If I wasn't such a procrastinator, I'd get a lot more done and feel better about myself." "If I quit smoking, I'd have a lot more money. I never realized how much I spend on this!"
- *Expressing optimism about change:* "I know it is going to be a lot of work, but I'm more ready to change now than I have ever been in the past. I think I can do it."
- *Expressing intention to change:* "I don't want to live like this anymore. I just need some help to figure out how to avoid slipping back into my old bad habits."

When change talk is not occurring, the therapist needs to help elicit these types of statements. There are many ways to do this, and we refer the reader to the book, *Motivational Interviewing: Preparing People for Change* (Miller & Rollnick, 2002) for a wealth of ideas and methods to help practitioners evoke change talk in their clients.

Client Satisfaction

Client satisfaction is an important part of any successful professional relationship. You want your clients to walk out your door with the sense that they have received a valuable service, worthy of their time and effort. Take time to check in with your clients about how the therapy process is going. Pay attention as well to satisfaction about how easy it is for them to contact you, the comfort of your office space, and your business practices. Take any complaints seriously; your practice will suffer if you do not address them effectively.

TIP
A satisfied client is more likely to tell others about a positive experience and help generate referrals by word of mouth.

Common Client Complaints

One common complaint that we hear from clients requesting to change practitioners is that the therapist was not properly prepared for the session. Clients make comments such as "It was obvious that she didn't read the chart. It was like we had to start all over again." Clients complain that they feel devalued if the practitioner does not take the time to prepare for the session. If the practitioner is ill prepared, it creates the impression of incompetence or disinterest. Repeated early occurrences of such therapist behavior are a predictor of client dropout. If you are aware that this has occurred, recognize it and apologize to the client. Keeping good notes with an indication of what to ask and work on in the next session can help with session-to-session continuity and client satisfaction.

Another complaint expressed by clients is that, ironically, practitioners do not listen! This is often paired with making a diagnosis without getting all of the information. Clients rarely go back to a therapist when this occurs. They need to feel that a practitioner can listen to their concerns and make sound judgments related to their care.

In addition, clients complain that practitioners do not return phone calls in a timely manner. When this occurs, clients feel that the practitioner does not consider the issue important enough to address quickly. You may have many clients, but it is important to remember that the client has only one therapist! It is challenging for a therapist to juggle multiple responsibilities. Strive to return phone calls within 24 hours. Successful practitioners set aside a specific time each day for office-related work, including phone calls. (See Chapter 5 for more on time management.)

Creating a Sense of Hope

Since the client has implicitly stated that the problem is one that he or she cannot solve, it is important for the practitioner to set a new definition that such a solution is possible.
—S. de Shazer, Clues: Investigating Solutions in Brief Therapy (1985)

He is the best physician who is the most ingenious inspirer of hope.
—Samuel Taylor Coleridge

It takes courage to admit that you cannot solve a problem alone and you need professional help. Clients often arrive with a sense of desperation and hope that the therapist can make sense out of what has been happening to them. Your client may never have been to a mental health practitioner before; or perhaps he or she has seen several. One of the most valuable things you can do during the beginning stages of therapy is to instill a sense of hope. Hope establishes the belief in the potential for change and helps the client realize that there are choices. Practitioners can convey, if true, that they have worked with similar issues before and have seen client progress in solving these problems.

Set realistic goals and create the anticipation that, by working together, improvement is possible and probable. This may be the first time the client has felt any hope of the possibility of change. The presence of hope is a good predictor that change will actually occur. Congratulating your clients on taking that first step or remarking how strong they must be to get to this point starts to give meaning to their struggle. Clients' realization that they have inner resources can be a great catalyst to get the therapy process started in a positive direction. Where there is hope, there is the possibility of positive change.

Eliciting the Client's Concerns

It can be easy to make assumptions about what brings your client to therapy. Consider this example.

> Lynn has a new therapist, Steve. She weeps throughout the first few sessions, making it quite difficult to do a thorough evaluation. Steve comes to the conclusion early in this process that Lynn is suffering from a pervasive depression. When he asks about recent stressors, Lynn replies, "It's always been like this." One day, Steve sees Lynn walking down the street with a group of friends. She is laughing and talking, seemingly the center of attention. Confused, Steve asks her at the next session (through her tears) how often she cries. She states that she cries only in therapy sessions. "That's what this is for, isn't it? To get out all the sadness?" Somewhat stunned, Steve discovers that Lynn has been coping with the recent death of her father. She has never wanted to burden friends or family with her emotions, so she has continued to function normally in her social interactions. Yet, knowing that her grief about her father continued to surface at times when she was alone, she decided to see a therapist "to get it all out." What Lynn really wanted from therapy was a cathartic experience to put an end to her grief. Steve thought Lynn might benefit from some cognitive-behavioral therapy to deal with not being able to ask for support from her friends and family, but Lynn's goal for the therapy was to have a place to cry. At the next session, Lynn said she felt better, that she had used the therapy time to feel her sadness, and thanked Steve for all his help.

Ask your clients directly, "What brings you here today?"; "How can I help?"; "What seems to be the problem?"; or "What are your expectations of therapy?" Repeat their concerns until you have an understanding of them. Write them down. Continue to elicit concerns throughout the course of treatment; some clients may want to change their focus midstream. Also, find out what is working and try to do more of it. If the client's expectation of treatment is not congruent with your style of therapy (e.g., you are a

The therapist is no longer seen as the sole expert in the room, observing and interpreting a patient's thoughts, feelings and behavior. Rather, he or she is part of a system, a two-person field, in which both participants co-create meaning and both observe the nature of what is being created.
—Barry A. Farber, "Self-Disclosure in Psychotherapy Practice and Supervision: An Introduction" (2003)

behavioral therapist and the client wants to continuously process childhood issues), it may be best to refer him or her to a therapist whose therapeutic orientation will provide a better match. (See Chapter 9 for more on determining what the client wants from therapy.)

Developing Collaboration with the Client

For there to be a true collaboration, there needs to be a free and honest flow of information between client and therapist. Unfortunately, many practitioners fail to encourage this flow in any explicit manner. The road to collaboration is paved with frequent client feedback. (See Chapter 6 for more on eliciting feedback.) Outcome and session rating scales keep practitioners on track by eliciting feedback from the client regarding the quality of the interpersonal relationship ("How are we working together?") as well as the quality of the sessions themselves ("How are the sessions going?"; "Are you getting what you need?"). Resources listed at the end of this chapter include contact information for two of

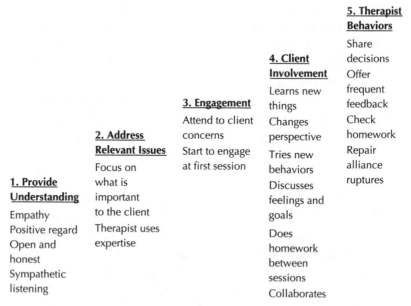

Figure 7.1   The Five Steps to a Positive Therapy Outcome (and How to Get There)

the most widely used instruments, one from Scott Miller, PhD, and Barry Duncan, PsyD, and the other from David Burns, MD.

Figure 7.1 illustrates five important steps for collaborating with clients to create a successful therapeutic outcome.

The Quest for Why: Insight versus Behavior Change

Clients come to therapy wanting to understand themselves better. They want to gain insight into their own lives. If the client is otherwise functioning well, this may be appropriate and helpful, at least in the short term. However, if the client is having difficulties in functioning (e.g., lack of sleep leading to job errors and risking employment), he or she may be better served by a more active, problem-solving approach. Understanding *why* the client is not sleeping may be less important than making behavioral changes to improve his or her sleep, at least initially.

Let's look at another example of this problem.

Jack starts therapy with Helen because he is plagued with self-doubt. He is nearing the end of college and is still unsure of what he wants to do with his life. He has researched a number of jobs but feels he wouldn't be good at any of them. He wants to understand why he has such difficulty planning for the future. After a thorough evaluation, Helen believes he has no serious pathology, but he does have difficulty making the normal adjustment from adolescence to adulthood. She suggests that they work on specific steps he can take to establish his values, goals, and strengths and to improve his decision-making skills. Jack, however, wants to spend each session reviewing his childhood, his relationship with his family, and his school experiences, trying to understand why he is having such problems. He resists any attempt to focus on the present and future.

If this is a private-pay situation, the client may be willing to pay and spend time exploring these issues. However, if you are expecting payment from a third party, you may need to step back and establish specific, measurable goals. Some clients are interested in the journey and gaining insight rather than changing behavior. This may or may not be compatible with your own personal style.

Setting Realistic Treatment Expectations

When clients do not have a clear sense of where they want to go, therapy can be reduced to a sightseeing trip of personal difficulty.
—Megrette Hammond

Clients may come to you expecting to make major changes in their life. They may expect you to totally transform their personality in a short time. It may help the therapy process if you can help clients to identify short-, medium-, and long-term goals. Help them to make the connection between small changes they can make in the course of a brief episode of treatment, and their larger goals.

For example, a client enters therapy with the goal "to have all the friends I want and a satisfying career." Validate these goals, then work to break them down into more realistic "bites" of work.

Long-Term Goals	Short-Term Goals
To have many friends	Identify communication strengths and weaknesses
	Learn and practice specific communication skills
	Invite three potential friends to an event
	Evaluate interactions with these three potential friends and problem-solve any difficulties
Have a satisfying career	Identify characteristics of a satisfying job
	Identify professional strengths and weaknesses
	Research three potential careers
	Take specific steps toward a more satisfying job

Consider another example, with a client whose therapy goal is "to stop feeling depressed."

Long-Term Goal	Short-Term Goals
Stop feeling depressed	Identify behavioral indications of depression (e.g., sleep, mood, activity)
	Determine probable contributing factors (illness, stresses, cognitions, relationships)
	Start medication evaluation and trial if appropriate
	Learn and practice three behavioral strategies for improving mood
	Develop a relapse-prevention plan

It is essential to be explicit in these goals. They will become the structure for your treatment plan. Write them down with the client, and review them frequently to be sure you are accomplishing what you set out to do. (See Chapter 9 for more on treatment planning.)

Challenge for the Practitioner

Large, long-term goals without short-term, specific steps can lead to lengthy, unproductive psychotherapy. Work with your clients to define a series of steps that they can do today that will lead to their long-term goal.

Summing Up

In this chapter we have looked at several important elements of therapist interactions with clients. Motivating clients, eliciting change talk, and establishing a sense of hope are all skills therapists should cultivate. Developing collaboration on the goals of therapy and setting realistic expectations for therapy can help you to bring the client closer to success with each therapy session. Review your clinical interactions in light of these elements when you find yourself engaging in unproductive and unsatisfying therapy sessions. Each session is an opportunity to interact skill-fully with your clients to create lasting change.

EXERCISES

1. How do you use motivational interviewing tech-niques in the first few sessions? How do you use them later in therapy?
2. How do you elicit change talk in your clients?
3. Practice using collecting, linking, and transitional summary statements.
4. Do you think your clients are satisfied with the services you provide? How can you tell? Do you have a systematic way to determine client satisfac-tion? How do you think client satisfaction affects your ability to get new clients?
5. How do you create hope in your clients? Do you believe a sense of hope is necessary for effective psychotherapy?
6. What do you think is the relationship between insight and behavior change? Which is most important? Why?
7. Identify long-term and short-term goals for the fol-lowing client scenarios:
   - George wants his family to get off his back.
   - Joan wants to never be lonely again.
   - Sylvia wants to stop doubting herself and go to graduate school.
   - Carl wants to be so organized and successful that he wins every sales contest at his company.
   - Susan wants to stop being afraid all the time.
   - Paul wants to get off heroin.
   - Rhonda wants to run her first marathon.
8. Use an outcome rating scale to measure how well you are collaborating with a client. How does it affect your interactions with the client? The outcome? The ease of treatment? The client's satisfaction? Your satisfaction?
9. Pay attention for a day to what your body language is saying to your clients.

Resources

Arkowitz, H., Westra, H. A., Miller, W. R., & Rollnick, S. (Eds.). (2008). *Motivational interviewing in the treatment of psychological problems*. New York: Guilford Press.

Miller, W. R., & Rollnick S. (2002). *Motivational interviewing: Preparing people for change*. New York: Guilford Press.

A free outcome and session rating scale can be downloaded from Scott Miller, PhD, and Barry Duncan, PsyD, at their web site, www .talkingcure.com. A variety of other fee-based tools to help the clinician with therapy effectiveness are also available at this site.

David Burns, MD, has a variety of assessment and treatment tools, including therapy session evaluation instruments, such as the Empathy Scale and the Helpfulness of Session tool that comes in a short, 5-item version as well as a full-length version. These instruments are part of his comprehensive Therapist Toolkit, which can be purchased through his web site: www.feelinggood.com/therapist's_toolkit.htm.

8

Understanding the
Change Process

What You Will Learn

- How the "processes of change" identified by Prochaska can be used by therapists to help clients move from one stage of change to another
- How to identify a client's stage of change and match your interventions to be most effective
- How a discrepancy between a therapist's interventions and a client's stage of change can be corrected
- The three client learning styles and how to enhance therapy by harmonizing with your client's style
- How to identify your client's "locus of control" beliefs
- How to identify "learned helplessness" and help your clients move toward "learned optimism"
- How to respond to clients' "secondary gains" and unconscious motivations
- The seven key abilities that lead to emotional resiliency and mental wellness

One of the great marvels of the modern world is that the simple act of talking with another person can affect deep and lasting change.

The collaboration between a client and a skilled practitioner can achieve:

- Insight that leads to behavior change
- Behavior change that leads to insight
- A visceral change in the way the mind/body interprets and reacts to the recall of trauma
- A change in the fear reaction that allows clients to do things that they could never do before
- A change in neurotransmitter levels that affects mood equal to the effects of medication
- The extinguishing of self-destructive behavior
- An improvement in relationship satisfaction
- The improvement of occupational functioning and sports performance

One of the greatest satisfactions a practitioner can have is being involved with clients as they successfully navigate this process and achieve these changes. It is, however, not always an easy process. One needs to ask the following questions:

- How do clients change?
- Are there any common patterns?
- How does a practitioner know how ready a client is for change?
- What is the best approach and technique to use with each client to help him or her change?

Prochaska's Model of Change

In the 1950s, James O. Prochaska, PhD, asked many of the same questions while studying to be a psychotherapist. During this time, his father suffered from alcoholism and depression and was very distrustful of the psychotherapy profession. After his death, Prochaska wondered why psychotherapy did not have a greater positive effect on him. Years later, in 1979, he published his book, *Systems of Psychotherapy: A Transtheoretical Analysis*, in which he did a comparative analysis of 18 major theories of psychotherapy and behavior change. He investigated diverse schools of thought espoused by some of the major influences in psychology, including Sigmund Freud, B. F. Skinner, and Carl Rogers.

His investigation indicated that despite the variations in approaches, methods, and viewpoints, certain common principles of change could be applied to any client. Self-changers used these methods to achieve their desired change by either applying them to their cognitive and emotional process or to their external environments.

These processes of change are a valuable addition to your tool kit. Prochaska, Norcross, and DiClemente (1994) have organized the processes used by self-changers. These processes can also be used by practitioners in therapy sessions to help clients move from one stage of change to another.

The Processes of Change Model

The processes of change model[*] details common methods people use to change.

Consciousness-Raising

Consciousness-raising involves becoming more aware of the nature and risks of unsafe behaviors. Raising consciousness can produce insight leading to a questioning of present behavior. Once this is brought into consciousness, there is more information available for decision making. You can then evaluate the positive and negative effects of the problem behavior and seek safer, more productive, and more satisfying alternatives.

Social Liberation

Social liberation occurs when the external environment supports beginning or continuing a change effort. For example, compared to 30 years ago, there is far less stigma attached to seeking mental health treatment. Many more people can now use insurance coverage for mental health disorders rather than having to pay privately. This gives more people access to the proper conditions to

---

[*]Adapted from *Changing for Good: A Revolutionary Six-Stage Program for Overcoming Bad Habits and Moving Your Life Positively Forward* (pp. 27–32), by John O. Prochaska, John C. Norcross, and Carlo C. DiClemente, 1994, New York: HarperCollins.

embark on a change process. Note that people in different stages of change may interpret these "social liberation policies" quite differently. For example, someone in a precontemplative stage, which we discuss later in this chapter, who has no desire to quit smoking may find public nonsmoking areas a nuisance, whereas someone who is trying to quit finds them helpful in avoiding the temptation to smoke.

Emotional Arousal

Emotional arousal is a powerful and dramatic emotional experience related to the problem. It can often jolt one into rapidly changing something that was previously very difficult to change. For instance, one of the author's spouses had her eye burned as a small child by the ashes from her father's cigar as he held it down by his side. It was so upsetting to him that he caused this injury to his child that he instantly gave up smoking cigars. The purpose of emotional arousal or cathartic experiences is to take that depth of emotion and create action and movement toward change. Public education announcements, movies, songs, and fear-based advertisements are examples of emotional arousal techniques used in the general culture.

Self-Reevaluation

Self-reevaluation involves looking at the pros and cons of changing the problem behavior. This requires an introspective look at yourself and the problem. How does your problem conflict with your values and the type of person you want to be? Can you see what kind of person you would be if you no longer had this problem? After a period of self-reevaluation, one often deeply feels that change is possible, and even preferable, to live a better life.

Commitment

Once someone decides to change, the next step is to accept the responsibility to do so. Two aspects to this commitment process have been identified. One is internal and private: the acknowledgment that only you can actually make these changes. The other is public: making a declaration to others that you have made a decision to change. Making this public commitment is more powerful than just keeping this decision to yourself. The act of telling others creates social pressure to keep commitments.

Countering or Counterconditioning

Countering or counterconditioning involves substituting healthy responses for unhealthy ones. For instance, someone feeling anxious might have the habit of taking a drink of alcohol. A counter to that urge could be taking a walk until the urge passes or listening to a relaxation tape. People who are anxious prior to giving a speech might do a relaxation exercise rather than pacing the floor. Any healthy activity will do. Finding the right activity can be a very creative process. This leads to a more effective outcome and empowering experience for the client.

Environmental Control

Countering changes a person's reaction to a stimulus; environmental control regulates the stimulus. This involves restructuring the environment so that exposure to what triggers the unhealthy behavior is limited. For example, if someone becomes very anxious while driving past a certain corner because of an accident that he saw there recently, he may choose to take a different route so that he is not exposed to the location that triggers the anxiety. One can also add stimuli that encourage positive types of behavior, such as a chart of daily exercises accomplished that is posted on the refrigerator.

Rewards

After the hard work of changing a particular behavior, many successful changers give themselves a reward. The reward may be internal, such as feeling a sense of satisfaction in achieving the goal, or external, in the form of an enjoyable gift. Finding what is meaningful to the client will have the most impact.

Helping Relationships

Support from family and friends provides positive feedback and inspiration to continue the change process. The use of a sponsor in

Only in growth, reform, and change, paradoxically enough, is true security to be found.
—Anne Morrow Lindbergh

Alcoholics Anonymous follows this principle. The sponsor provides caring, understanding, and acceptance. Similarly, a relationship with a mentor may help a person keep on track at school or work.

It is important to remember that these are processes of change. Each process may have many different types and varieties of techniques to help clients change.

Assessing Stages of Change and Matching Interventions

How do practitioners identify their clients' readiness for change, and how does one help them manage the process of change? Further research by Prochaska et al. (1994) revealed that people went through various predictable stages of change.

TIP

By properly assessing what stage of change the client is in, the practitioner can tailor interventions to match the process that is the most useful for each stage.

When the practitioner's approach does not match the client's stage of readiness for change, the client may feel forced into a change that she does not want to make, or she may feel that the practitioner does not fully understand her problem or needs. The likelihood of dropping out of therapy increases with this type of mismatch. However, when therapists understand the change process, they can help their clients through it more efficiently with less trial and error and less distress. When done well, this feels like a very natural process for both practitioner and client.

Occasionally an "a-ha" moment occurs, when the lightbulb goes on and you can see the client make a series of connections and gain sudden insight. However, most of the time change is a process, with all of its pitfalls, failures, and successes. The process of change can occur in a single session, but it is more likely to occur over a series of sessions, or even over several episodes of care. You may encounter clients who are unwilling to change or do not seem capable of changing. Some will tell you outright that they have no intention of changing! In this case, any attempt on your part to encourage change will produce strong resistance.

The Stages of Change Model

Stage 1: Precontemplation

Clients at this stage often do not believe they have a problem. They are not very interested in help. Why should they be? They don't have a problem! They have not thought very much about it. Any negative consequences are not associated with the "problem." These clients can be quite defensive if pressured to change. They are often in treatment at the insistence of someone else: a spouse, parent, boss, or even the court system. Precontemplators want to change everyone else around them. They may have some insight but have such a poor history of self-change that they do not want to address the issue in any way. They feel it is hopeless, so why bother?

TIP

Recipe for failure: jumping from precontemplation to action. Sometime precontemplators are coerced into changing by someone else, and they give it a halfhearted attempt without understanding how it will benefit them or being committed to the change. Upon failure they can then turn around and say, "See, I tried and it didn't work!"

Client Language
- "I don't have a problem."
- "I'm just here because they said I had to come."
- "I tried before but it didn't work, so why bother?"

There is a lot of appeal in being a precontemplator. In this case, ignorance really is bliss. It is a very safe place. Without having to worry about changing, there is no possibility of failure. It is a mental environment free of guilt, peer pressure, and time demands. Common defense mechanisms of precontemplators are denial and minimization, rationalization, projection, and displacement (Prochaska et al., 1994). Precontemplators may view their problems as character flaws, which eventually destroys their ability to initiate a change process.

Practitioner Strategy
- Engage in nonthreatening, open discussion.
- Encourage thought, examination, and looking at the situation from different viewpoints.
- Raising ambivalence can help move the client to the next stage by increasing the sense that there may be a problem.

Practitioner Questions
- "What would have to happen for you to know that this is a problem?"
- "What warning signs would let you know that this is a problem?"
- "Have you tried to change in the past?" (Miller & Rollnick, 1991, pp. 191–202)

It takes a lot of courage to release the familiar and seemingly secure, to embrace the new. But there is no real security in what is no longer meaningful. There is more security in the adventurous and exciting, for in movement there is life, and in change there is power.
—Alan Cohen

One clue that a client is moving from precontemplation to contemplation is that the pros of changing start to increase in number (Prochaska et al., 1994).

Stage 2: Contemplation

During this stage, the client is aware there is a problem and has spent some time thinking about it. The problem has caused some negative consequences, and the client is considering changing at some time in the future. Although the client would like to change, he or she is ambivalent about it.

These clients are unsure whether they want to make the effort and do everything that changing would entail. They may focus on negative ramifications of the change, and they are not sure that it is worth the effort. The cost of changing may be too high. They may not want to give up certain things to make the change. The long-term benefits of change may not outweigh the short-term consequences. This stage can last from a few weeks to a lifetime. Some people never progress beyond this stage.

Client Language
- "I would like to change but . . ."
- "I'm just not sure I want to do that right now."
- "I've been thinking about changing when . . ."
- "I feel like I'm kind of stuck."

Client Struggles
- These clients struggle with ambivalence and doubt about whether they can change. Some search to understand their problem better. When they reach this high level of understanding, they will be ready to act, usually sometime off in the future.
- As a practitioner, be aware of the disease of chronic contemplation. These clients often need to look at things in minute detail and will leave no stone unturned in their quest to understand why they have this problem. Some will spend years in this state. They would rather live in the joy of the possibility of change than in the struggle of action. They equate thinking with action.

Practitioner Goal
- Be empathetic, validate their struggles, and offer encouragement that change is possible for them.
- Get clients thinking about making a change and what that would mean in their lives.
- Strengthen their confidence that they have the ability to make the change.

Practitioner Questions That Help to Elicit Change Talk
- "Why do you want to change at this time?"
- "What are the reasons for not changing?"
- "What would keep you from changing at this time?"
- "What are the barriers that keep you from change?"
- "What might help you overcome those barriers?"
- "What people, things, or programs have helped you overcome things like this in the past?"
- "What would help you now?"
- "What do you think you need to learn about changing?" (Miller et al., 1991, pp. 191–202)

Our dilemma is that we hate change and love it at the same time; what we really want is for things to remain the same but get better.
—Sydney J. Harris

The gem cannot be polished without friction, nor a man perfected without trials.
—Chinese proverb

One of the clues that a client is moving from contemplation to preparation is when the client's language and thoughts change from talking about the problem to focusing on the solution. The client may also become more future-oriented, rather than living in the past. The cons of changing decrease (Prochaska et al., 1994).

Stage 3: Preparation

This stage involves clients making plans to take specific action to change. They have made a commitment. They may experiment with small changes at first as a way to test their readiness.

When you make a commitment, the universe conspires to assist you.
—Barbra Streisand

Client Language
- "It really has gotten out of control. I need to do something about this."
- "This is it. What can I do to get started?"
- "So maybe if I did this, then that would not happen!"

Client Struggles
- These clients are preparing emotionally to make the change but are still unsure how to go about it.

Practitioner Goals
- Help clients gather information about what they need to change their behavior. Encourage them not to skip this phase.
- Encourage spending time assessing what it will take to change and seeking support from others who have made similar changes.
- Help them devise a specific workable plan of action.

Practitioner Questions
- "What strategies will you use to change?"
- "What resources are available for you to change?"
- "Who can be your advocate, buddy, or support system to help you through this?"

Prior planning prevents poor performance.
—Jordan Barrett

Stage 4: Action

These clients have thought about making a change, have prepared for it, and are ready now to take practical steps to make it happen. This stage often involves teaching and supporting a variety of techniques to help the client change.

Client Language

- "I am ready to work on this now!"
- "I'm mentally ready now. I know I can do this."
- "When do we get started?"

Client Struggles

- These clients are dealing with initial difficulties that may seem too hard to overcome.

Practitioner Goals

- Help clients set realistic goals and develop practical methods to achieve them.
- Reexamine their commitment to the process and help them develop a clear sense of what they want to accomplish.

Practitioner Questions

- "When you have achieved the change that you want in your life, what will you do differently?"
- "How can you avoid a slip?"
- "If you do relapse, how can you get focused again?"
- "What kind of rewards will you give to yourself to keep going?"
- "Who can give you support right now?"
- "Whom should you avoid right now?"

Knowing is not enough; we must apply. Willing is not enough; we must do.
—Bruce Lee

Stage 5: Maintenance

Clients are doing what they have prepared for in the other stages. Their new goal is to maintain the gains they have made so far. They are able to anticipate high-risk relapse situations and have integrated new coping skills into their behavioral repertoire.

Client Language

- "I can't believe how far I've come!"
- "Why did it take me so long to do this?"
- "I've still got a ways to go, but I really like where I am right now."

Self-conquest is the greatest of victories.
—Plato

Client Struggles

- These clients have to work hard to avoid slipping back into the old behavior.
- They may fear that if they do slip back, they have failed.

Practitioner Goals

- Remind clients of how much progress they have already made.
- Encourage them to learn new skills to maintain their gains.
- If a relapse occurs, recognize the discouragement but help them realize that this is normal and part of the process. Most people do not take a straight line on the road to change but take some twists and turns, and even a few detours.

Practitioner Questions

- "What would throw you off track right now?"
- "How can you avoid that?"
- "If you can't avoid it, how will you get back on track?"

TIP

Dealing with relapse: When clients relapse they often feel a sense of failure, which undermines their confidence regarding overcoming the problem. Remind them that relapse is not a final destination but an opportunity to examine why and how the slip occurred and a chance to learn new skills. The likelihood of relapse is so high that clients should not only prepare for it, they should expect it!

Stage 6: Termination

Clients who have overcome their problem have maintained the desired behavior for an extended period. The issue is no longer a problem in their life. These clients often have a clear sense of the old life and the new life. Going back to the old way of being seems very strange, even undesirable. Terminators have a lot of confidence that they won't relapse. There is some controversy in the field about whether any problem can be completely overcome, or if there is always a danger of its return (perpetual maintenance).

Client Language

- "How did I ever do that? I never want to go back there again."
- "I can't even see myself doing that anymore."

- "I can't believe I used to do that. The new me doesn't even find that attractive."

Client Struggles

- These clients are dealing with the results of the change in their lives, which may include having to let go of old friends who are still doing the undesirable behavior, treating others differently, or being treated differently by others.

Practitioner Strategy

- Congratulations are in order! Support continued self-development, and offer the opportunity to return to therapy if the need arises.

TIP

Knowing how people change influences your actions as a psychotherapist. The emphasis is not necessarily on changing clients' behavior but helping them move from one stage of change to the next so they change their own behavior. This concept alone can be very liberating for the practitioner!

Which Change Processes Make a Good Match for the Various Stages of Change?

It is important for practitioners to match the process they use with the client's stage of change. For instance, consciousness-raising and social liberation are very effective during the precontemplative and contemplative stages (Prochaska et al., 1994). During the preparation stage, it is helpful to revisit the client's sense of commitment so that there is clarity of purpose. However, when more goal-oriented stages occur, it is more effective to change tactics and help clients counter their behavior, control their environment, and rely on social supports.

We have reviewed literally thousands of treatment plans in our duties as utilization managers of outpatient psychotherapy for a managed care organization and health plan. The vast majority of practitioners guide their clients through this process well. The therapists who do not tend to mismatch the process to the stage of change. In particular, they usually focus on the consciousness-raising aspects over the other processes, regardless of the stage of change of the client. They believe that if their clients just have another insight, it will propel them into change. (See Chapter 7 for more on the difference between insight and behavior change.) They either fail to recognize when clients are ready to move to the next stage, or they fail to support them by helping them use the stage-appropriate process to move to the next stage. Consciousness-raising is a lot more interesting for these practitioners. The process of helping clients to counter and control their environments may not be as "glamorous," but it is this practical aspect of therapy that clients often need to help them continue their journey toward change.

This mismatch often causes the client to drop out of treatment; in some cases, it helps perpetuate the problem. We often see a client become quite dependent on the therapist who is providing very ineffective treatment. If, at a later date, the client works with another practitioner who has the same approach, he or she can have another unproductive episode of care. When this occurs repeatedly, it can adversely affect clients' sense of self-mastery over their own ability to change and lead to the belief that they can never be well.

Understanding Clients' Learning Styles

It is helpful for practitioners to understand their clients' learning styles. How do they process information? What is the best method to help them learn? Through the therapeutic exchange of words, ideas, feelings, and visual images, clients learn how to change themselves. Matching the language, metaphors, and type of homework assignments to each client's learning style will greatly increase the practitioner's effectiveness. There are two ways you can determine a client's learning style: directly and indirectly. The direct method is simply asking! Most people know what style is most comfortable for them. The indirect method involves listening to their language for cues. Client responses such as "I see what you mean" and "I hear what you are saying" can help you identify the learning style that is most comfortable for your client.

Let's examine the three main styles of information processing:

1. Visual
2. Auditory
3. Kinesthetic

Visual Learners

Visual learners may give you an indication of their learning style by the language they use in session: "I see what you are saying"; "Every time I think of that situation I can't help seeing . . ." If you are working with a visual learner, the client may benefit by your using more visual material. For instance, rather than talking about the stress cycle, a practitioner may want to use a handout with a visual representation of how thoughts, feelings, and body sensations all interact. This may be much more effective with this type of client than just talking about it. In this case, a picture may truly be worth a thousand words. Likewise, a practitioner's metaphors should be visual in nature to be effective. These clients may respond well to guided imagery.

Auditory Learners

Auditory learners are likely to need to talk a lot. For some practitioners they are the perfect client! They process information out loud. They may need to process issues repeatedly. Repetition helps to solidify the concept in their minds. Having them explain a possible solution to their problem as if they were explaining it to a third person can be a useful intervention. Because auditory learners are usually good at remembering songs, jingles can be used to remind them to engage in a behavior that has been difficult for them. For instance, a client who is a workaholic could be assigned a popular jingle: "You deserve a break today, so get up and get away. . . ." This is a much more powerful intervention than just asking the client to take a break now and then. The client will remember the jingle and will do something different. This can be a very effective way to help a client break an entrenched behavioral pattern.

Kinesthetic Learners

Kinesthetic learners learn by doing. They need a hands-on approach. They may not respond as well to auditory or visual clues.

They need to get their body involved and "feel" whatever it is they are involved in. Showing them how to relax their body by relaxing their shoulders is much more effective than having them visualize a comfortable place. Kinesthetic learners respond well to doing something, so homework assignments that require a task work very well.

Although these learning styles seem very obvious, they are often overlooked. Matching your interventions with the client's learning style can produce a powerful and lasting change that feels natural for the client. It may seem silly for the practitioner and the client at times, but it does work!

Locus of Control

A competent psychotherapist must keep in mind the concept of locus of control. The theory of locus of control was developed by the psychologist J. B. Rotter (1966). Derived from social learning theory, it "describes the degree to which individuals believe that reinforcements are contingent upon their own behavior" (Swick & Graves, 1986, p. 41). People with an internal locus of control believe that what they do affects outcomes in their lives. People with an external locus of control believe that other people or events control outcomes. These beliefs develop over time, beginning in childhood, and have a subtle but profound effect.

Try listening to how your clients explain why things happen as they do.

> "It's not fair! Every time I get close to my goal, something always interferes! I guess it doesn't matter if I try or not. I'm never going to get what I want."

> "I've noticed that when I stop paying attention to my sleep and exercise patterns, all my relationships start going downhill. Usually if I start taking better care of myself, my relationships improve, too."

Clients who have an innate internal locus of control may be easier to help. They will listen to suggestions and try them out. They can see a clear cause-and-effect relationship between their own behaviors and their results. If this belief system is taken too far, however, these clients may come to think that everything happens because of their own behavior.

> "I was thinking negatively about that camping trip all week. No wonder it rained! I must have brought it on myself somehow."

You may need to help these clients develop a more balanced and accepting attitude toward life.

Clients who have an external locus of control can be challenging. They may have no hope that anything they do will affect their situation. They will tend to reject suggested changes, or try them halfheartedly just so they can show you why they will not work. (See Chapter 12 for more on working with resistance and avoidance.) These clients can benefit from cognitive interventions. Making locus of control beliefs explicit and then testing them in real-life situations can be useful. Identifying the experiential source of external locus of control beliefs can have some benefit, but ultimately you must help the client develop, test, and refine new beliefs in order to have a genuine effect.

Learned Helplessness and Learned Optimism

The concepts of learned helplessness and learned optimism are related to locus of control. In learned helplessness (Peterson, Maier, & Seligman, 1993, p. 148), people believe that bad events are:

- *Global:* "It affects everything I do."
- *Stable:* "It happens all the time."
- *Internal:* "It's my fault; my character flaws make everything go badly."

In contrast, people with a learned optimism explanatory style (Seligman, Reivich, Jaycox, & Gillham, 1995, pp. 52–63) believe that bad events are:

- *Specific:* "She didn't like that particular comment I made."
- *Temporary:* "This is a problem for me right now."
- *External:* "My parents are fighting because of their own relationship problems, not because of what I said" (though this does not preclude taking responsibility for one's own actions accurately: "I didn't do well in that presentation because I did not prepare for it enough").

Examining clients' explanatory styles can help to identify pervasive errors in thinking. Learned helplessness beliefs are often the result of real experiences of powerlessness, such as child abuse, domestic violence, or other victimization. Help clients understand that their current situation is an attempt to adapt to a very negative experience. It is important to validate how such beliefs originated and that they can be unlearned in favor of more optimistic beliefs. (See Chapter 12 for more on core beliefs.)

Now that your clients' perceptions have changed, you can help them learn new skills.

Secondary Gains

Some clients appear to have all the elements in place necessary for change: They say they want to, they have done all the necessary preparation, and their environment is conducive to change. Yet they do not change. When this occurs and a client does not change, think secondary gains. There is usually some positive payoff behind all of the seemingly negative repercussions of the behavior. For example, perhaps, because of her problem, she gets extra attention from family members, or gets special accommodations at work. To change, this client needs to give up these positive secondary gains.

Clients often pay a great price to get the positive payoff. This is usually beyond the client's conscious awareness. Seeing this repeated pattern, the practitioner can help to bring this issue to the conscious awareness of the client. Once this is in conscious awareness, the focus can be shifted to helping the client develop more appropriate methods of getting the positive payoff without denying herself the opportunity to change.

When a client is deliberately exaggerating symptoms for some kind of personal gain and manipulation of others, this type of behavior is malingering.

One area that is much overlooked is the concept of tertiary gain, in which a client may unconsciously exaggerate symptoms to please the practitioner. In this case, a client's report of symptoms may be more pronounced in session when compared to what happens between sessions. Assessing functional impairments at intervals may help the therapist uncover this pattern.

Unconscious Motivations

Unconscious motivations can sometimes drive the outcome of the change process. Energy psychology approaches, such as thought field therapy, are particularly adept at uncovering and working with unconscious motivations. In the energy psychology approach, when a client consciously states that he wants to change but unconsciously believes that he doesn't, he is said to be "psychologically reversed." This psychological reversal can be the root cause of why some clients are unable to change behaviors and lose weight, stop using substances, or have better relationships. These clients have a deep-seated unconscious belief that is contrary to what they are consciously expressing, so they end up sabotaging themselves. These beliefs are usually related to themes such as "I don't deserve good things to happen to me"; "It is not safe to change (some other bad thing will happen if I start doing the new behavior)"; "It's not possible to change this behavior"; "If I change this behavior someone I care about will be hurt"; or "I will lose my identity if I get over this problem" (a common theme with some Vietnam-era vets).

Mental Wellness—What Is It?

As practitioners we most often focus on the deficits or problems of our clients. The *Diagnostic and Statistical Manual of Mental Disorders* provides the definition of mental illness. But what about mental wellness? How should this be defined? The physician Daniel Siegel has asked over 55,000 mental health practitioners to define mental wellness, and only 5% have ever considered the question (Hammond, 2006). How can we as practitioners help our clients if we do not have a concept of what mental wellness is?

Why does one person grow through adversity, and another in similar circumstances does not? What does each person do differently? Resiliency involves being able to bounce back from adversity and challenge by using certain skills to deal with the stressors of life. If illness is defined as disease, then wellness indicates the presence of healthy behaviors and attitudes. Although the concept of resilience is very broad, it is generally agreed that resilience rests on the idea of achievement of positively (or the avoidance of negatively) valued outcomes in circumstances in which adverse outcomes would normally be expected (Kaplan, 2006).

Revich, Gillham, Chaplin, and Seligman (2006) have identified seven key interpersonal factors or abilities that appear to increase overall resilience:

1. *Emotional regulation:* Being able to understand what you are feeling and why you are feeling it and expressing it in an appropriate way.
2. *Impulse control:* Being aware of your reactions and slowing down the process of expression in order to make conscious choices that are appropriate to the situation.
3. *Causal analysis:* Making sound, accurate judgments about the causes of your problems.
4. *Realistic optimism:* Having an optimistic and realistic viewpoint.
5. *Self-efficacy:* Having confidence in yourself that you can solve problems and cope with a broad range of life situations.
6. *Empathy:* Being able to see things from someone else's viewpoint, understand their emotional state, and connect with them on a genuine human level.
7. *Reaching out:* Having the ability to connect with others during stressful times and receive support when you need it.

In addition, we would add mind/body integration, or the ability to gain insight from somatic experience and the use of physical activity to increase mental stamina. This mind/body balance is a sign of mental wellness. Many clients enter treatment lacking many of these resiliency skills. These aspects of resiliency can be part of your treatment plan for them. Teaching emotion regulation skills, using mindfulness to examine cause-and-effect relationships, and practicing problem-solving skills help promote the kind of resilience that will enable your clients to function successfully.

Summing Up

In this chapter we have seen how several different aspects of the change process can be used to identify the stages of change of your clients and how best to help them through the process. You may choose to incorporate some of these concepts into your evaluation and treatment planning forms so that you will be reminded to pay attention to them. You may also want to review these concepts whenever you are feeling stuck with a client in an unproductive therapy episode.

EXERCISES

1. What have you needed to change about yourself in the past 5 years? How did you do it? What "processes of change" did you use?

2. Have you ever been in a "precontemplation" stage of change? How do you recognize this in your clients?

3. Have you ever misread a client's stage of change? How did this affect the course of therapy? Were you able to move the client to a different stage of change? Did you change your own approach to better match the client's stage of change? Why or why not?

4. Read the following scenarios and determine:

   • What is the client's stage of change?

   • What are the client's struggles?

   • As a practitioner, what would be your strategy and what types of questions would you ask?

A 14-year-old girl comes into therapy at the insistence of her parents, who have just learned that she is sexually active.

A client comes in wanting to overcome her fear of flying in order to go on a vacation with her family in 2 months.

A client knows that he needs to learn assertiveness skills. He is tired of being taken advantage of. He has tried a few things, but they haven't worked out well. He just doesn't know what to do next.

A client is referred by her physician to make some lifestyle changes. She has been thinking about making some changes for a while now. Although she understands that she would be healthier if she made the changes, she is not so sure now is the right time to begin.

(Continued)

A client has made dramatic changes regarding overeating and has been able to sustain that for quite a while. He is going through a very stressful time right now and will be going to a wedding in a few weeks. He is afraid he might slip.

5. What is your own preferred learning style (visual, auditory, or kinesthetic)? How do you recognize learning styles in your clients? How do you modify your therapy techniques to better match those of different clients?

6. What is your definition of mental wellness? What aspects of resiliency do you most embody? How did you get there? Have you seen clients develop more resiliency?

9

Beginning Treatment

What You Will Learn
- How to determine what your client wants
- How to recognize pathology
- How to use the *DSM* to establish an accurate diagnosis
- How to guard against overpathologizing your clients
- The elements involved in taking a comprehensive history
- How to establish a diagnosis and discuss it with your client
- The importance of determining functional impairments and functional goals
- How to develop a case conceptualization
- Useful questions for developing a case conceptualization
- How to use "the miracle question"
- How to set the stage for treatment with focused treatment planning
- Why it is important to pay attention to the client's stage of change during treatment planning
- How to define measurable goals
- How to set realistic treatment expectations
- Why termination planning starts now

In this chapter we examine the elements of a successful first few sessions with a new psychotherapy client. It is important to develop a clear focus for therapy, integrating your own unique style of interaction. That sense of focus means a plan of action for each client. This will ensure that you:

- Accurately assess the client's needs and goals.
- Have a mutually agreed upon treatment plan.
- Set up a time frame (see Chapter 10) to accomplish those goals.

Having a clear focus means that you can justify the time and expense of psychotherapy to your client and any insurance plan that may be paying for treatment. An explicit treatment plan and informed consent will help protect you from any allegation of malpractice. Because you cannot predict adverse events, a competent evaluation and plan is needed for every client.

TIP

It is much easier to create a clear treatment plan at the beginning of treatment than to try to construct one after treatment is already under way.

Determining What the Client Wants

Practitioners and clients have many different views of the purpose of therapy (see Chapter 1). Most clients enter therapy with an idea of what they want from treatment. Examples of common expectations follow.

"I just want to feel better."
"I think we should talk about all of the trauma in my life, and this will resolve everything."
"I want some advice about how to deal with my problems."
"I want you to fix my relationship with . . . "
"I want you to analyze my dreams and tell me what they really mean."
"I want to learn more about how to handle my emotions."
"I want to understand why I always . . . "

There are several effective ways to determine what your client wants. The first is to simply ask directly:

"What led you to call now for therapy?"
"What would you like help with most?"
"What would you like to get out of therapy?"
"What would you like to be able to do that you don't feel you can do now?"

An important component at the beginning of every episode of psychotherapy is establishing the client's expectations. You may want to ask some brief questions about the client's expectations on your initial client history form, which can be a very effective way of gathering information. Try to ask the question in two or three different ways; it may take a new client several tries to get at the heart of what he or she wants to accomplish. A symptom checklist may be useful at this point as well. You are likely to get a more extensive history and more thoughtful comments if you send the history form to clients in the mail a week before your first meeting than if you have them fill it out in the waiting room 15 minutes before the session. When you are able to review the history before the session, it is easier to discuss how it affects the client's symptoms. Then the interaction occurs in a meaningful way during the first session, rather than simply taking a report of information.

Recognizing Pathology

What is pathology?

psy·cho·pa·thol·o·gy

1. The study of the origin, development, and manifestations of mental or behavioral disorders
2. The manifestation of a mental or behavioral disorder (Psychopathology, n.d.)

Psychopathology is a set of experiences and/or behaviors that cause a person some level of observable impairment, distress, or disability that is thought to originate in some abnormality in the neurocognitive system. These symptoms often set the person apart from his or her peers.

As mental health practitioners, we are interested in the descriptive nature of pathology. What are the symptoms? Do they have any observable pattern? Can they be grouped together to indicate a recognizable diagnosis? Sometimes symptoms are pathological signs that do not necessarily indicate a definitive diagnosis. For instance, consider a 70-year-old woman who is displaying signs of confusion and hallucinations. Is this a psychotic disorder, or is the origin of this pathology a urinary tract infection? If it is an infection and it is treated with antibiotics, the symptoms will disappear and the client will return to her previous level of functioning. (See Chapter 15 for more on medical conditions that have mental health symptoms.)

Consider these common client presentations:

- Jim is a 14-year-old boy who frequently gets into fights, punches holes in walls when angry, and cannot read.

- Kathy is an 8-year-old girl who is refusing to go to school, cannot tolerate being away from her mother, and wakes up frequently with nightmares.

- George is a 35-year-old man who is unable to get out of bed in the morning, has stopped going to work, and hears voices telling him to kill himself.

- Jill is a 56-year-old woman who has a long history of profound depression, with frequent periods of increased activity, decreased sleep, and broken relationships.

Each of these clients has significant behaviors that lead to alienation from others. Each has a great deal of difficulty functioning in his or her roles in life, as students, family members, workers, and friends, and each has an identifiable pathology that can be treated with psychotherapy.

Pathology stems from biological, social, and environmental stressors. Jim may have a Conduct Disorder, Intermittent Explosive Disorder, and/or a Learning Disability. What is the source of 8-year-old Kathy's nightmares? Has she been abused or traumatized? Has she been in a recent motor vehicle accident? Is she being bullied at school? Does her mother have a life-threatening illness and Kathy is acting out? As a psychotherapist, you want to identify the pathology, possible causes, and consequences of the pathology. It helps to bring a sense of curiosity to the evaluation, rather than jumping to a diagnosis prematurely. In the example of Jim, for instance, you want to find out:

- When Jim's angry behavior started
- Whether there have been any recent changes in the behaviors
- What trouble he has with reading and other schoolwork, and when it started
- Whether he has any medical problems that could be contributing to his behaviors
- Whether he is abusing any substances
- What Jim thinks the problems are
- What his parents and teachers have tried to do about the problems so far

The answers to these questions will reveal the precise shape of his pathology.

Using the Diagnostic and Statistical Manual of Mental Disorders

One tool that is essential in evaluating pathology in your clients is the *Diagnostic and Statistical Manual of Mental Disorders* (DSM), which has been available from the American Psychiatric Association in various editions since 1952. The DSM identifies mental disorders, including incidence, criteria for diagnosis, and criteria for identifying variants. It is important to get in the habit of consulting your DSM during the evaluative process for each client. You will use the DSM to determine if your client has a disorder or a problem of living. You will also use it to determine if your treatment has been effective over time. For example, a client may come to you with seven of the nine of the criteria for a Major Depressive Episode, with five required for diagnosis (American Psychiatric Association, 2000, p. 356). After several months of treatment, he may meet only three criteria, thus showing significant improvement. On the other hand, over time he may meet an increasing number of criteria. You may discover that another diagnosis best explains the client's symptoms, and you will need to change your treatment strategies.

Guarding against Overpathologizing

A sense of curiosity in the evaluative process, as well as knowledge of *DSM* diagnostic criteria, will help to identify pathology. But guard against overpathologizing your clients and medicalizing normal human experience (Travis, 2007). Not everyone who enters therapy has a diagnosable disorder. A wide range of human behavior may be considered normal in any given culture. Overpathologizing is influenced by relying too strongly on the medical model, managed care's emphasis on treating a disorder if coverage is to be accessed, and exuberant therapists. The harm that can result from overpathologizing can follow a client for a lifetime. This harm is not always recognized by therapists, or the effect of the harm is accepted by therapists as unavoidable. A client who is diagnosed with major depression may later be denied a job or health insurance because of the diagnosis. If the diagnosis is inaccurate, the client will be unnecessarily harmed. Personal suffering can occur for reasons that have nothing to do with pathology. Consider the following examples.

- Sally is unhappy with how her best friend is treating her. She has been feeling increasingly angry and has even started having trouble sleeping at night due to rumination.

- George comes to therapy because his wife thinks he should have more hobbies lined up before he retires next year.

- Melissa's parents have brought her to therapy because she does not seem to be enjoying school and has become moodier in the past few months.

- Frank has a vague sense of dissatisfaction in his life and wants to find out why he is not enjoying everyday activities.

While you certainly want to explore whether symptoms of a mental disorder are present in these clients, they may not meet criteria for any disorder at all. Most can be helped in a few sessions without pathologizing what may be normal transitions in life. Avoid the temptation to keep digging until you find a diagnosis. If the client wants to pay for therapy with health insurance benefits, you may need to explain that no diagnosis is both good news and bad news: The client is likely to feel better quite soon, but health insurance is not likely to cover the therapy. It would be unethical to try to "up-code" to a *DSM* diagnosis to obtain coverage. (See Chapter 2 for more on the ethics of up-coding a diagnosis.)

Taking a Comprehensive History: The Structured Interview

After getting a clear idea of what your client wants from therapy, it makes sense to get more information to formulate a diagnosis, form a case conceptualization, and develop a treatment plan. It is useful to have a written format so that you are sure to get relevant information with each client. Introduce the client to what you are doing, saying something like "I want to be sure I get all the information that I need to make sure we will be going in the right direction."

There is an art to doing the initial interview in a way that gets all the relevant information, does not take too long, and, at the same time, begins to establish rapport. Take time to reflect back to the client what you have heard and ask for clarification. Write down some of the client's own words, which will help you clarify your own understanding of the material as well as demonstrate to the client that you are truly listening.

Important areas to explore in the structured interview are:

- Client's statement of the problem and goals
- Family history (parents, siblings; any family history of mental illness or substance abuse)
- Childhood (significant events, illnesses, school functioning, friends)
- Adolescence (as above; and dating, career planning, education)
- Adulthood
- Vocation
- Military service
- Marriage/relationship history
- Children
- Religious or spiritual orientation
- Significant events

- Health history and current health status (including chronic pain)
- Medication history
- Abuse history
- Current behavioral functioning
- Strengths
- Previous coping strategies
- Mood symptoms
- Anxiety symptoms
- Psychotic symptoms
- Interpersonal problems
- Other symptoms

Once you have all the information you need, let the client know that you will review it carefully before the next session to make sure that you have a clear idea of what the problem is and what you can do to help. (See Chapter 4 for more on documentation of the initial interview.)

TIP

As a psychotherapist, you have an obligation to treat your clients with the most effective, efficient, and ethical treatment available. You wouldn't want to call a plumber who wanders around your house for hours before finding out what pipe is leaking, or who recommends tearing out all the plumbing to fix one leaking pipe, or who continues to charge you $100 an hour to tell stories about other pipes he's fixed in the past. Unfortunately, consumers of therapy are not always informed enough about the process of psychotherapy to know when the equivalent is being done to them. Endeavor to provide therapy to your clients with at least the level of professional competence that you would expect from your plumber!

Setting the Stage for Treatment: Accurate Diagnosis

Your next step is formulating an accurate diagnosis. At times, the diagnosis will be quite clear in the initial interview. If it is, you may want to begin communicating this with the client.

Discussing the Diagnosis with Your Client

One of the reasons clients choose to meet with psychotherapists is that we have specialized knowledge. They want to know the answer to "What's wrong?" Psychotherapists have the training, skills, and technical knowledge to diagnose disorders. Consider these factors when discussing a diagnosis with your client:

- Your level of confidence in the diagnosis
- The client's own assessment of the problem
- The client's level of psychological sophistication (some may need specific and detailed information; others may just need the highlights)
- The necessity of diagnostic clarity if the client is using health insurance to pay for services
- Your confidence in your ability to treat the disorder

Some clients come into the session telling you their diagnosis. Respect their assessment, but remain open to other possibilities as well. Be wary of jumping to conclusions too quickly. Some clients, especially those who have seen many practitioners, pick up another diagnosis with each episode of treatment and may present to you with multiple diagnoses. They are usually overwhelmed and quite confused. The first step with these clients may be establishing some diagnostic clarity. Consider the following example.

A 38-year-old woman comes to see you after a series of unproductive therapy episodes with a variety of practitioners over the course of 15 years. With each treatment episode she picks up a new diagnosis. She states that her current diagnoses are Attention Deficit Disorder (Inattentive Type), Generalized Anxiety Disorder, Dysthymia, and Posttraumatic Stress Disorder. A friend of hers notices that sometimes she is inactive and sometimes she seems more animated but anxious. The friend thinks she might be bipolar.

In the course of taking the history you find out that the woman had a series of traumas starting in early childhood and was in an abusive marriage. As you complete your assessment, some of the pieces of the puzzle start to come together. As a result of a long history of verbal abuse and physical threats, she became unsure about herself and her ability to act independently. Any behavior that fell outside of the "acceptable" limits placed by her husband caused her a great deal of anxiety, until she became anxious in nearly every situation. After years of living a life filled with a high level of anxiety, it became very difficult for her to concentrate and sleep. She has periods of great fatigue but later cannot stand to be inactive any longer and tries to catch up on things that she has left undone for a long time.

Clinical Considerations

If you see separate clusters of symptoms rather than a client undergoing an integrated experience, you may be inclined to add a new diagnosis. If you strive to view the client's symptoms as having some integrated but yet undiscovered meaning, you can get a more comprehensive understanding of your client's experience. This approach gives you a better chance of focusing on the one thing that may give the client the most benefit. In some cases, it may be the lynchpin that holds the other symptoms in place.

Some practitioners are eager to diagnose without taking a longitudinal view of the client's symptoms. Reconsider the case of the 38-year-old woman with a multitude of diagnoses. This woman's trauma has gone untreated for a long time and has gotten increasingly worse over the years, until she experiences incapacitating anxiety affecting almost every facet of her life (Generalized Anxiety Disorder). Eventually, the high level of trauma and anxiety has led to disturbed sleep and problems with concentration and focus (Attention Deficit Disorder). After years of living an unchosen life, this client has become chronically sad about her state in life and all of the things she has been unable to do (Dysthymia). However, despite all that she has gone through, she has a resilient spirit which tries to break though now and then to be more active in her own life. For brief periods she becomes more active, but her anxiety eventually overtakes her, returning her to an unsatisfying and restricted life. Some therapists will see this cycle as a possible Bipolar Disorder, but if seen in the context of her total experience, it could be a "flight toward health" that is eventually overcome by her anxiety symptoms.

This type of case conceptualization is important because it greatly influences the treatment plan. If one follows the multiple layered diagnostic route, it is likely that this client will end up taking a stimulant (which may exacerbate her anxiety), a mood stabilizer, and sleep medication, with a focus on helping her manage a variety of symptoms. If, however, the focus is on treating her trauma and anxiety with the goal of reducing the anxiety so that she has a wider range of behavioral options available to her, it is possible that there will be improvements in focus, attention, sleep, and mood. The domestic violence issue will need to be addressed as well.

After the session, look over your structured interview notes carefully. Make some hypotheses about the probable diagnosis. Then review the client's symptoms against the criteria in the most recent edition of the *DSM*. Ask yourself whether a different diagnosis might better explain the symptoms, and review criteria for that diagnosis. Be cognizant that a client may have more than one diagnosis.

If the diagnosis is clear to you, move on to treatment planning. However, if it is not clear what the diagnosis is, or it is a complex case, consider consulting with a colleague. You may end up with several "rule-outs" until you are able to get more information from the client over time. A first episode of depression may go on to be a Major Depressive Disorder, Recurrent, or it may be the first sign of an emerging Bipolar Disorder. Being clear about what the disorder is likely to be, as well as alternatives, will help you focus treatment in a logical and sequential manner. Be sure to consider possible personality disorders, as these can complicate the treatment of other disorders. (See Chapter 13 for more on personality disorders.)

What if the client appears to have no serious pathology? The client may still have symptoms or problems that can be a focus of therapy. Remember that down-coding and up-coding of diagnoses is unethical and can have serious consequences. Calling a V-code an Adjustment Disorder or a major mood or anxiety disorder to obtain insurance payment for treatment can lead to an ethical dilemma for you and diagnostic confusion for your clients. An inaccurate diagnosis can linger long after your work with a client is completed.

Conversely, what if the client appears to have a serious disorder, but you are reluctant to acknowledge this to yourself, your client, or third-party payers? This, too, can lead to significant problems, including legal liability if an adverse event occurs. Your best protection is to look objectively at the symptoms presented and the criteria listed in the current version of the DSM. If the symptoms match, that is your diagnosis. If they are close to a match but do not completely match, you can diagnose a rule-out. Be prepared to give your client information about the diagnosis, including symptoms, criteria, and prognosis. In certain cases, you may want to mention your hesitation to make a diagnosis until you have more information. Clients will appreciate the thoroughness of your work and that you are not jumping to conclusions without a complete understanding of the symptomatology.

Some clients choose to pay for treatment privately rather than have the diagnosis appear in their medical record. Do not be pressured into down-coding; remember that your liability in the case of an adverse event can be significantly impacted if it appears you missed a serious diagnosis and were treating a less serious one instead. (See Chapter 3 for more on the ethical and legal risks of up-coding and down-coding.)

Assessing Functional Impairments and Functional Goals

One of the most important things you can do to ensure effective and efficient treatment of your clients is to pay attention early in treatment to functional impairments and functional goals. As part of your DSM 5-Axis diagnosis, you will need to establish a beginning Global Assessment of Functioning (GAF) score. This scale evaluates functioning in three spheres: psychological, social, and occupational. The scale is described in the latest version of the DSM, along with examples of various types of functional impairments. For example, a GAF score of 51 to 60 means "moderate symptoms (e.g., flat affect and circumstantial speech, occasional panic attacks) OR moderate difficulty in social, occupational, or school functioning (e.g., few friends, conflicts with peers or coworkers)" (American Psychiatric Association, 2000, p. 34). Be sure you understand how to use this scale and practice making accurate assessments.

Functional Impairments

A functional impairment is the inability to function at a level normally expected of a person of the same age, education, and social environment. Some examples of functional impairments are:

Psychological Functioning
- Symptoms of mental disorders that interfere with daily life

Occupational Functioning
- Inability to go to work at expected times
- Inability to do the work expected
- Difficulty getting along with coworkers
- Odd or bizarre behavior that impairs work activities

School Functioning
- Inability to go to school or stay at school
- Inability to get schoolwork done
- Conflict with peers or teachers
- Odd or bizarre behavior that impairs school activities

Social Functioning
- Conflicted relationships with family or friends
- Isolating from family or friends
- Odd or bizarre behavior that impairs social activities

Health Functioning
- Behaviors that harm one's health
- Inappropriate use of medical professionals (overuse, underuse)
- Failing to treat serious illness

It is important to note that to be considered in the GAF score, these impairments must be related to psychological symptoms and not solely to medical problems. For example, the impairment of a worker who is often absent from work due to severe migraine headaches would not be included, but the impairment of a worker who is often absent from work due to incapacitating anxiety would be included.

As you are doing your initial client assessment, be sure to note specific examples of functional impairments. Some impairments may be disturbing to your client ("I keep having these awful arguments with my sister"), or they may be disturbing only to others ("Sure I get sent to the principal's office every day, but that's just because my teacher has a grudge against me"). You can ask your client "How does symptom X get in the way of you doing what you want to do?" or "What would you like to be able to do or accomplish that you cannot do now because of symptom X?"

Functional Goals

Functional goals should be clearly understood by the client. Explain that by establishing functional goals, you and the client will be able to see how therapy is progressing and when it is time to complete your work together. You may need to negotiate some goals that you see as important but your client does not. For example, you may negotiate a functional goal of "know how to get my teacher and principal off my back and be able to do it." This functional goal has two aspects to it:

1. *Insight:* "Knowing how to get my teacher and my principal off my back"
2. *Behavior:* Doing something different as the result of the insight gained

Whenever possible, try to make at least some of these functional goals measurable. This makes the goals achievable. While the goal "never have any arguments with my sister" may be impossible to achieve (and may lead to years of unproductive treatment), the goal "spend 2 hours per week with my sister without having serious arguments" or "have fewer than three arguments with my sister every month" is much more achievable. A client who has a functional goal may remember what was said in session and alter his or her behavior outside of the session. After all, isn't this the intention? A functional goal reminds clients of behavioral parameters and can influence their decisions when you are not present. As you move into the treatment planning stage, these functional impairments and functional goals will become the building blocks of your work together.

Case Conceptualization

Your next step in beginning treatment with a new client is to form a coherent case conceptualization. A case conceptualization answers these questions:

- What are the client's presenting problems and symptoms? What are the intensity and duration of the symptoms?
- What are the client's strengths?
- How did the client's problems develop?
- What is the impact on the client's functioning?
- What are your goals for treatment?
- What treatment will be most useful in attaining these goals?

The client's problems and strengths will be evident from your initial interview and client history. Your diagnosis will inform your assessment of the causes of the client's problems, along with relevant history that the client has shared. Your therapeutic orientation is important. Remember Marcia in Chapter 1, who visited 11 therapists with 11 different approaches? Each thera pist had a unique assessment of what caused Marcia's anxiety and sleep problems. Each orientation brought to light different aspects of her problems. Understanding your own philosophy of psychotherapy is crucial in becoming a competent therapist. We all have our own preferred way of explaining people's problems. (See Chapter 1 for more on understanding your own philosophy of therapy.)

In forming your case conceptualization, you have several options:

- *Explain your particular therapeutic orientation to your clients in the early stages of treatment.* If you practice cognitive-behavioral therapy, let them know you will be looking at how their thoughts affect their emotions and actions. If you are biologically or medically inclined, let them know you will be looking primarily at possible biological causes and solutions. If you are relationally oriented, let them know you will be examining how their previous and current relationships impact their problems. There is a lot to be gained from being expert in one or two psychotherapies, but you have a responsibility to explain that you are approaching problems through a certain filter, and that other filters might generate other theories about what will be most helpful.

- *Examine your clients' problems through several different approaches, and develop a case conceptualization that takes all of them into account.* Look at the biological, cognitive, and relational aspects of each client. Be open to the possibility that a particular approach may have the best likelihood of success with a particular client, whether or not it is your favorite approach. Be open to using several different treatment approaches simultaneously or starting with one and then moving to another (e.g., sending a depressed client with vegetative signs to his primary care physician for consideration of starting antidepressant medications, and then examining cognitive and behavioral solutions). Always explain what approaches you believe will be most helpful, and why.

A case conceptualization does not have to be long and wordy. It does help to write it down concisely in your clinical record, as part of your initial assessment. The following is an example.

 Marcia comes to therapy for help in dealing with anxiety and insomnia. She has a history of early trauma and a more recent car accident. She has a cognitive style that tends to be self-critical and has difficulty communicating her needs to her family. She also has some signs of depression and may benefit from an antidepressant. She will also benefit from practicing improved communication strategies and challenging unhelpful thoughts. She is willing and able to improve her self-care. If these approaches are not successful, a short course of a trauma desensitization treatment program may be needed.

Useful Questions for Generating a Case Conceptualization

A therapist needs to ask the right questions to understand the client's issues in the context of his or her total experience.

The following is a script used by the psychologist Donald Meichenbaum (2005, p. 12) to gather the relevant information to form a case conceptualization.[*] Notice that the choice of language and clarifying questions helps to draw out more information from the client that is quite detailed.

1. Background information and reasons for referral

"Let me see if I understand, what brings you here is . . ."
   (distress, symptoms, present and in the past)

2. Presenting problems and level of functioning

"And it is particularly bad when . . ."
"But it tends to improve when . . ."
"And it is affecting you . . ." (how . . . in terms of relationships, work, etc.)

3. Comorbidity

"In addition, you are also experiencing . . ." (struggling with . . .)
"And the impact of this in terms of your day-to-day experience is . . ."

4. Stressors (past and present)—Current, ecological, developmental, familial

"Some of the factors (stressors) that you are currently experiencing that seem to maintain your problems are . . . or that seem to make them worse are . . ." (current, ecological stressors)
"And it is not only now, but this has been going on for some time as is evident by . . ." (developmental stressors)
"And have other family members experienced something similar?" (family stressors)
"And the impact on you has been?" (family psychopathology)

---

[*]*Source:* ENRAGED! Addressing Violent Behavior toward Self and Others in Adult Psychiatric Patients, handout presented at the Institute for the Advancement of Human Behavior workshop, Bellingham, WA, October 2005. Reprinted with permission from Donald Meichenbaum, PhD.

5. Treatments received (current and past): Check efficacy, adherence and satisfaction

"The treatments you have received were . . ." (note time, type, by whom)

"And the one that worked the best was . . ."

"Was there any treatment you had trouble following through with?" (adherence history)

"And some of the difficulties (barriers) in following the treatment were . . ."

"But you were particularly satisfied with . . ."

6. Strengths—Individual, social and systemic

"But in spite of . . . you have been able to . . ."

"Some of the strengths (signs of resilience) that you bring to the present situation are . . ."

"Some of the people (resources) you can call upon to help are . . ."

"And they can be helpful by doing . . ." (social supports)

7. Summary risk and protective factors

"Have I captured what you have been saying?" (summarize risk and protective factors)

"Of these different areas, where do you think we should begin?" (begin to collaborate on developing a treatment plan)

8. Goal attainment—Short term, intermediate and long term

"As a result of our work together, what would you like to see change in the short term?"

"How are things now in your life? How would you like them to be? How can we work together to help you achieve these goals?" (short term, intermediate and long term)

"If you achieved your goals, what would you see changed?"

"Who else would notice these changes?"

9. Barriers—Individual, social, systemic

"Can you foresee anything that might get in the way, any possible obstacles or barriers to achieving

> *your treatment goals?" (Consider with the client possible individual, social, systemic barriers. Do not address the potential barriers until some hope and resources have been addressed and documented.)*
> *"Let's consider how we can anticipate, plan for and address these potential barriers."*

Meichenbaum (2005) recommends reviewing the case conceptualization with clients so that they fully understand it. Have clients put it into their own words. Involve significant others in the treatment plan by asking for their input and feedback.

The Miracle Question

It can be difficult for some clients to articulate what they want. These clients often say that they want to "feel better," but they can't always put into words what that means in tangible terms. In these cases, practitioners can use the solution-focused brief therapy technique known as "the miracle question": "Suppose that one night, while you were asleep, there was a miracle and this problem was solved. How would you know? What would be different?" (de Shazer, 1988, p. 5).

Clients who previously had a hard time articulating what changes they want to make often say, "Oh, that's easy. I would wake up relaxed from a good night's sleep and feel confident in my interpersonal relationships. I'd meet my girlfriend for a cup of coffee and spend the day skiing!"

So what have we learned from this statement of what "feeling better" means to this client? It means:

- Being relaxed
- Getting a good night's sleep
- Having self-confidence in interpersonal relationships; perhaps overcoming loneliness so that he can share his life with others
- Engaging in meaningful recreational activity

Now that we have a definition of what feeling better means to this client, we can work collaboratively to design a treatment plan that helps achieve those goals.

Setting the Stage for Treatment: Focused Treatment Planning

Having completed your assessment, established a diagnosis, defined functional impairments and goals, and developed a case conceptualization, you are now ready to develop a treatment plan. The treatment plan should be documented in the file and discussed and agreed upon with your client. You should develop a form for this so that it is quick and easy to accomplish for each client. The treatment plan should be discussed with and given to the client. To get the client fully engaged in treatment, it is important that there is an understanding of what you are working on together, how you will do it, and why you think it is important. Do not assume that your intentions are known to the client. A clear plan will help immensely in any utilization review you may have with insurance companies, as well as in communication with other professionals who are working with your client. (See Chapter 5 for more on utilization review.)

A wealth of ideas for treatment planning can be found in treatment planner books and software. For example, *The Complete Adult Psychotherapy Treatment Planner*, fourth edition (Jongsma, Peterson, & Bruce, 2006), contains detailed behavioral definitions, long-term goals, short-term objectives, and therapeutic interventions for problems such as anxiety, depression, eating disorders, and psychosis. This book contains possible *DSM* diagnoses for each problem area and numerous evidence-based practices for many of these diagnoses. All the elements in the treatment planner can be individualized and adapted to meet the requirements of each client. We suggest you consult treatment planners often in the beginning and middle stages of treatment, being careful to individualize your plans. Remain flexible in adapting treatment as needed throughout the course of treatment.

Pay Attention to Stages of Change

Make sure that you match your initial approach to the stage of change of the client. Forty-five percent of people who start therapy drop out after only a few sessions. Prochaska et al. (1994) looked at dropout rates due to mismatched stages and processes and found that they could predict with 93% accuracy which clients would drop out based on mismatched therapeutic treatments and stages of change. (See Chapter 7 for more on the stages of change.) Consider the following.

> A 42-year-old man has been sent to a psychotherapist by his primary care physician because he has a heart condition, smokes, and has very high anxiety. He says he wants to quit smoking but realizes that he uses his smoking to control his anxiety. He can't imagine what he would do without it.

If this client was set up with an action plan to quit smoking, it is likely that he would drop out before even starting, or fail in his attempt. This client still has ambivalence about quitting and has not committed to doing so. Helping this client move from the contemplation stage to the preparation stage by using processes such as emotional arousal, self-reevaluation, and commitment is more likely to keep the client engaged in treatment. Once that occurs, an action plan can be set up to control his anxiety and quit smoking.

Define Measurable Goals

If you have conducted a thorough initial interview, you will have a considerable amount of useful clinical material to develop a treatment plan. Setting measurable goals can help demonstrate progress in treatment. Regardless of your philosophy of treatment, if you have established functional impairments, you will be able to determine measurable goals. Having a few, clearly measurable goals is more helpful than having many vague goals, such as "feel better about myself, increase my self-esteem, and be a better person." Your list of functional impairments will give you a baseline of how you will measure each goal. Here are some examples of measures:

Count a Behavior
- Reduce panic attacks from three per day to fewer than two per week.
- Participate in at least three social activities per month for 3 months.

- Apply for four jobs per week.
- Attend school at least 4 days per week.

Counting a behavior helps clients realize that they are making progress.

Rate a Behavior
- Reduce depressed mood from 5/5 to 2/5 or less, at least 5 days per week.
- Reduce general anxiety from 4/5 to 1/5 or less.
- Reduce suicidal ideation from 3/5 to 1/5 or less, at least 25 days per month.

These are subjective measures by the client, and each client will define them differently. Rating a behavior helps a client notice and describe subtle differences in feeling states. It also helps clients to see shades of improvement.

Percentages
- Demonstrate 80% completion of schoolwork per week.
- Decrease being absent from work from 50% to 10% of days scheduled.

Measurable goals should be linked to functional impairments. For example, "Decrease depressed mood from 5/5 to 2/5 to improve work performance and attendance." (See Chapter 13 for more on developing measurable goals.)

Set Realistic Treatment Expectations

Most of us would like to have perfect lives, perfect performance, perfect calm, and to be happy all the time. However, we know that these are unrealistic goals and that perfection is a desired state not necessarily achieved. Some degree of imperfection in our lives keeps things interesting. For a client with a significant disorder, some level of persistence in symptoms may be acceptable. We all need to establish an internal way to measure "enough." It is important to negotiate with clients about realistic goals. Goals that are too high or too low can undermine even the best treatment. If needed, set stepwise goals (e.g., 80% attendance this month, 90% the next, 100% the next). Goals can be modified over time if you find that they were unrealistically high or low. (See Chapter 10 for more on reexamining goals.)

TIP

Setting the expectation that therapy will end within a particular time frame is important in promoting your clients' ability to focus on attaining specific goals.

Termination Planning Starts Now

Every episode of care has an end. Being "in therapy" is not a normal state. Our goal should be to help our clients learn to leave us behind. The ultimate goal of therapy is to end therapy. Despite possible financial incentives to keep a client in treatment, we need to begin planning termination from the very beginning. The thought of endless therapy may be disheartening to some clients; for others, it may be a convenient way to avoid developing satisfying relationships in the real world outside of therapy. We want those with whom we work to become healthy individuals, not perpetual clients. Communicating from the beginning that your work together is time-limited is an essential element of providing focused treatment to your clients. Talk with your clients at the beginning of therapy about what time line they think is appropriate, and negotiate this as needed. (See Chapter 10 for more on setting up time frames.) Discuss with your client what you see as the focus of treatment, how you will work together, and how many sessions you think it will take. Take your client's input and arrive at a plan and time line. You can say something such as the following.

"I see that your anxiety can cause a lot of disruption in your social and occupational life. Our plan is to do a systematic desensitization over a period of time so that your anxiety around this situation (or experience or object) is lessened until it is no longer affecting you and keeping you from doing what you want to do. Let's see how we do in 10 sessions, and then we can reevaluate. Does that sound like a reasonable plan?"

Most clients really appreciate having a road map and a sense of what to expect along the way. Without a mutual understanding of the general plan and time line, client and practitioner may have different expectations. The practitioner may have a 20-session plan in mind, but if the client is paying privately and has an expectation of paying for eight sessions, treatment will end prematurely. (See Chapter 5 for more on discussing fees with clients.) The client will not feel that she accomplished what she had hoped for, and the practitioner will be left with a sense of incompleteness. This can be avoided with mutual understanding of a defined plan. Please remember, however, that a plan is a living, breathing document that can change. It is not rigid.

Clients will be able to focus on the positive progress they are making only if termination is part of the plan from the beginning. We discuss more about termination in a later chapter, but remember to include termination planning from the start.

Summing Up

In this chapter we reviewed all the steps necessary to begin an episode of treatment with a client. The process of establishing an accurate diagnosis, identifying functional impairments and functional goals, and establishing a clear treatment plan is essential to providing effective and ethical treatment to your clients. Get in the habit of following a consistent process of evaluation and treatment planning. The rest of the psychotherapy will flow smoothly if the start of the episode has set the stage.

EXERCISES

1. Assess your intake process. Are you are getting enough information to fully understand the client's problem and make an accurate diagnosis? How could you enhance your process? List all of the elements you think are needed for an adequate evaluation.
2. How do you keep from overpathologizing or underpathologizing clients? Which way do you tend to go? Have you ever had a negative outcome to therapy because you've over- or underpathologized a client?

(Continued)

3. Practice explaining the following diagnoses to a new client (using your *DSM* as reference):
   - Anxiety Disorder Not Otherwise Specified
   - Dysthymia
   - Major Depression, Recurrent
   - Bipolar II
   - Posttraumatic Stress Disorder
   - Psychosis Not Otherwise Specified
   - Schizophrenia
   - Obsessive-Compulsive Disorder
   - Anorexia
   - Attention Deficit Disorder, Combined Type
   - Oppositional Defiant Disorder
   - Borderline Personality Disorder
   - Avoidant Personality Disorder

4. Define three measurable behaviors that could be targeted for each of the above diagnoses. How could you measure each one?

5. Define three potential functional impairments and improvements for each of the above diagnoses. How could you measure each one?

6. Choose one of the above diagnoses. Write up a short case conceptualization. Practice explaining your case conceptualization to the client.

7. Do you prefer to explain your particular preferred therapeutic orientation to clients, or to look at the problems through several different lenses and choose a treatment plan that seems to best match the client's needs by incorporating aspects of different orientations?

8. How do you assess your treatment plan to make sure that the plan is one that your client understands, agrees with, and believes is achievable?

Resources

Jongsma, Jr., A. E., Peterson, L. M., & Bruce, T.J. (Contributing Ed.). (2006). *The complete adult psychotherapy treatment planner* (4th ed.). Hoboken, NJ: Wiley.

TheraScribe® is a treatment planning and clinical record software management system with standardized language that allows you to quickly and easily create effective treatment plans. You simply point and click to choose from the built-in set of behavioral definitions: *DSM-IV-TR* diagnoses, goals, objectives, and therapeutic interventions. Available through Wiley & Sons, Inc. at www.wiley.com/legacy/therascribe/default .htm, TheraScribe® consultants are available at (866) 888-5158. Call them to see if this software fits your practice needs.

10

The Middle Phase of Treatment

What You Will Learn
- How to determine the most appropriate frequency of sessions
- How to determine the most appropriate modality of therapy
- How to set up time frames
- How to identify and work with client strengths and exceptions
- How to identify intervention points
- How to address and resolve common client behaviors that interfere with therapy
- The two sides of catharsis
- How to work with transference and countertransference
- How to recognize and change practitioner behaviors that interfere with therapy
- What to do when therapy isn't working
- How to recognize and respond to the iatrogenic effects of therapy

So, you have met with and assessed your new client. You have established a diagnosis, determined functional impairments, and created a treatment plan with clear goals and a proposed time frame. What next? In this chapter, we examine the middle phase of treatment and some of the issues that may arise as you work with your client to implement the treatment plan.

Frequency of Sessions

With some clients, the optimal frequency of sessions will be obvious. A client with suicidal or homicidal ideation and intent may need to be hospitalized for safety. If intent is not present, weekly or even biweekly sessions, with possible phone check-ins, along with an agreed-upon safety plan, may be needed. Similarly, a client with a current crisis that is expected to resolve quickly may be best served by weekly sessions, perhaps with further sessions spaced out monthly before termination.

The frequency of sessions may be negotiable. Momentum may be lost when sessions are spaced too far apart. When there is too much time between sessions, it is hard to develop therapeutic continuity. Guard against doing the second session over and over again, which can happen if there is a long time between sessions. Initially, if a client is trying to develop new behaviors, it is best to have sessions spaced fairly close so that the therapist can monitor and encourage the change process and keep relapse to a minimum. With other clients, meeting once or twice a month is helpful, as the client has plenty of time to implement new behaviors and complete homework assignments. Spacing sessions out to once a month or longer can be part of a process of "weaning" from therapy. These sessions may also be useful in maintaining behavioral changes. Some clients who do not have confidence in their new behaviors want to maintain that "lifeline" with the therapist until they truly feel that they can do it on their own. Others may need support through ongoing circumstances, such as a terminal illness, caregiving for another, or a divorce. The client's ability to pay for sessions, whether privately or through insurance, may also be a factor.

Challenge for the Practitioner

Clients who have dependency issues can transfer those issues to the therapy process. Ultimately this is not healthy for the client. It may be preferable and even therapeutic to see the client less often (with more homework), even though this is counterintuitive to what the client wants. More is not always better!

Factors to consider when deciding on frequency of sessions include:

- Safety of client and others: Schedule frequent sessions when risk is greater.
- Urgency of current crisis: Schedule frequent sessions to allow for quick resolution.
- Leave time between sessions to allow practice of new behaviors and integration of new insights.
- Client preference should be balanced with treatment needs.
- Therapist preference should be balanced with individual client needs.
- Affordability is based on client needs.
- Health care coverage: A client may have a limited number of sessions per year. What is the best use of these sessions? Is it best to schedule weekly or with less frequency?
- If the client is paying privately, his or her financial situation should be balanced with treatment needs.

Ultimately, you need to negotiate the frequency of sessions with each client you see. Communicate your recommendation and solicit your client's feedback. Be alert to unfocused treatment that continues from week to week without direction and of treatment that simply fades away without any sense of accomplishment or finality. These treatment episodes will ultimately be unsatisfying for both you and your clients.

Modality

Determining whether your client would be best served in individual, family, or group therapy is another crucial decision that must be made early in therapy. Your assessment of the client's functional impairments is an important factor. A client who may benefit by peer feedback and social interaction may be encouraged to participate in group therapy. A client who has significant conflict with family members might benefit from spending a portion of the treatment in family sessions. If you do not have the expertise and interest in a modality that is needed, be willing to recommend another psychotherapist. In certain situations, a second modality may be a useful adjunct, such as doing individual work focusing

on dialectical behavior therapy while your client is also involved
in a group with the same focus. (See Chapter 13 for more on dialectical behavior therapy.)

Another factor to consider is how the client functions within
the family system. Frequently family members with multiple issues
are engaged in treatment. Consider the following example.

The mother is depressed, the father is abusing substances,
and the teenage son is having behavior problems (according to others, of course!). The parents approach you to
work with the teenager, but in the course of your evaluation you uncover father-son conflicts bordering on verbal
abuse due to the father's alcohol use and parenting difficulties on the part of the mother due to her depression.
They request individual therapy to help "fix their son."

It is unlikely that progress can be made with the teenager without addressing what is going on in the family.

So what do you do? Given the severity of the problems with
the parents, it is unlikely that family therapy would be successful
at this time. Perhaps working with the parents together and sep-
arately may be necessary initially. Assess their awareness of how
their unique issues affect the family system and may be contributing to their son's acting-out. A chemical dependency evaluation
for the father and a meeting for the mother with her doctor for
a physical workup and antidepressant trial may be helpful. There
may be various levels of motivation and willingness on the parents' part to pursue this course of treatment. Once the parents are
in treatment, there is a greater likelihood of success in working on
the interpersonal issues without the interference of the substance
abuse and depression problems. It is likely that various combinations of individual therapy with the teenager, meeting with the
parents, perhaps the parents pursuing help for their own issues
with other practitioners, and ultimately family therapy may be the
most help.

Not everyone in the family may be willing to follow your
suggestions. Some practitioners will not see a family unless all
members are willing participants. Others will work with whom-
ever is willing, with the idea that if you change one dynamic
in the family system, the relationships will be affected without

having to work with everyone directly. Practitioners need to be flexible to work with the client's family dynamics and environmental changes.

Setting Up Time Frames

"I don't want to force my client into doing something" is a common phrase heard among practitioners who feel uncomfortable setting up time frames. Time frames are often misunderstood as being coercive because the focus is mistakenly placed on the feeling state rather than a behavioral marker. Feeling states are subjective and established by the client. They cannot be forced. For instance, one cannot set up an initial time frame specifying that in 3 months the client will no longer feel anxious. This will likely increase anxiety because, prior to treatment, the client cannot conceive that not feeling anxious is even possible. Time frames are determined by behavioral markers that are designed by both the practitioner and the client based on the client's stated goals. If the focus is on setting up a time frame for a behavioral marker rather than the feeling state, the anxiety reaction can be managed so the client can make progress. Consider the following scenario.

> Stan is a 20-year-old college student who has had an escalating problem with anxiety since his parents divorced when he was 9 years old. He found solace in isolation, and this pattern has persisted. Now that he is in college, however, isolation is no longer satisfying and is interfering with his ability to interact with others socially, academically, and occupationally. He has avoided social situations, and even getting a job. The act of asking a question in class feels impossible. He would like to interact with others in these settings without paralyzing anxiety.

A skilled practitioner can collaborate with Stan to use time frames quite effectively. It is often easier to cross a giant chasm by jumping from one ledge to another in a series of small jumps rather than taking one giant leap. A time frame can help the client get from one ledge to another. It can be something to work toward.

Some of the most successful clients are those who come into therapy with a time frame of their own. For instance, a client is going on a trip in 2 months and wants to get over his fear of flying. The time frame focuses energy and provides motivation for sustained effort.

The practitioner can use the collaborative process to set a reasonable time frame that feels comfortable to the client. In the case of Stan, one could set up a time frame for doing some role-plays in session. Once this is established, another time frame is set up for him to ask a grocery clerk in the supermarket where a particular item is located. Each stage builds on the skills and comfort level of the stage before. The interesting thing about time frames is that clients usually overestimate the time it will take for them to reach their goal because they do not have a concept regarding how they will do it. Once you work with them on building skill in the particular area, they often achieve their goal much earlier than expected, which can be a great boost to their confidence. As long as you pick an incremental, reasonable, achievable goal, all the elements related to the problem can be worked with in a manageable way. Without this kind of focus, the problem can loom very large. Using a hierarchy of small, manageable steps accompanied by time frames can help clients achieve goals they would not believe are achievable in such a short time. (See Chapter 7 for more on setting realistic treatment expectations.)

Clinical Considerations

When working with anticipatory anxiety, the method of talking without doing can sometimes prolong the problem. It is actually much more compassionate to help a client manage anxiety leading up to action than to avoid action and perpetuate and strengthen the anxiety.

Steven enters into therapy to deal with his fear of public speaking. As a young adult, his fear is starting to interfere with his occupational choices. He would like to change, yet he is focused on his sense of inadequacy. This sense of inadequacy often acts as a barrier to overcome his fear. His focus is on talking about all the situations in which he experienced a negative outcome. Over time, he has avoided getting himself into situations in which he has to speak in front of large groups. It becomes clear to the therapist during the initial sessions that he is quite eloquent talking one-on-one; however, when he starts to talk about having to speak in front of a large audience, his anxiety level increases dramatically. Every time this happens, his fear seems to be strengthened. Instead of repeating this pattern over and over in the course of treatment, it may be helpful to teach him various relaxation and behavioral management techniques so that he has a means of managing his anxiety. Without this type of intervention, it is likely that his fear will continue to grow.

Working with Client Strengths and Exceptions

As part of your assessment process, focus a portion of your attention on determining your client's strengths. This can be done through observation and direct discussion with the client. However, the fog of the presenting problem often obscures the client's strengths and resources: What skills and insights has she developed as a result of working with this issue? Who are her allies and support system? Is she motivated to change? Many clients are not able to identify their strengths and resources initially. It can be worthwhile to help your clients take an honest inventory. Their strengths are often the building blocks of successful interventions. A support system can provide inspiration that they are not alone in facing this problem.

It is important to make those strengths a part of each session. Psychotherapy that focuses only on problems and symptoms will not generate much hope in your client. (See Chapter 7 for more on creating a sense of hope.) Many clients who are depressed or anxious have difficulty generating and acknowledging strengths. Sad and fearful emotions, thoughts, and self-doubt can crowd out all sense of their positive attributes and strengths. As a therapist, part of your function is to remind clients of their own strengths and successes. Clients who can verbalize and practice their own strengths will develop self-efficacy skills and make faster progress in therapy.

Challenge for the Practitioner

Be aware that although every client will have some strengths, not all will have the skills and knowledge it takes to solve problems and change behaviors. Some strengths may need to be taught, practiced, and reinforced during the therapy process.

Solution-focused brief therapy pays attention to client strengths and exceptions as a way to solve problems in living. Asking a client "How have you coped with this in the past?" can help generate solutions based on the client's own strengths.

Statement of complaint

Search for exceptions

Yes

Describe differences between exceptions and complaint

Redefine complaint and change view of solution

Set goals

Do more of what works!

Figure 10.1   The Solution-Focused Brief Therapy Model of Working with Exceptions
Adapted from *Clues: Investigating Solutions in Brief Therapy*, p. 131, by S. de Shazer, 1988, New York: Norton.

Some clients generalize their complaint as always occurring; for example, a client may say, "I am always anxious" or "I am depressed all of the time." With thorough discussion, a practitioner may find that there are exceptions to the client's complaint and there are times when the complaint is not active at all. Figure 10.1 illustrates a solution-focused brief therapy model for working with clients who say that their complaint occurs "all the time."

Steve de Shazer, one of the founders of solution-focused brief therapy, was a master at uncovering exceptions that redefine the problem and thus create a new solution. Consider the following scenario, in which a young woman comes to therapy with the complaint that she feels depressed "all the time":[*]

Session 1

A young woman's *main complaint is that she is feeling depressed all the time.* The therapist defines the complaint as occurring all the time and then starts to search for exceptions when she is not feeling depressed. As a result, both client and therapist discover that there are quite a few exceptions that are defined in behavioral terms. The feeling state starts to become clearer when the client acknowledges that she feels the way she does because of her relationships with the various men in her life.

- *Redefining the original complaint:* By the end of the first session, the original problem was redefined as "I am feeling depressed due to the problems I have with men." This was done by focusing on the exceptions.

- *Therapist's thoughts:* Help the client find her strengths and develop a different perspective by focusing on the exceptions when she was *not* depressed.

- *Task given by the therapist:* Pay attention to what is going on when the exception occurs and notice what is different about those instances.

---

[*]Adapted from *Clues: Investigating Solutions in Brief Therapy* (pp. 116–118), by Steve de Shazer, 1988, New York: Norton.

TIP

Listen for absolutes in the client's language, such as "always," "all the time," "never," and "every day." This language is a clue that probing deeper to find the exceptions will help deconstruct the original complaint and find a new solution.

Session 2

At the next session the young woman gave details about her observations but stated that things were not better and actually seemed worse. However, doing the task gave her an insight that she was really *just* depressed about her relationship with her boyfriend. She was not depressed about anything else. She did not want to give up on her relationship. She thought the problem was that he needed to change so that she and her boyfriend could have a better relationship, but he was not interested in coming to counseling. She, however, was interested in helping him change.

- *Redefining the original complaint:* "I am depressed about my relationship with my boyfriend."
- *Therapist's thoughts:* Continue to help her find her own solution by doing something different. The task was not specific. The therapist wanted her to choose what she would do differently.
- *Task given by the therapist:* "Do something different in how you relate to your boyfriend."

Session 3

She called her boyfriend and asked him to go with her to her office picnic, which, as in the past, he refused to do. He told her that if she was going to nag him, their relationship was over. She reacted by crying and thinking this was the end of the world. The next day, however, she did not think it was so bad. She remembered her report from session 2 that everything else seemed to be going okay in other areas of her life, and she started to feel better. She thought, "Nothing could make me take him back." She went to the picnic without him.

- *Therapist's thoughts:* There is a possibility that she will now be depressed about the breakup with her boyfriend.
- *Task given by the therapist:* "Between now and the next time we meet, pay attention to what you have to do to overcome any urges you might have to feel depressed about the breakup."

Session 4

She decided not to succumb to her ex-boyfriend's attempts at getting back together, which helped pull her out of a tendency to become depressed. The task assignment helped her discover that moving to a different room or getting out of the house or leaving her desk at work helped her to change her tendency to become depressed. This was a great improvement from the patterns of her past, but she decided to make a follow-up appointment for 6 weeks later.

6 Weeks Later

She called and canceled the appointment, stating that even though she felt lonely at times she was not depressed. She was much more active and doing things with her girlfriends.

This is a good example of the importance of exception finding. In this case, the redefining of the problem *and* the solution was hidden in the exceptions! The original narrow problem was generalized to a feeling of depression about everything. Without an exploration of the exceptions, it would be easy to assume that this client was depressed, maybe even in need of an antidepressant. It is likely that antidepressants would have been of little help to her because even though she said she felt depressed, she did not show signs of a clinical depression. Her feeling state changed after clarifying the problem and thus finding new solutions. This case description also highlights the importance of how the therapist views what the problem is and thus the solution. (See Chapter 1 for "A Trip to the Therapist's Couch.")

Identifying Intervention Points

The art of psychotherapy involves being continuously aware of intervention points as they arise in therapy. Some interventions will, of course, be outlined in your treatment plan. Referring to your treatment plan (before and after a session) can help to determine if you are on track. However, you must continue to be "awake," to notice new or surprising elements in your client's behavior in each session. Competent therapists are light on their feet in responding to client's in-session behavior. You may need to point out what you are noticing, as the client may not be aware of the implications of his or her behavior. This need not be confrontational; bring a spirit of interested inquiry and wondering to this intervention.

Interventions can be varied. Often just pointing out a client's statement is enough to bring about a new insight and potential new behavioral adaptations. At other times, you may see an opportunity to teach a new skill and practice it within the session. You may spontaneously come up with a new idea for a homework assignment and need to generate client enthusiasm for it, or you may simply note the behavior and plan how to intervene in the future.

Many issues come up in sessions that require skillful intervention. Taking a passive stance can result in a poor outcome, client boredom, and therapist boredom. It can also result in therapy that either goes on indefinitely with no progress, or therapy that fades away without any resolution of the problems that the client came seeking help with in the first place. If your work is subject to utilization review by an insurance payer, you may be asked why there is no demonstrable progress, or how you could have missed an obvious intervention opportunity. (See Chapter 5 for more on utilization review.) You may also develop a reputation among clients and other professionals as a therapist who does not produce results.

Client Behaviors That Interfere with Therapy

Marsha Linehan (1993a, pp. 131–141) identifies a number of behaviors—of both the client and the therapist—that interfere with therapy effectiveness. These behaviors can lead to ineffective therapy or termination before the client makes progress. Although Linehan is looking primarily at treating Borderline Personality Disorder, the concept of therapy-interfering behaviors can be generalized to nearly all forms of therapy and client diagnoses. Developing the ability to recognize these behaviors as they occur, intervene in some way, and overcome the behaviors is essential to the effective and ethical practice of psychotherapy.

Self-Sabotage

Clients may come to therapy with the best intentions, but circumstances conspire to make the therapy ineffective. Clients are usually not aware of how they are sabotaging therapy. For example, a client may come to therapy seeking help for anxiety around attending college classes. But he may spend all of the therapy sessions complaining about professors, other students, and the cost of college (and therapy!). He may resist the therapist's attempts to focus on anxiety precipitants and cognitive styles and learn specific relaxation techniques. A client like this must be firmly reminded of the focus of therapy and the tasks outlined in the treatment plan; the therapist may need to bring the focus back to solutions to the problem of anxiety again and again. This is where a written, agreed-upon list of target problems or behaviors can be useful.

Self-sabotage behaviors by a client are often a reflection of behaviors that interfere with many other aspects of functioning. A client who wants to talk nonstop during therapy sessions may do the same thing when going out to dinner with friends, thus jeopardizing other relationships. A client who sits sullenly during therapy sessions and responds in monosyllables may be similarly uncommunicative in other relationships. A client who is

15 minutes late for every therapy appointment may be in trouble at work for being late to every meeting. Ignoring these issues, or hoping they will magically go away on their own, is neither kind nor effective. You will be giving your client a gift by speaking up and addressing the behavior openly in therapy sessions.

Boundary Issues

Boundary problems come in all sizes and shapes. Linehan (1993a, p. 135) describes these behaviors as "pushing the therapist's personal limits." Like self-sabotage, boundary issues often reflect behaviors that cause problems in the client's life outside of therapy. A key concept (again from Linehan) is that of "observing limits": Therapists must learn to observe or notice their own reactions to the client's behaviors, rather than imposing an arbitrary, judgmental "boundary." This approach can be modeled to individual clients, who may find it helpful in their relationships outside of therapy.

The following is a simple process for identifying and responding to boundary issues within sessions (adapted from Linehan, 1993a):

1. Notice your own emotion (sad, fearful, angry).
2. Notice the client behavior that occurred just before your own emotion.
3. Describe your emotion and the client behavior to the client (nonjudgmentally, of course).
4. Describe the behavior you'd like the client to do instead.
5. Ask the client to do that behavior (and listen to the answer).
6. If needed, offer reinforcers (both for complying with your request and for not complying).

Let's look at an example of observing limits.

 Susan comes to her therapy session 20 minutes late, without apology or explanation (for the third time in a row). Janice, the therapist, notices that she is feeling mildly angry at Susan and associates it with her behavior of coming to sessions late.

Janice says, "You know, Susan, I notice that I'm starting to feel a little angry when you come into the session late.

It makes it hard for us to do the work that we've agreed to do together. I'd really like it if you'd make an effort to get here in time. Would you agree to do that?"

Susan replies, "But you know I have to rush here after work! I can't help it! I'm late everywhere I go. I'm just a late kind of person. If you can't deal with it, maybe I should find a different therapist."

Janice says, "I sure hope it doesn't have to end that way. It sounds like being late causes problems in other areas of your life, too. Let's see if we can work together on a plan for getting here on time. If it works here, it may work in other areas of your life as well. If you can improve on this, I think we can continue with the work we are doing together. If you choose not to work on getting here on time, we may need to take a break for a while until your schedule loosens up."

Noncompliance

In almost every episode of therapy, you will be asking your client to do something. You may ask clients to come to sessions as planned, to call 24 hours in advance of cancellation, to pay their bills promptly, to focus during sessions, to answer questions truthfully, to try new behaviors, to do homework. We assume that clients who initiate therapy are ready and willing to comply with these requests. What about those clients who aren't willing?

First, it is important to point out the problem to the client (and not just ignore it). The client may not be aware of the behavior, or may just think he can get away with it. He may be fearful of doing what is asked, or he may not be motivated to change at this time. He may be more interested in getting into a power struggle with you (especially if this is how he copes with other relationships).

Next, clarify the client's goals. Does the client want help with something? Is this reflected in the treatment plan? Have the client's goals changed? Can the client recommit to the goals established? Or can the therapist agree to changed goals? (See Chapter 7 for more on eliciting the client's concerns.)

You will need to establish accountability; in some situations, the natural consequences of noncompliance can be explicit and effective. Getting a bill for a no-show can help improve attendance.

Not focusing on the problem at hand during a session can result in not getting the help wanted and living with uncomfortable symptoms for another week. For other types of noncompliance, you may need to establish reinforcers. For example, for a client who is argumentative during sessions (to the point that it precludes any progress), you may let the client know that you will stop sessions if she does not stop arguing after two reminders. Another technique is to have the client save her arguments for the last 10 minutes of the session, when she can argue freely for the allotted time.

Poor Attendance

Clients who continually skip sessions can be frustrating to the therapist. Clients who are not willing to schedule appointments in advance, but just want to be able to call you any time they are in crisis are also frustrating. These clients are often stuck in the "crisis mode" and unable to think ahead. They have a habit of reacting rather than being proactive. Establishing expectations early in treatment can help to prevent some of these problems. Establish a no-show and late cancellation fee and include this in your initial paperwork and discussions. (See Chapter 5 for more on establishing no-show fees.) You have reserved a time for the session and deserve to be at least partially compensated if your client does not attend. Some therapists offer one free late cancellation but charge for all others. You can use your discretion about whether to charge a fee for a late cancellation that you deem unavoidable (such as a sudden illness or a family emergency). Be wary, though, if "unavoidable" cancellations or no-shows become a habit; this may indicate the presence of a therapy-interfering behavior which must be addressed. Discuss with the client your opinion about how often sessions should be scheduled for optimal progress. If the client is unwilling to schedule and attend sessions often enough to make progress toward treatment goals, you may find it necessary to end the treatment episode and recommend another therapist or plan of action.

 Sally calls a new therapist, John, for a crisis appointment. Her anxiety has reached new heights, and she feels unable to cope with it another day. John happens to have a cancellation that day and can fit her in. He offers her some relaxation, breath work, and cognitive exercises to assist in the crisis and proceeds to do a complete evaluation. At the second session, she reports some relief in her anxiety and agrees to a treatment plan to address longstanding Posttraumatic Stress Disorder and Obsessive-Compulsive Disorder symptoms. However, she cancels the next two appointments, saying she is too busy to come and is feeling fine anyway. Three days later, Sally calls, again in crisis, and demands an immediate session. John agrees to see her the next day, but she cancels again, saying she is fine. John calls to talk with Sally about this pattern, but she is clear that she wants to see him *only* in emergencies.

John has a choice to make at this time. He may choose to remain available to Sally for crisis appointments, hoping that in time she will come to see the necessity for regular appointments to address her long-term symptoms. Or he may choose to tell her (ideally in person, followed up by a letter) that he is unwilling to work with her in this manner, and that if she is not able to commit to regular sessions, he will decline to treat her when she is in crisis. He may suggest other resources that may be a better fit for what she is willing to do.

Practitioner Behaviors That Interfere with Therapy

When Linehan (1993a, p. 138) discusses therapy-interfering behaviors, she includes behaviors of the therapist. She describes two major categories of therapist behaviors that interfere with therapy:

1. Behaviors that create a therapeutic imbalance
2. Behaviors that communicate disrespect for the client

Behaviors That Create a Therapeutic Imbalance

Consider this example of a behavior that creates a therapeutic imbalance.

A client comes to therapy feeling devastated by the news that she has just lost another job. She spends the hour talking about how terrible she feels and that she believes she will never get a new job. She leaves the session feeling more discouraged than when she came.

While the therapist was appropriately validating of the client's feelings and thoughts, he did not offer any change strategies that could give her hope. This imbalance between acceptance and change strategies left the client with little benefit from the therapy session.

An imbalance can occur in many different ways. It is easy to push your clients into changing behaviors without balancing this with accepting clients as they are. Likewise, we can be so validating and accepting that we don't challenge our clients enough. This practitioner behavior can lead to early termination of therapy or an unsatisfying therapeutic experience.

Linehan's (1993a) work is based on dialectical tension: the balance between seemingly opposite characteristics, such as that between flexibility and stability. Our clients want to have clear expectations of the therapy experience: to know the rules, to understand how therapy is going to help them, to know what to expect from you. If you don't create a stable environment for your clients, they may not be able to feel comfortable and secure in their work with you. However, they may also need flexibility at times. They may want to change appointment times, or to focus for a session on an issue that is not part of your core treatment plan. If you are not able to be flexible in these situations, your clients may not feel that they can work with you.

An imbalance can also occur between nurturing and demanding behaviors. Most therapists can respond naturally to a client's need for nurturing within the therapy relationship. Encouraging your client, providing comforting words, offering a cup of tea are all nurturing and can enhance the therapy. However, part of the work of therapy is to invite change. We want our clients to take their own problems seriously and to practice new behaviors outside of therapy sessions. Work to develop a therapeutic atmosphere in which it is possible to work together on solutions.

For example, having a casual conversation at the beginning of the session to establish rapport and demonstrate some humanness is a generally accepted practice. However, some practitioners have a hard time switching into therapy mode and continue the casual conversation 20 minutes or more into the session. While it can be a pleasant experience for both, it uses valuable time that detracts from the real focus of therapy: to help clients change.

One of the keys to an effective therapeutic relationship is an awareness of balance. Notice what you are doing and saying in sessions, and notice your client's reactions to you. Ask your clients directly if they feel you are pushing for change too much, or not enough. Be aware of your own preferred position in the dialectic. You may be quite comfortable in nurturing your clients but have a harder time challenging them to change. Practice your weaker position, and learn to remain light on your feet in responding to imbalances that arise.

Behaviors That Communicate Disrespect for the Client

Some practitioners are very informal in their attire, sitting cross-legged in the chair or even taking their shoes off in a session. While this might be acceptable for some clients, others may feel that this atmosphere is too informal and is disrespectful.

Behaviors that indicate a lack of respect for the client are numerous and common (Linehan, 1993a, p. 141). Some clients will be more sensitive to them than others. To avoid these behaviors, you must pay attention to what your clients say and do, respond to them compassionately and nonjudgmentally, and maintain a professional appearance and environment. (See Chapter 5 for more on creating a respectful office space.) Be open to feedback and encourage your clients to point out when they feel disrespected by you. Work to repair the relationship by taking responsibility for your own behavior and agreeing to make acceptable changes.

Joe enters therapy with Caroline to work on increasing outbursts of anger in his workplace. At his second session with her, she is joined by her dog; the dog is not feeling well, and she wants to have him with her during the day. Halfway through the appointment, the veterinarian calls; Caroline answers and talks with the vet for about 5 minutes about the dog's diagnosis and treatment. When she returns her attention to Joe, he is visibly angry with her. Caroline has been worried about her dog, but realizes that she has been disrespectful of Joe by focusing more on the dog than on Joe. Joe fumes that she has wasted his time and has been unprofessional; he starts to get up to leave. Caroline recognizes that her behavior had been disrespectful, regardless of her intentions. She apologizes to him and takes the dog out to the receptionist (who happens to enjoy spending time with him). She asks Joe if she can make up the time to him and promises to give him her complete attention. When the veterinarian calls again, she lets the call go to voicemail. Caroline does not blame Joe for his reaction or see it as a pathological expression of his anger problems.

Respect for your clients is a crucial part of your interaction with them. Remember that respect can be expressed differently in different cultures, and that your clients are the best source of information on what respectful behaviors are and what they expect from you.

The Two Sides of Catharsis

One of the uniquely positive aspects of therapy is that it provides a safe environment for clients to have a cathartic experience. Catharsis, however, can have two sides. The positive side is that clients can relieve emotional and psychological pressure by freely expressing themselves to an active and caring listener. By relieving this burden, clients often change their perspective on the problem, discontinue the emotional drain, and can psychologically free themselves to see new solutions. (See Chapter 1 for more on the benefits of catharsis.) Clients often report feeling "lighter" after a session of this type. Therapy provides the setting for the cathartic experience, which can be very healing. The act of catharsis can often relieve physical symptoms, such as fatigue.

The negative side of catharsis is that some clients get stuck in this phase. The act of continually focusing on having a cathartic experience can, in some cases, be emotionally draining and can act as a psychological barrier to seeing new solutions. This type of client has the same experience as the previous client—only it has the opposite effect. It is difficult to say where that tipping point is, but it is something that practitioners should be aware of.

Transference and Countertransference

Some psychotherapies focus heavily on working with transference and countertransference issues within therapy. Others do not use the concept at all. Transference refers to a client's feelings about the therapist (which may mirror feelings the client has about other important people, usually family members). Countertransference refers to similar feelings the therapist may have about the client (which may reflect the therapist's personal life).

In practical terms, this concept encourages self-reflection and careful observation. If you notice that your client seems to be relating to you in a way that is parallel to the client's other important relationships, it is important to point this out.

"I notice that you seem to expect me to disapprove of your decisions, sort of like how you expect your mother to react to you. I wonder if you can see me as a completely separate person, who will have my own reactions to you and your choices. I wonder if you also expect other people in your life to react to you like your mother does."

This can help the client increase awareness of how expectations of other people's reactions may not always be accurate and can point the way to changing these expectations. It is important to give this kind of feedback in a gentle and nonjudgmental way.

The concept of countertransference can encourage therapists to be self-reflective about their own feelings toward clients. It is important not to blame the client for your emotional reaction. We all react emotionally to people and events; this is a normal part of being human. Our reactions come from a variety of sources, including our own history; the behavior of the people we interact with; whether we are ill, hungry, or tired; and our current relationships. The key is self-awareness of these emotional states and the many possible contributors to them.

If you find yourself having strong or unusual emotions about a particular client, examine the factors that may be contributing to them. Notice your own behavior in the therapy: Are your emotions interfering with competent psychotherapy? If so, it is very important to seek consultation with an experienced peer. You may need to change the focus of the therapy and your interventions; you may need to change your response to the client; or you may need to (gently) suggest another therapist who may be able to be more effective with that particular client's presentation. As a general rule of thumb, it is not advisable to share your problematic emotional reaction with the client, as this may do more harm than good. An experienced peer or supervisor can help you examine your feelings and identify the triggers in your own experience without exposing the client to your own process.

Reexamining Goals

In the previous chapter we discussed the process of eliciting and formalizing your client's goals for therapy. During the middle phase of therapy it is often helpful to revisit these goals together. Are they still current? Have they been met? Are other goals now more important to the client? Are the goals too ambitious, or too easy? Sometimes what a practitioner thinks is happening with the client is not actually how the client is feeling. Renegotiate your client's goals as needed to maintain a clear focus to the treatment.

As a therapist, you must also take time to review your goals with each client you see. In some of the clinical charts we have audited, the practitioner states the goals in the initial sessions and then fails to address them later. Checking your chart notes *before sessions* can help keep you on track regarding continuity and what to address next; asking the client about progress *in sessions* can give you valuable feedback on how the client feels the therapy is progressing.

What to Do When Therapy Isn't Working

In the middle part of therapy, you may begin to feel stuck. Perhaps the client isn't making progress as fast as you anticipated. The client may spend all session arguing with you about why therapy is not working, or may sit passively and wait for you to "fix" her. Or the therapy may just be fading away with fewer sessions and little expectation for change. The client's primary care physician or parents or teachers may call you to ask why the client is not getting any better—or is even getting worse.

When this happens, reevaluate your diagnosis, goals, and treatment plan with the following questions:

- Was your original diagnosis inaccurate?
- Is another diagnosis now more likely?
- Are the client's goals realistic?

- Is the treatment plan adequate?
- Are there suggestions you have made to the client that he or she has not agreed to or followed up on?
- Is there an underlying substance abuse problem that is stalling treatment and needs to be addressed?
- Is there an underlying medical problem that needs to be evaluated by a physician?
- Does the client need medications, or more effective medications?
- Has the client made as much progress as he or she is capable of?
- Does the client need a different approach or a different therapist?

After pinpointing the problems with your current treatment plan, discuss them with your client. Ask clients what they think is slowing progress. Discuss possible solutions. Bring other significant supports into the process, if appropriate. Your new plan may include:

- Revising and/or reprioritizing goals
- Revising treatment strategies
- Referring for chemical dependency evaluation and treatment
- Referring to a primary care physician or psychiatrist for medication review
- Taking a break from therapy
- Referring to a different therapist with a different style or expertise
- Gaining more commitment from the client to complete homework and behavioral practice
- Gaining support from or changing the behaviors of other professionals or family members involved in care
- Scheduling sessions more frequently or less frequently

Agree to revisit the plan after implementing solutions to see if they are helping. Consider consulting with a peer or supervisor if improvement does not occur.

Iatrogenic Effects of Therapy

Therapists hate to think that what they do can harm their clients, yet therapy can have iatrogenic effects. Some clients actually do better when they are *not* involved in therapy. At times, it is helpful to take a break from therapy and evaluate the outcome. Remember that the wrong approach, misinterpretation of symptoms, and inappropriate interventions can potentially have harmful consequences for clients in certain circumstances (Lilienfeld, 2007). Frequently monitoring your client's functional impairment, via the GAF score or through direct feedback, is necessary to ensure that your client is making progress. A meta-analysis by Lambert et al. (2003) found that client feedback reduced the rate of symptom deterioration by 4% to 8%. Therapists who use client feedback can then make a treatment correction and avoid further decline. (See Chapter 6 for more on eliciting client feedback.) If you start to see functioning deteriorate, a serious review of treatment is required. Be willing to consult with a peer or supervisor and make some changes in your approach.

Consider the following example of iatrogenic treatment.

Stella was a 55-year-old woman who had seen the same therapist, Carl, for the past 8 years. She was frequently suicidal, had tried several medications with little positive effect, and had frequent arguments with family members. She had three psychiatric hospitalizations in the past 30 years and believed that she was quite fragile. Carl, too, thought that Stella was fragile. He worried about her risk of suicide and often suggested or agreed to sessions two or three times per week. When he tried to space her sessions out to one or two sessions per month, Stella would call him in crisis and he would increase the frequency of sessions again. Carl felt stuck. He was aware that Stella was not getting any better, and he felt that the best he could do was to try to prevent a suicide or hospitalization. He had a suspicion at times that she was in fact getting worse with more therapy, but for the most part he felt that by helping her cope, he was doing the right thing.

At one point Stella planned a trip out of the state with her husband to spend time with one of their children and their grandchildren. Her husband was recently retired, and they planned to stay for 2 months. Carl was quite concerned that Stella would decompensate during the trip and would need to be hospitalized. In the weeks before the trip, Stella's chronic suicidality continued. When Stella returned in 2 months and went to her first session with

Carl, she reported that she and her husband had had a wonderful time and that her mood was better than it had ever been. Carl began to think that it was time to consider tapering down and then terminating therapy, since she had done so well. However, by the next session Stella was again suicidal, miserable, and demanding two sessions per week. Carl complied. The following winter, the same pattern repeated itself, and again the next summer when Stella and her husband took another long vacation.

This scenario is a good example of how it is sometimes important to shift the focus in therapy. In this case, Carl's focus on Stella's inability to cope actually reinforced this behavior. This focus created less autonomy and fostered an unhealthy reliance and dependency on the therapy process. An alternative approach would have been to focus on the exceptions to her mood states that occurred on her yearly trips. (See the section in this chapter on working with client strengths and exceptions.) Why were things better on her vacations? What was she doing differently? Could she do that at other times? Some practitioners are reluctant to shift the focus of treatment at a time when they perceive the client as fragile, but sometimes this is just what the client needs to guide him or her to healthier behaviors.

Working Toward Termination

In the next chapter we look at the process of ending therapy in more depth. However, it is important to keep in mind that therapy is not meant to be an ongoing, everlasting process. Most clients expect to get better. Your job is to help them to complete therapy successfully.

Summing Up

In this chapter we have reviewed some of the common steps used to move the therapy process forward. Determining the optimal timing and modality of sessions will impact the client's ability to make changes and improve functioning. We have also discussed how to work with client strengths and exceptions and how to identify key intervention points in psychotherapy. We have reviewed the most common problem areas that can arise during an episode of therapy and effective ways to respond to them.

EXERCISES

1. How do you determine the most appropriate spacing of sessions for each client? What factors do you consider?
2. How do you establish a realistic time frame for goal attainment with your clients?
3. Describe the solution-focused brief therapy model of searching for exceptions and working with strengths. How have you used this model with your own clients?
4. How do you tend to cope with boundary violations with clients? What boundary problems have you experienced most often?
5. Discuss an example of client noncompliance. How did you respond to it?
6. Have you had a client whose catharsis proved to be unhelpful in the therapy process? Why do you think it was not helpful?
7. What kind of strong emotions have your clients aroused in you during therapy sessions? How do you address transference and countertransference in therapy?
8. What behaviors that communicate disrespect for clients have you observed in yourself or other therapists? Have you ever felt disrespected by a personal therapist? How did you respond?
9. What do you do when therapy feels stuck and no progress is being made? How do you discuss this with clients?
10. Identify where you tend to feel most comfortable in these dichotomies:

    - Acceptance versus change
    - Nurturing versus demanding
    - Structured versus flexible

(Continued)

11. Practice your weaker position. For example, if you are comfortable being very nurturing with your clients but do not feel very confident setting challenging goals, practice that!

12. Examine how you might respond to the following behaviors of a client:

- A client you are treating is habitually late. Because of this, you do not have enough time to adequately deal with the client's clinical issues. The client wants to continue the session past the scheduled time, and you have other clients waiting.

- A client complains that she does not seem to be making progress, yet she rarely does the homework you have given.

- A client calls you in crisis and you shuffle some appointments to see him. Once the crisis has ended, he starts to miss appointments. A week later, he calls you in crisis and wants to be seen right away again.

Resources

Cohen-Posey, K. (2000). *Brief therapy client handouts*. New York: Wiley.

11

Ending Treatment

What You Will Learn
- How to help clients live life between sessions
- How to identify the three signs that a therapy episode is nearing its end
- How to set up a relapse-prevention plan
- The lessons of relapse
- The importance of the final session
- How to cope with incomplete endings

Many therapists have difficulty with the termination of therapy. In this chapter, we discuss ways to approach the end of an episode of psychotherapy in a compassionate, professional, and effective manner.

Helping Clients Live Life between Sessions

Most clients see their therapist for about 1 hour per week. Some may be seen more or less frequently, depending on their level of acuity, preferences, and the therapist's style of practice. This leaves 167 hours of life between sessions. How should clients spend this time?

What the client does between sessions is almost always more important than what happens in session. Therefore, what happens between sessions should be a major focus of psychotherapy.

How will you, as the therapist, address this? If you have done a thorough evaluation, identified functional impairments, and created a treatment plan that addresses these impairments, you are well on your way. Functional impairments are usually related to the client's daily life. The client may have difficulty initiating or maintaining friendships, attending to health needs, or completing work tasks. Part of each session should focus on the previous week's specific functioning. Ask clients "Did you call a friend to plan an activity?"; "Did you make an appointment with your doctor?"; "Did you take medications as prescribed?"; or "Did you complete the report that was due on Wednesday? If not, what symptoms or behaviors got in your way? What can we do today that might help remove these barriers?" Breaking down the tasks into attainable steps, discussing how to address obstacles, and motivating commitment to the goal are all part of the therapy session. (See Chapter 7 for more on setting realistic treatment expectations.)

This is not to say that process-oriented therapy does not have a place in your sessions. You may begin and end your sessions with discussions of daily functioning but spend time in the middle of the session working with the client in a process-oriented fashion. Your therapeutic style and techniques are at the core of what you do as a psychotherapist. It is important to keep track of what is going on in your client's daily life. This attention to detail lets you know you have made a difference and helps you know when and how to terminate treatment.

Positive Termination Strategies: How to Know When You Are Done

Termination planning starts at the first session. Few clients want, and can afford, open-ended treatment. As you discuss your philosophy of care, assessment, and treatment planning method, communicate that psychotherapy is a finite process with a beginning, middle, and end. Completion of therapy depends on the client's symptoms, your therapeutic style, and the client's progress.

Psychotherapy is best thought of as episodic. Think of your own therapy experiences. Most of us would agree that we are never really "done"—so psychologically healthy that we will never need therapy again and will live our lives in total bliss. Most of us enter therapy because we are in crisis or at a crossroads and cannot find a way out of our personal suffering. We eventually leave therapy when we feel "good enough," knowing that there may be further suffering ahead. Being explicit with clients about the episodic nature of psychotherapy can go a long way toward encouraging effective, efficient, and focused therapy. A client who believes that therapy can go on forever may not be very committed to making each session count; there is always next week to confront the problem. Meanwhile, the client has a supportive, caring, and sympathetic person who will spend time with him or her each and every week. The very nature of the therapeutic relationship can be soothing and satisfying. Some clients think, "Why bother with relationships in the real world when such a person is available in the therapy office? Why bother changing my behaviors when I am already totally acceptable to my therapist?"

How do you know when an episode of therapy is nearing its end?

- Symptoms have decreased.
- Functioning has improved.
- Goals have been met or modified.

If you engage in regular feedback with your clients, your work together will have a natural ending. Your clients will work toward a successful termination *with* you. When feedback occurs regularly, clients often initiate their own termination. (See Chapter 6 for more on eliciting feedback.)

Setting Up a Relapse-Prevention Plan

As your client nears the end of a treatment episode, work to develop a relapse-prevention plan. Review your initial treatment plan. What is the client doing differently now? What will it take to continue to do these things?

Teresa had been in therapy with Paul for about 3 months. She initially started therapy because of severe depression. She had difficulty getting out of bed in the morning, had difficulty going to sleep at night, and had pervasive sadness and suicidal thoughts. Paul encouraged her to see her primary care provider for a trial of medications. He worked with the thought patterns that contributed to her depression and helped her develop more effective problem-solving techniques. He also taught her some emotion regulation and distress tolerance skills, so that even when she felt sad she could take steps to improve her mood and stay safe.

When both Teresa and Paul began to think that she had accomplished her goals for therapy, they worked together on a relapse-prevention plan. They listed the positive steps that Teresa was taking in her daily life: taking medications as prescribed, using a daily thought and emotion chart to monitor her moods and thinking patterns, and practicing specific emotion regulation and distress tolerance skills daily (especially morning walks, listening to music, and spending time with friends).

Teresa and Paul also listed her relapse signals: insomnia, pessimistic thinking, and suicidal thoughts. They created a plan for Teresa to continue monitoring and responding to these signals and a plan for when she should consider returning to therapy.

The important elements in a relapse-prevention plan are:

- Symptoms and behaviors to monitor (and how)
- Specific behaviors to continue
- Warning signs and steps to take if symptoms become troublesome again

Be sure to write down your plan, and give a copy to your client. Your client may also choose to give a copy to a trusted friend or family member to help him or her stay on track. Relapse is a very common occurrence in the change process. The road to change is not a straight line and is often paved with bumps and detours. Clients should be prepared and have a plan to deal with relapse should it occur. To ignore the possibility is to be ill prepared. Relapse can be a time to help clients reevaluate what led up to the relapse and what did and did not work for them. This can be especially helpful before embarking on another change effort. Clients who have already done a lot of work do not necessarily need to go back to the beginning of the change process. After a short period of reevaluation they may quickly go through the contemplation stage and back into an action plan. Others may decide, after some contemplation, that this is just not a good time to make this particular change. (See Chapter 8 for more on working with stages of change.) Table 11.1 shows the important lessons that clients can learn from relapse and related practitioner interventions.

Table 11.1 The 10 Lessons of Relapse

	Lessons of Relapse	Practitioner Interventions
Lesson 1	**Few changers terminate the first time.** Most people do not overcome their problem with just one effort. Many try repeatedly before succeeding. However, many clients expect to succeed the first time.	Let clients know that they are normal (not failures). This is a great step toward strengthening their next effort.
Lesson 2	**Trial and error is inefficient.** Many clients set out to change without having any kind of a plan or road map. They try many different things. Some work and some don't. This can be very time consuming and frustrating. Each relapse often brings more feelings of inadequacy or hopelessness.	Help clients rely on the stages and processes of change rather than trial and error.
Lesson 3	**Change costs more than you budgeted.** Many people who try to change on their own underestimate how much time and energy it will take. It can be expensive too. Many problems take years to develop, so it is unrealistic to think that they can be changed quickly. Prochaska et al. state that it takes about 6 months of concerted effort in the action phase before someone is ready to move into the maintenance phase.	Help clients use a variety of the processes of change so that they have a healthy substitute for the behavior they are trying to change. Help clients assess their level of commitment. Help them learn to pace themselves, so that they do not move too quickly into the maintenance phase, which can increase their likelihood of relapse.
Lesson 4	**Using the wrong process at the wrong time.** Sometimes people use the processes of change incorrectly: they act on faulty information, they think they just do not have enough willpower, or they replace one problem with another.	Inform clients about tested methods of change. Some things cannot be changed by willpower alone. Environmental control techniques are necessary during the action and maintenance phases to be successful.
Lesson 5	**Be prepared for complications.** Change does not occur in a vacuum. Sometimes changing one problem can make another one worse.	Help clients transfer learned skills to new problems. Many skills learned in overcoming one problem can be used in another.

(Continued)

Table 11.1 (*Continued*)

	Lessons of Relapse	*Practitioner Interventions*
Lesson 6	**The path to change is rarely a straight line.** Many people who attempt to change take detours and are subjected to time delays. Things don't always happen in the order that they should.	Help clients see their starts and stops as part of a developmental process. Starting the change process again doesn't mean that they have to start back at the beginning and that all of their effort has been for naught. Each effort brings them closer to their goal.
Lesson 7	**A lapse is not a relapse.** In the course of changing, it is easy to fall back into old habits. Believing in absolutes can help turn a lapse (missing a trip to the gym, cheating on a diet, etc.) into a full-blown relapse. Some clients believe that if they trip they might as well fall all the way. Once guilt and self-blame get involved, a full-blown relapse is usually not far behind.	Help clients avoid catastrophizing and to quickly resume their usual routine without self-blame.
Lesson 8	**Mini-decisions lead to maxi-decisions.** Most relapses are not conscious but the result of small decisions that have negative consequences. ("I think I'm doing pretty well so I'll just skip . . ."). Before you know it, things are changing for the worse and heading toward relapse.	Increase client awareness that the small decisions they make can sometimes contribute to a relapse without ever making a conscious decision to do so.
Lesson 9	**Distress precipitates relapse.** Some types of distress (in the form of anxiety, anger, depression, loneliness, or other emotional problems) are the precursors to relapse.	Dialectical behavioral therapy techniques such as distress tolerance and emotional regulation skills can be used to manage distress.
Lesson 10	**Learning translates into action.** At some point, you have to take what you have learned and put it into action.	Help clients realize that action without intent and preparation decreases the likelihood of success. Time spent clarifying commitment and preparing for action is time well spent. Taking the leap of action is easier if the pros outweigh the cons of changing.

Adapted from *Changing for Good: A Revolutionary Six-Stage Program for Overcoming Bad Habits and Moving Your Life Positively Forward*, (pp. 223–231), by J. O. Prochaska, J. C. Norcross, and C. C. DiClemente, 1994, New York: HarperCollins.

One of the most frequently shared examples of the relapse and relapse-prevention process is this poem by Portia Nelson:[*]

Autobiography in Five Short Chapters

By Portia Nelson

Chapter One

I walk down the street.
    There is a deep hole in the sidewalk.
    I fall in.
    I am lost. . . . I am helpless.
    It isn't my fault.
It takes forever to find a way out.

Chapter Two

I walk down the same street.
    There is a deep hole in the sidewalk.
    I pretend I don't see it.
    I fall in again.
I can't believe I am in the same place.
    It isn't my fault.
It still takes a long time to get out.

Chapter Three

I walk down the same street.
    There is a deep hole in the sidewalk.
    I see it is there.
    I still fall in . . . it's a habit . . . but,
        my eyes are open.
It is *my* fault. I get out immediately.

Chapter Four

I walk down the same street.
  There is a deep hole in the sidewalk.
  I walk around it.

Chapter Five

I walk down another street.

The Importance of the Final Session

A successful termination is often dependent on the content of the final session. The final session is a natural place to create or review the relapse-prevention plan, review accomplishments, and express feelings about the end of the therapy relationship. Both therapist and client may feel some sadness, fear, or anger about the termination, as well as hope or happiness. Talk about these honestly, and in the end say clearly "Good-bye." Learning and practicing how to say "Good-bye" is an extremely helpful skill for both client and therapist. Life is full of endings, and to be comfortable in expressing this reality is a great gift.

It is important that the positive work of the client is summarized and reviewed. The last session is a great time to do this. It is easy for some clients to lose perspective and forget what life was like when they first started. Pointing out how far they have come and the changes they have made can help to solidify their positive experience so that they leave the last session feeling satisfaction that they have accomplished something. Leaving the last session feeling confident and hopeful will help clients face future adversity and challenges with a new skill set.

Incomplete Endings

What happens when your client simply stops coming to therapy? Sometimes a client changes therapists without telling you. Sometimes clients feel that therapy is complete and don't want to spend more time saying good-bye to you. Sometimes clients feel that the therapy wasn't helpful. Sometimes the money or insurance runs out, and the client does not want to incur a debt to you. There are times when a client's family or friends may feel the therapy is harming the client (or their relationship with him) and encourage him to stop coming to sessions. Incomplete endings can be difficult for the therapist, and it is important to acknowledge this. You may want to consult with a colleague if this becomes troublesome to you. If it happens often, you might want to reevaluate your treatment planning and communication with clients about the expected course of treatment.

If you have concerns about the client's safety, you should attempt to contact him and encourage him to return, at least to develop a safety plan. In some situations, you may need to contact the client's primary care provider with recommendations for further treatment or family or law enforcement if you have concerns regarding the client's danger to self or others. (See Chapter 3 for legal issues around client safety.) Be sure to document in the client's chart all attempts to contact the client or others on his behalf.

Summing Up

In this chapter we have discussed the importance of approaching therapy termination with a plan. Identifying when an episode of therapy is nearing its end and setting up a specific relapse-prevention plan can help therapy come to a positive conclusion. Use your last session to celebrate progress made and prepare for further growth outside the therapy process. If you have set the stage from the beginning by identifying clear goals for therapy and using focused interventions, both you and your client will approach termination as a natural ending to a positive process.

EXERCISES

1. How do you assess whether client functioning is improving? Have you experienced times when client functioning declined? How did you respond?
2. What clues do you look for that signal that an episode of therapy is coming to an end?
3. Write a sample relapse-prevention plan for a client with:
   - Major Depressive Disorder, Recurrent
   - Generalized Anxiety Disorder
   - Posttraumatic Stress Disorder
   - Adjustment Disorder
   - Bipolar Disorder
4. What kind of "incomplete endings" have you experienced in your personal or professional life?
5. How do you feel when a client terminates treatment abruptly?

12

Working with Common Themes

What You Will Learn

- How to define self-esteem and work with clients to improve it
- A behavioral model for working with low self-esteem
- How core beliefs influence clients' self-esteem and behavior
- How to use motivational interviewing to address client resistance and avoidance behaviors
- How to use "joining the resistance," restraining, and reframing to reduce resistance to change
- How to work with forgiveness and acceptance
- The importance of humor and laughter in psychotherapy

An active psychotherapy practice is full of a multitude of client presentations, challenges, and solutions. In the next several chapters we look at some of the common themes that occur in a practice. Entire books have been written about each of these topics. We focus here on some clinical nuggets that you can use right away. In this chapter, we examine self-esteem, core beliefs, dealing with resistance, working with forgiveness, and using humor in psychotherapy.

Self-Esteem

A major bane of psychotherapy utilization reviewers is the ubiquitous mention of "low self-esteem" as a problem and "improve self-esteem" as a goal—usually without any specific objectives to bridge the gap. Let's examine exactly what self-esteem is and how it can be enhanced.

Self-esteem is one of the more common, yet misunderstood, concepts in the field of mental health. Clients spend time lamenting that they do not have it and looking for it without knowing what they are looking for. They cannot explain what it is; they just know that whatever it is, they do not have it! Often, practitioners identify clients who have poor self-esteem, spend a lot of time talking with them about it, yet also may lack a way of helping their clients achieve higher self-esteem.

Is self-esteem an all-or-nothing proposition? Can someone have some self-esteem but need more? Can someone have it but not know it? A person's self-esteem is intricately involved with his or her own sense of worthiness. How do you measure worthiness? David Burns (1993), MD, psychotherapist and author of *Ten Days to Self-Esteem*, helps clients see the fallacy in trying to measure their worthiness. If you measure worthiness based on accomplishment, there will always be someone who you perceive as accomplishing more. Does that mean you are less worthy? If so, does this mean that if someone is the best at something, all others are worthless by comparison? Everyone can do something of value. Dr. Burns works with clients to help them stop trying to measure their value in comparison to others. Burns recommends rating our traits, but not ourselves.

Viewing self-esteem in this way can help clients get out of an all-or-nothing mind-set. Many clients who have poor self-esteem grew up in a dysfunctional family environment filled with active abuse or passive neglect. Some of these children perform admirable behaviors but live in an environment where these behaviors are never recognized. These children are not validated for positive behaviors, accomplishments, and successes or praised for their innate qualities. Conversely, they are often told that they are stupid, cannot do anything right, and will not amount to much. Is it any wonder that this type of environment becomes the breeding ground for self-sabotaging core beliefs? Some clients spend their entire lifetime feeling bad about themselves and dealing with these issues. Validation from another is such an important aspect of self-esteem that it is unlikely that it can exist without it, particularly in the formative years. Many grow up with a validation deficit.

There are two aspects to helping a client develop self-esteem. Both need to be present in order to achieve self-esteem:

1. Something needs to be done, a specific act or behavior.
2. Someone needs to observe this behavior and validate it directly.

There is more hunger for love and appreciation in this world than for bread.
—Mother Teresa

Helping clients with low self-esteem develop the ability to see their strengths rather than their weaknesses is often the best place to start. The specific act or behavior can be almost anything. It doesn't need to be achievement-oriented; it can simply be an act of kindness to another or taking good physical care of oneself and feeling good about it. The important thing is that it needs to be meaningful to the client. Both elements need to be present in helping clients develop self-esteem: They need to do something, and the therapist or another significant person in the client's life needs to validate it. In this way a new personal history is written and can be the stepping stone to developing self-esteem.

Self-esteem will come as a result of accurate self understanding, appreciation of one's genuine skills, and the satisfaction of helping others.
—Dr. Michael Miller

A common pitfall of therapists who are trying to help their clients develop self-esteem is that both elements are not present. They may try to validate something that has not occurred, and thus it feels very empty and meaningless to the client. It is not believable. The client thinks of himself as being unable to achieve anything worthwhile, so jumping ahead and validating is too great a leap to make.

Rarely can clients develop self-esteem by talking about how they lack it. They need to create new experiences and be validated in doing so. This can be a powerful intervention for clients who feel inadequate, and an extremely important first step. (See Chapter 10 for more on working with client strengths and exceptions.)

A Behavioral Approach to Increasing Self-Esteem

Most clients come to psychotherapy because something is not working in their life. They usually feel bad about their own behaviors and emotions or others' behaviors and the impact it is having on them; often they feel bad about both. Many clients want to change the outside world to match their internal needs—an extremely difficult task! It is important to help clients focus on what they can learn to control.

Sharon arrives at her first psychotherapy session and presents George with a carefully typed list of problems. She says she can't sleep well at night because she is worrying about her terminally ill mother. She had a panic attack last week at the grocery store. She feels bad all the time about what she's doing: When she is at work she wishes she could be with her mother; when she's with her mother she worries about missing important work deadlines. She says she hears a voice in her head all the time—her mother's voice, she thinks—saying "What a bad daughter you are!" Sometimes she thinks she is "going crazy." George reviews these problems with Sharon and shares that she may have an Adjustment Disorder with depressed mood and anxiety. He normalizes her experiences, explaining that most people with a terminally ill mother and a demanding job would have similar reactions. He reviews some important self-care strategies to help her improve overall functioning, including ways to improve sleep. When he asks about her relationship with her mother, Sharon says, "She never really loved me—she wanted a career and got stuck being a mother. She always told me that I would be the death of her!"

George empathizes with Sharon's experience with her mother and the mixed feelings she may have about her mother's impending death. He suspects that she has chronic low self-esteem due to her mother's critical statements. He suggests that they begin working on improving her self-esteem at the next session.

What does low self-esteem look like? How will clients know when they have more self-esteem? How is it expressed? Let us examine self-esteem in behavioral terms:

High Self-Esteem	Low Self-Esteem
Thinks positive and pleasant thoughts about oneself	Thinks negative and unpleasant thoughts about oneself
Says positive things about oneself to others	Says negative things about oneself to others

(Continued)

Feels pleasant emotions (love, joy, calm) when thinking about oneself	Feels unpleasant emotions (hate, sadness, fear) when thinking about oneself
Makes decisions and choices based at least partly on one's own needs and wants	Makes decisions and choices based primarily on others' needs and wants
Frequently engages in activities which give one enjoyment	Seldom engages in activities that give one enjoyment; often does behaviors that cause oneself harm

How can a therapist assist a client in moving from low self-esteem to high self-esteem? First, help clients define the thoughts and emotions that influence their self-esteem.

George helps Sharon make a list:
I think "I am a bad daughter."
I think "I can't do it all."
I think "I should have never been born."
I feel guilt, shame, sadness, and fear when I think about myself.

Next, help the client see the connections between thoughts, emotions, and behaviors.

I agree to visit my mother twice a day despite an already busy schedule and then say to my mother, "I'm sorry I couldn't get here sooner." I think "I am a bad daughter."

I agree to take on new projects at work despite feeling overwhelmed already and then say to coworkers "I'm sorry I didn't get this done."

I think "I can't do it all" and then stay up late at night to finish work and household tasks, and then feel too keyed up to sleep.

I skip lunch so that I have more time to finish work projects.

I eat an unsatisfying fast-food dinner so that I can go to see my mother after work.

I have stopped going for pleasant Saturday walks with my friend.

Now we have tangible ways to define what low self-esteem is for this client. The intent is to work with the integrated system of thoughts, feelings, and behaviors. Focusing on feelings alone creates a sense that they occur in isolation and that there is nothing to do about them. It is very difficult to establish control over feelings. However, breaking the situation down into cause (thoughts) and effects (behaviors) provides some opportunities for insight *and* interventions.

Next, help the client determine a way to count or measure these behaviors for 1 week.

> Count how many times per day you think "I am a bad daughter."
> Keep a list of everything you do after 9 PM.
> Count how many minutes you spend eating lunch and dinner.

You may need to be creative to find a way to measure behaviors consistently—forms, charts, or worksheets may help. (See Chapter 9 for more on how to define measurable goals.) The purpose of counting is to provide an increased sense of awareness. ("I never realized that I was eating on the run all the time. No wonder my stomach always feels upset!")

Help your client to identify thoughts that indicate high self-esteem.

> I will think "I am doing the best I can for my mother."
> I will think "I can feel some joy in my life despite my mother's illness."

Once there is a change in thinking, what will the client be doing differently? Help clients determine what that will look like in terms that are meaningful for them.

> I will change my schedule and visit Mom once per day.
> I will say no to new work projects for 1 month.
> I will eat one healthy meal per day lasting at least ½ hour, and breathe deeply between each bite.
> I will go for a walk every Saturday.

Encourage your clients to make a commitment to initiate one or more of these behaviors to substitute for their low self-esteem behaviors. This will give them an opportunity to rewrite their future. Again, determine a system for counting or measuring their success. Remind them that it may take a while to completely replace their low self-esteem behaviors with high self-esteem behaviors, but now that they have a road map, they can continue to do so even after therapy ends.

The significant problems we have cannot be solved at the same level of thinking with which we created them.
—Albert Einstein

Core Beliefs

It is no accident that we follow the section on self-esteem with one on core beliefs. Clients with poor self-esteem often have negative core beliefs. We all have beliefs, both conscious and unconscious, that drive our actions and reactions in everyday life. As practitioners, we often treat the symptoms that bring a client into therapy: depression, fear, eating problems, anger, and self-defeating attitudes. The root causes of unhealthy behaviors and self-esteem issues can be negative core beliefs. Most people are not aware of their core beliefs, yet they are the underlying driver of many of their actions.

A negative core belief can be as simple as "I don't deserve good things in my life." This belief can be incredibly powerful and can encompass a person's entire approach to life. The person's job, personal relationships, choice of partner, finances, and general living conditions can be affected by this belief. Is it any wonder that when something positive happens, the effects do not last long? Clients who have these negative core beliefs often engage in self-sabotaging behavior. The negative result fulfills the negative core belief and causes an even deeper reinforcement of the idea that they do not deserve good things in their lives. The core belief can be the underlying cause of the symptom and help to perpetuate it.

If clients have difficulty doing something positive for themselves, suspect a negative core belief. Negative core beliefs usually originate in childhood. Children often believe that they are the cause of problems that occur in the family. Abuse or neglect are fertile ground for the development of negative core beliefs. Alice J. Brown (2007, pp. 3–4), a psychotherapist and the author

They say the chains of habit are too light to be felt until they are too heavy to be broken. The chains you put around yourself now have enormous consequences as you go through life.
—Warren Buffett

of *Core Beliefs Psychotherapy*, writes about the origin of negative or mistaken core beliefs:

> When children come to believe that something is fundamentally wrong with them and develop mistaken core beliefs, another significant process happens; they begin to suppress their real selves and develop coping selves. The real self is who people really are: their real feelings, needs, style, dreams, talents and personality. The coping self develops as children attempt to become whoever they believe they must be in order to fix the problems in the family and get their needs met. Coping selves look to the environment for cues that will tell them how they should feel, think and behave. It is a very painful and unsatisfying way to live. It also leads to unhealthy, superficial and codependent relationships.
>
> The coping self develops at the same time as the mistaken core beliefs develop, for the same reason. A child's thinking goes like this: problems exist, they are my fault, something must be wrong with me so I need to be someone else. Conversely, when the mistaken core beliefs are corrected, the person is able to let go of the coping self and reconnect to the real self.

Working with negative core beliefs can be a rewarding experience for both therapist and client. Helping clients change these beliefs can fundamentally change their total outlook on themselves and how they view and act in the world. Cognitive-behavioral techniques can help bring these beliefs to conscious awareness, and techniques such as eye movement desensitization and reprocessing and those of energy psychology work directly on the unconscious beliefs themselves, unraveling the connection between negative thoughts, somatic experience, and behavior.

Working with Resistance and Avoidance Behaviors

It can be frustrating for psychotherapists to work with clients whose resistance and avoidance seem to block every attempt at progress.

- Emily carefully explains that she cannot do anything different in her life; she expects therapy to "fix" her without any effort on her own part.
- Frank declines to get an evaluation and treatment for his daily cannabis use, but wants to continue to talk about his depression ad infinitum.

- Hannah is late for every appointment and then expects the session to extend into the next hour.
- Eric is willing to talk about his day-to-day life but resists any attempt to look at his history of childhood abuse as it may relate to current relationship problems.

You can prevent some of these problems of resistance and avoidance by giving adequate attention to a thorough initial evaluation and treatment plan. It is best to discover early in treatment if there is a discrepancy between your client's expectations of the therapy process and your own. Be very clear at the beginning of treatment about what you expect of the client and what the client can expect of you. Gain a level of agreement on the goals and methods of treatment so that if resistance or avoidance occurs you can address it immediately and directly. (See Chapter 7 for more on developing collaboration with clients.)

"I have noticed recently, Linda, that you seem to be rejecting every suggestion I make. This is pretty frustrating to me, and I wonder if you may be frustrated by our lack of progress in improving your depression. I think we should review our treatment plan and see if we have gotten off track from our original agreement or check to see if the goals have changed."

Sometimes resistance can be caused by the client's disagreement with your assessment of the problem. A client with panic attacks may not agree that learning more about the physiology of anxiety can help her cope with panic. A client with depression may not agree that episodic use of alcohol and drugs may be worsening his symptoms. A client with difficulty concentrating and focusing attention may not agree that developing time and task structures will be helpful in improving work performance. This is best approached directly: Review your assessment of the problem and treatment goals, and ask for the client's thoughts and feelings about them. If the disagreement is significant and is blocking treatment effectiveness, strive to find some common ground and work from there. The problem may be solved as you work together on the common goal.

Clinical Considerations

Motivational interviewing (Miller & Rollnick, 2002) views resistance as a signal of dissonance. It is a way for clients to communicate that they do not agree with the direction the therapist is going. When this occurs it is an opportunity to stop, try to understand it, and do something different. Resistance often occurs in response to something that the therapist is doing.

Some clients have a wall of resistance that prevents them from getting to the other side of change. They may not want to talk with you because they are there involuntarily, have been court-ordered to therapy, or have been pressured to attend by a parent or a spouse. Others may be in therapy voluntarily and have less conspicuous forms of resistance that create a barrier to change. In any event, working with this resistance is the first priority and must be addressed before proceeding with anything else. This resistance can come in a variety of forms:

- *Hostility:* "Why are you even talking with me? I'm not interested. I'm here just because they said I had to be. Are we done now?"
- *Excuses and avoidance:* "I just didn't have time to do the homework."
- *Apathy:* "I didn't do the homework. I've already tried so many things and none of them has worked, so why bother?"
- *Self-labeling:* "I have _____ so I can't do that."

Despite all of the wonderful knowledge you may possess as a therapist, not everyone is ready to hear it directly. A variety of techniques can be used to address these behaviors. The least effective is direct confrontation. This often just fuels the resistant behavior and makes it stronger. As skilled therapists, we can more effectively address resistance indirectly by accepting clients for exactly where they are at the moment, joining with them, and helping them define their own problems.

Do not lecture. Instead, ask questions in an attempt to understand who, what, and why clients are resisting. Once you understand this, it is likely that you and the client can find some common ground to work from. It is helpful to determine the client's stage of change and match your approach to the process that will move the client to the next stage.

Clinical Considerations

Clients who have a high degree of resistance respond best to a nondirective approach; however, clients who have low resistance and are cooperative often have a better outcome with precise direction and guidance from the therapist.

Joining the Resistance

Joining the resistance is a very helpful technique, particularly with hostile clients. When you give permission for the resistant behavior, you take the payoff away. Resistant clients often believe that you are a part of the system that does not understand them and will force them to do something that they don't want to do or that they view as unreasonable or unnecessary. Resistance is often present to combat this, and your failure in trying to confront their resistance is their reward. If you join that resistance, it is no longer attractive to maintain it. When that occurs the resistance may dissipate, and a constructive interaction can begin. Let's look at an example.

Brian is a 16-year-old boy who is brought into the session by his parents, who are complaining of his surly attitude and his lack of respect when interacting with other members of his family. He sits slumped in his chair, looking away from the therapist.

Therapist: I understand that your parents wanted you to come here.
Brian: Forced me, more like it. How long is this going to last?
Therapist: I don't really know.

Brian: Hmm. I don't know that I can sit here and listen.

Therapist: That's fine. Your parents have paid for the time so we need to do something. Any ideas?

Brian: I don't know. You're the counselor. (Pause) Don't you ever get tired of that?

Therapist: Tired of what?

Brian: Listening to other people's problems. (He turns to face the therapist.)

Therapist: No, it's usually pretty interesting. Everyone's got a different story.

Brian: Well I've got one for you.

Therapist: I'd love to hear it. So what's your story?

Brian: My parents are always on my back. They won't let me do what I want to do.

Therapist: Like what?

Brian: You know, go out at night, see some of my friends. . . .

Therapist: What happens then?

Brian: Well, I get pretty nasty. I admit it. I don't like it when they tell me what to do.

Therapist: If we could figure out a way to get your parents off your back, would you be interested in working on that together?

Brian: Yeah. That would be great.

Therapist: Tell me more about when that happens.

Brian: Well . . .

Clinical Considerations

The power of counterintuitive thinking: There is a great story about the hypnotherapist Milton Erickson that illustrates how effective counterintuitive thinking can be. As a child Erickson was observing his father trying to get a very stubborn donkey into the barn. His father tried pulling the donkey from the front by the harness and then tried to push the donkey into the barn from the rear. No matter what he did, he could not get the donkey into the barn. Observing that the donkey seemed to move in the direction opposite of the force applied, Erickson went over to the animal and started to pull his tail in an attempt to pull him *away* from the barn. The donkey then reacted by moving *into* the barn.

Restraining

Restraining is another technique that can be effective when a client always seems to forget or cannot quite get around to the assigned homework. This involves telling clients that they are not ready to do the assignment; perhaps it is too soon or too complex for them. The goal is to attempt to hold the client back, looking for some rebellion and flight into healthy behavior.

Peter is an independent businessman who is successful in his work life but has a lot of difficulty with interpersonal relationships.

Therapist: Peter, we have been meeting now for quite a few sessions and I notice that whatever homework assignments I give you, they never seem to get done.

Client: I've been pretty busy. This is a very hectic time in my business.

Therapist: Sure, I understand that. I have wondered if you spent the same amount of effort in your personal life that you spend on your business, if you would achieve the kind of results you are looking for.

Client: Hmm . . .

Therapist: This may be too big of a step for you, and you may not be ready to do the homework I have given you. We may need to focus on something more basic.

This approach can be quite provocative but often works well when used sparingly, in appropriate cases. Interestingly, some clients, when told that they are not ready for the assignment, need to disprove it to you by actually doing it. Because Peter is a very results-oriented person in his business life, he is an ideal candidate for this approach. Clients will often come in the next week reporting that they did the homework they hadn't been able to do. Once this occurs it provides a lot of material to work with.

Therapists should ask these clients "What happened? What were the results? How did that feel?"

Reframing

Reframing is used to give clients a different perspective on personal qualities they see as negative: "Would this trait be valuable if used in another situation or in a different way?" The meaning of the trait remains the same, while the reframe illustrates that it may be helpful in another context. The change in the client's perception often causes a change in the meaning of the perceived fault. A perceived deficiency can be reframed as a strength. This technique can help to prevent a client from slipping back into old, familiar, and destructive habits that lead to resistance. Reframing can help clients move forward with the realization that they already possess the personal qualities needed for healthier behaviors.

Virginia Satir, known for her pioneering work in family therapy, was a master in the art of reframing. She believed that the presenting issue itself was seldom the real problem; rather, how people coped with the issue created the problem ("The Top 10," 2007). A good example of reframing is seen in her work with a male parent who came into therapy concerned about his daughter's stubbornness. During the course of discussion with the father, Satir was able to reframe the daughter's stubbornness as a positive trait that would be valuable to protect her from destructive influences and to help her achieve her goals. As it turned out, stubbornness was also a trait of the father. By helping the father realize that they shared this trait in common, Satir was able to reframe it so that he needed either to recognize the value of her stubbornness or deny the value of his own (Veryard, n.d.).

Forgiveness and Acceptance

Many clients enter psychotherapy with a backlog of unresolved feelings of anger, grief, and hurt over events in their lives. These events may be current, ongoing, or from many years ago. Some clients come to therapy for the sole purpose of rehashing these events in excruciating detail, hoping to get some validation from the therapist about how awful life has been. These clients are stuck in a loop of blaming these events for every past and current problem in their lives. They may feel hopeless about ever recovering from these events and use therapy to stay stuck in the past.

These clients embody age-old existential and spiritual questions:

- Who am I?
- Why do I exist?
- Where do I fit in?
- Why is there suffering in the world?
- Why didn't someone save me?
- How can I go on?

As a psychotherapist, you will be asked to struggle with these questions again and again. Make sure you have at least some answers for yourself, in your own life, so that your clients' struggles will not constantly trigger your own unanswered questions and cause unnecessary suffering. Although you do not want to prescribe your own philosophy of life to your clients, it is important to communicate from your heart that you believe in something that gives you strength to move forward in life.

What are the options in responding to the reality that cruel, unpleasant, and unfair events have occurred and may continue to occur in one's life?

- *Stay stuck in the pain:* Realizing that this is a choice can be enormously liberating. Making a choice moves power back to the individual. Even if this realization is all that comes out of an episode of psychotherapy, your client may be able to go forward with a renewed sense of self-efficacy.
- *Learn to ignore the pain:* This can be a precursor to healing, as it allows new experiences to gradually take over. Again, the concept of choice is crucial. Choosing to ignore pain is different from numbing it or dissociating oneself from the painful experiences. Choosing to focus on creating new, pleasant experiences can cause past or current unpleasant experiences to fade in memory and importance.
- *Attempt to draw an apology, retribution, or restitution from individuals or groups who have harmed you:* This option may involve careful preparation for confronting the originator of the events.

Clarity of purpose, safety, and determination must all be addressed in this preparation. Your client must also prepare for the possibility that the person confronted will deny, minimize, or attack in response to the confrontation; your client may not get the payoff desired. Preparation must therefore also entail a "Plan B" for a negative outcome. Indeed, even if the desired outcome is attained, your client must still create a future life with a different focus.

- *Attempt to forgive the individuals or groups who have harmed you:* Often motivated by religious beliefs, this option can be effective if it can be broken down into specific behavioral expressions. It may require communicating the forgiveness directly, or it may involve communicating it by proxy through service to others. Like acceptance, forgiveness does not imply that harm was not done, only that it is relegated to the past and its results are not deliberately carried forth into the present or future.

- *Learn to accept the harm that was done:* This approach is rooted in mindfulness traditions and practice. It is an important element in dialectical behavior therapy (Linehan, 1993a, 1993b). (See Chapter 13 for more on dialectical behavior therapy.) Acceptance involves being aware in the moment, rather than dwelling in the past or future. Acceptance is often attained slowly: "You have to turn your mind and commit to acceptance over and over and over again" (Linehan, 1993b, p. 176). Through gentle, in-the-moment, guided mindfulness practice (though not necessarily formal meditation), a client can gradually lose focus on the painfulness of the past and begin to focus on creating a satisfying life in the future.

He who cannot forgive others destroys the bridge over which he himself must pass.
—George Herbert

Note that all of these options are pointed toward future thoughts, emotions, and actions of the client. Keep this outcome in mind as you and your clients explore different ways to respond to unpleasant events. If a client is suffering due to chronic pain, the illness or death of a loved one, or other unpleasant events, many of these same strategies can also be useful.

If a client is suffering due to current abuse by others, you must take steps to help your client move toward safety. Provide opportunities to acknowledge and name the abuse, to develop skills and safety plans, and to access resources needed to change the present abusive situation.

The Role of Laughter and Humor

Laughing and crying are two innate indicators of emotional reaction. As practitioners, we are probably more comfortable working with a client who is crying than integrating humor and laughter into a session. Clients often lose their sense of humor and the ability to laugh as their problems increase in intensity and they become more socially isolated. Regaining that ability is also one of the first signs that therapeutic progress is being made. For the astute practitioner, the presence or absence of humor can provide therapeutic clues and, in certain circumstances, act as a helpful intervention. Be aware that humor is regional, familial, and cultural. What may be humorous to one may not be to another.

Some uses of noticing the presence of humor and laughter in clients:

Humor—the ability to laugh at life—is right at the top, with love and communication, in the hierarchy of our needs.
—Sara Davidson

- *As an indicator of mental status:* Clients with mood disturbances have often lost their ability to have any varied affect. In other clients, the presence of laughter is incongruent with what they are saying and is socially inappropriate. For instance, a client may be laughing when describing someone being injured. In these cases, the presence of laughter may be an indication of a serious antisocial personality trait or a psychotic disorder.
- *As a defense mechanism:* Sometimes humor can be used to defuse uncomfortable feelings and to decrease anxiety. In these situations, laughter can be an indicator that a practitioner can use to further explore the topic.
- *As an avoidance mechanism when dealing with conflicting emotions:* Sometimes humor is used by a client to avoid facing uncomfortable realities. Humor can be an effective way of distracting others from your true feelings. If done often enough, people can spend years avoiding issues. Everyone is familiar with the "class clown" who uses humor to mask unresolved hurt. A skilled practitioner who sees this humor as an indicator can investigate a topic further once the mask of humor has been peeled away.

Both Carl Rogers (1961) and Abraham Maslow (1961) recognized the importance of humor as an indicator of a fully functioning person. Humor is often used by people who are coping well.

Laughter is a
tranquilizer with
no side effects.
—Arnold Glasow

They are able to recognize the seriousness of their situation, yet lessen the anxiety associated with it by using humor and laughter.

Recent research from Missouri Western State University (Miller, 2008) showed a clear relationship between humor and mental health. The results indicated that study participants who had an elevated sense of humor had less difficulty coping with daily life and had better mental health. In the counseling relationship, humor can be a tool to build relationships, facilitate communication, and strengthen the therapeutic alliance (Sultanoff, 1992).

The Physical and Psychological Benefits of Laughter

If you can laugh
at it, you can
survive it.
—Bill Cosby

There are many positive physical and psychological effects of laughter. In fact, laughter can instantly achieve (or reflect) many of the effects we are trying to attain in therapy: physical and emotional release, relaxation, a change in perception, and a way to socially connect with others. Laughter can also strengthen the immune system, decrease stress, and enhance mood!

Humor has many benefits that promote well-being in clients. However, good timing and integration of humor is very complicated. If used effectively, humor can put the client at ease, open the door to deeper work, and demonstrate the practitioner's humanness. If misused or misinterpreted, it can cause significant disruption to the therapeutic alliance.

The purpose of this discussion of humor is not to demonstrate how to insert laughter in therapy sessions, but to bring to the awareness of practitioners the possibility of including humor in their work with clients. Practitioners who don't use humor run the risk of depriving their clients of a valuable tool that they can use in their ongoing struggle for change and emotional balance. You need to find your own comfort level and ways to integrate humor into your work with clients.

Summing Up

In this chapter we examined some common trouble spots in psychotherapy. We looked at self-esteem both conceptually and behaviorally and suggested ways to help clients improve their self-esteem. We discussed the importance of identifying a client's core beliefs. Undoubtedly, you will have plenty of opportunity in your career to work with client resistance and avoidance behaviors using motivational interviewing and other techniques presented. Tackling tough issues of forgiveness and acceptance of troubling life experiences involves having a clear sense of your own perspective on these issues. Last, we discussed the important role of humor and laughter in psychotherapy.

EXERCISES

1. Define what low self-esteem means to you. How can you recognize it? How do you think it develops? How can low self-esteem be expressed behaviorally? What steps might you take to help a client improve self-esteem? Why?

2. Set up a behavioral approach to work with this client with poor self-esteem:

Sally is a young adult who states that she does not have any self-esteem. She thinks it comes from not getting any positive feedback as a child. She states that she has thoughts that she is not good enough for her boyfriend. She finds that she often ends up doing things for others that she does not want to do, and then feels bad about herself later.

3. You receive a court-ordered referral for a client who has anger problems. It is obvious that she does not want to be in session and is transferring her anger at the system to you. What can you do?

4. What negative core beliefs have you encountered in clients? How do you identify and work with core beliefs?

5. Give an example of each of the following techniques for responding to client resistance. How do you tend to respond to resistance in clients?
   - Joining the resistance
   - Restraining
   - Reframing

(Continued)

6. How do you work with acceptance and forgiveness in your personal life? Discuss a difficult client situation in which acceptance or forgiveness was a focus of therapy.
7. How do you use humor in therapy? Why?

13

Working with Challenging Cases: Chemical Dependency and Personality Disorders

What You Will Learn
- How to determine your role in treating clients with chemical dependency problems
- How to use the Alcohol Use Disorders Identification Test (AUDIT)
- How to recognize clients with personality disorders
- How to identify specific behavioral targets that cause distress to clients with personality disorders
- An introduction to dialectical behavior therapy (DBT)
- How to do a behavior chain analysis of target behaviors
- How to teach mindfulness skills to clients
- How to use DBT with clients with a history of trauma

In this chapter we discuss two of the most challenging clinical presentations. In the course of a psychotherapy practice, you will see clients who are using a variety of substances. For instance, you may see a couple for marital therapy and discover that one of the partners has a drug or alcohol problem (which may be the source of their difficulties). Another client may be referred for anger management treatment, and you learn that he is drinking heavily and regularly. Other clients may be using a depressant such as alcohol to control their anxiety. The focus of our review of chemical dependency problems is to clarify your role and provide tools to identify substance use problems and develop an approach to working with these clients.

Some of the most challenging clients you will work with are those with personality disorders. These disorders are often poorly understood, difficult to recognize, and difficult to treat. It is common for psychotherapists to ignore mounting evidence that a client has a personality disorder and continue to ineffectively treat other problems. The purpose of our discussion of personality disorders is to give the practitioner confidence and a better understanding of how to work with this challenging group of clients. Even if you choose not to work with this diagnosis as a specialty, you are likely to have clients with a personality disorder whether you recognize it or not, so it is helpful to have a plan for when that occurs.

Treating Clients with Active Chemical Dependency Problems

What is your role in these cases? Research indicates that mental health problems are the first associated feature of someone with a chemical dependency problem. It is very difficult to treat the mental health symptoms while the use of substances is ongoing. As a psychotherapist, you are treating the mental health symptoms: anxiety, anger, depression, and so on. The use of substances may exacerbate these symptoms. The dynamics are complex, as the client may not be aware of the connection between the symptoms and the substance use. Other clients are aware of the connection and use substances to control their symptoms. Often, the substance use is causing increasing negative consequences in their relationships and/or with the legal system.

Certain mental health practitioners have expertise in working with chemical dependency problems, but many others do not. If your services are being paid for by an insurance company, the client usually has two different benefits, one for mental health issues and one for chemical dependency problems. Although you cannot ignore the influence of the client's use of mood-altering substances, it is not always advisable to specifically treat the substance abuse issue, especially if this is not your area of expertise. If you have a contract with an insurer to provide mental health services, they may not reimburse you for chemical dependency treatment. In these cases, helping to identify the possibility of a chemical dependency problem and making a referral for a formal chemical dependency evaluation is the best course of action. Coordinating your approach with the chemical dependency practitioner can help to assure a better therapy outcome. Being aware of what the other practitioner is doing can help you avoid efforts that may be counterproductive to the overall therapy process.

One of the most common pitfalls of mental health practitioners treating clients who have both mental health and chemical dependency problems is a failure to recognize the influence of the substance use on the mental health symptoms. For example, a young adult is being treated for mild depression, with symptoms of poor motivation and lethargy. He also reveals chronic daily use of marijuana. Using cognitive-behavioral techniques will likely have limited effect if the symptoms are continually being fueled by the substance use. We have seen cases in which practitioners continue to ask for more psychotherapy sessions because of poor client progress, yet fail to recognize the influence of the substance or to address this issue with the client.

Why should the use of alcohol by clients be of interest to the mental health practitioner? According to *Understanding the Effects of Alcohol*, a patient education publication by Group Health Cooperative (2007, adapted with permission):

- Alcohol abuse can cause or make conditions such as depression, anxiety, sexual problems, and a variety of physical problems worse.
- Drinking alcohol can have harmful interactions when taken with prescription medications such as pain medication, anti-anxiety medication, antidepressants, and some antihypertensives, as well over-the-counter medications.

- Alcohol use can cause someone to make unsafe decisions about driving a car or boat or operating machinery, increasing the risk of injury to self and others.
- Excessive alcohol use can hurt family and friends, affect relationships with coworkers, and affect the ability to perform and keep a job.
- Drinking while pregnant can lead to serious problems for the baby, including miscarriage and birth defects such as fetal alcohol syndrome.
- Excessive alcohol use can contribute to making unsafe decisions about sex, increasing the risk of getting a sexually transmitted disease or having an unplanned pregnancy.

You should also be aware of typical gender differences in the use of alcohol as shown in Table 13.1.

Table 13.1 Gender Differences Regarding Alcohol Use

	Women	Men
Moderate consumption of red wine for health benefits	1 glass	2 glasses
Influence of alcohol problems on everyday quality of life	Internalize problems	Externalize problems
Emotional and behavioral effects	Depression and guilt about use	Fighting, increased drinking, and tolerance
Course	Develop problem later than men, but once there is a problem, it heightens at a faster rate	Slow progression

Based on information from "In Living Well: Gender Differences about Alcohol Are Sobering," by B. Condor, April 30, 2007, *Seattle Post-Intelligencer*. Retrieved July 15, 2007, from http://seattlepi.nwsource.com/health/313508_condor30.html.

The use of substances is a powerful emotional manager (T. C. Portman, personal communication, November 29, 2007). You can use your knowledge of the change process to help clients make the connection between their current mood state and their substance use. (See Chapter 8 for more about the change process.) Your goal should be to help clients recognize the need to take a closer look at this connection as part of the overall treatment for their presenting problems. Then you can make a referral to a chemical dependency professional for an evaluation. It is easier to do this if you see yourself as part of an integrated health care system rather than a sole practitioner having to do it all. The mental health practitioner can then work as part of the multidisciplinary team.

Using the Alcohol Use Disorders Identification Test

One quick and easy way to determine if a client has a significant alcohol problem is the Alcohol Use Disorders Identification Test (see Table 13.2; World Health Organization, 2001). This is a public domain instrument developed by the World Health Organization to help people learn about their drinking habits and determine whether they have a problem. This instrument has been tested in a wide variety of settings with people from all over the world. It was developed for use in a primary care medical practice but can easily be adapted for use by mental health practitioners in an outpatient private practice setting. An article in the *Brown University Digest of Addiction Theory and Application* ("More Studies Validate AUDIT," 2007) reviews some of the latest literature on and confirms the validity of the AUDIT as a screening tool for alcohol use disorders in a variety of settings and with diverse populations. Another tool, the CAGE, has been used quite extensively to identify those with a serious alcohol problem. The CAGE is an acronym based on four questions about:

Cutting down drinking
Annoyed by people asking about your drinking
Guilt about drinking
Eye-opener drink needed in the morning

Table 13.2 The Alcohol Use Disorders Identification Test

The Alcohol Use Disorders Identification Test: Interview Version

Read questions as written. Record answers carefully. Begin the AUDIT by saying "Now I am going to ask you some questions about your use of alcoholic beverages during this past year." Explain what is meant by "alcoholic beverages" by using local examples of beer, wine, vodka, etc. Code answers in terms of "standard drinks". Place the correct answer number in the box at the right.

1. How often do you have a drink containing alcohol?

   (0) Never [Skip to Qs 9-10]
   (1) Monthly or less
   (2) 2 to 4 times a month
   (3) 2 to 3 times a week
   (4) 4 or more times a week

6. How often during the last year have you needed a first drink in the morning to get yourself going after a heavy drinking session?

   (0) Never
   (1) Less than monthly
   (2) Monthly
   (3) Weekly
   (4) Daily or almost daily

2. How many drinks containing alcohol do you have on a typical day when you are drinking?

   (0) 1 or 2
   (1) 3 or 4
   (2) 5 or 6
   (3) 7, 8, or 9
   (4) 10 or more

7. How often during the last year have you had a feeling of guilt or remorse after drinking?

   (0) Never
   (1) Less than monthly
   (2) Monthly
   (3) Weekly
   (4) Daily or almost daily

3. How often do you have six or more drinks on one occasion?

   (0) Never
   (1) Less than monthly
   (2) Monthly
   (3) Weekly
   (4) Daily or almost daily

   Skip to Questions 9 and 10 if Total Score for Questions 2 and 3 = 0

8. How often during the last year have you been unable to remember what happened the night before because you had been drinking?

   (0) Never
   (1) Less than monthly
   (2) Monthly
   (3) Weekly
   (4) Daily or almost daily

4. How often during the last year have you found that you were not able to stop drinking once you had started?

   (0) Never
   (1) Less than monthly
   (2) Monthly
   (3) Weekly
   (4) Daily or almost daily

9. Have you or someone else been injured as a result of your drinking?

   (0) No
   (2) Yes, but not in the last year
   (4) Yes, during the last year

5. How often during the last year have you failed to do what was normally expected from you because of drinking?

   (0) Never
   (1) Less than monthly
   (2) Monthly
   (3) Weekly
   (4) Daily or almost daily

10. Has a relative or friend or a doctor or another health worker been concerned about your drinking or suggested you cut down?

   (0) No
   (2) Yes, but not in the last year
   (4) Yes, during the last year

Record total of specific items here

Scoring:

0–7: Low risk for problems caused by drinking alcohol.

8–15: Could be at risk for problems caused by drinking alcohol. Making changes in drinking habits can lower risk.

Above 16: Scores above 16 could mean drinking alcohol is causing life problems.

Source: The Alcohol Use Disorders Identification Test: Guidelines for Use in Primary Care, second edition (p. 17), by T. F. Babor, J. C. Higgins-Biddle, J. B. Saunders, and M. G. Montiero, 2001, Geneva, Switzerland: World Health Organization, Department of Mental Health and Substance Dependence. Retrieved February 26, 2008, from http://whqlibdoc.who.int/hq/2001/WHO_MSD_MSB_01.6a.pdf. Reprinted with permission of the World Health Organization.

Because alcohol comes in a variety of forms—beer, wine, and hard liquor—it is helpful to use a common language to determine exactly what is meant by one drink and its various equivalents:

Beer or Wine Cooler	80-Proof Distilled Spirits	Wine	Liqueur, Sherry, or Aperitif
12 oz	1.5 oz	5 oz	4 oz

The CAGE is very good at identifying those with an already existing alcohol dependence problem, but it often overlooks those who may have an alcohol abuse problem or who may be at risk for more serious problems.

The AUDIT is able to identify those who are at an earlier stage of alcohol use and are at high risk of developing a dependence problem. Psychotherapists can use it in their practice as a screening tool and a conversation starter with their clients. By identifying risky alcohol behavior, you may be able to help clients make the connection between their alcohol use and mental health symptoms and perhaps prevent a more serious problem.

Axis II: Personality Disorders

Every therapist should become familiar with the various personality disorder descriptions and criteria in the latest version of the *DSM*. These disorders are indicated by long-standing behavior patterns that lead to ineffective and unsatisfying relationships with others. It is likely that they are caused by a combination of biological and early life environmental factors. Contrary to popular opinion, effective treatments are available, particularly for Borderline Personality Disorder.

Many clients with personality disorders also have significant Axis I disorders. Therapists must do a thorough evaluation and identify these disorders, which should be treated either before or during treatment for personality disorders. Mood disorders, Attention-Deficit/Hyperactivity Disorder, and anxiety disorders are common. Appropriate medication and behavior treatments for Axis I disorders should be offered and supported. In addition, some medical conditions may cause or increase common personality disorder symptoms; for example, clients with chronic pain or various endocrine diseases may be incorrectly diagnosed with a personality disorder. (See Chapter 15 for more on medical conditions that have mental health symptoms.)

As with other diagnostic categories, you should begin with a detailed evaluation, assessment, and treatment plan. It is quite useful to elicit the client's goals and expectations of therapy. Discuss your diagnosis and the specific criteria you believe your client meets. If you are hopeful that treatment can be successful and nonpejorative in your description of the diagnosis, your client is unlikely to be offended by it. It is interesting to note how many therapists refuse to diagnose personality disorders because they feel it is a derogatory category. Many clients are relieved and reassured when they finally have a name for what has caused them pain for most of their life. An accurate diagnosis can give meaning to their struggle and provide a rationale for the difficulty they have had managing their emotions and behaviors.

Traditional psychoanalytic psychotherapy generally prescribed a long and intense course of treatment with a goal of complete personality restructuring. Although this can be helpful in some cases, it is quite costly both monetarily and in continued suffering by the client. This type of treatment is generally not covered by medical insurance, so it is out of reach to any but the wealthiest clients.

A more practical, and arguably more compassionate, approach to treating individuals with personality disorders involves identifying specific behaviors that cause the client or others pain. This is best done as a collaborative process. Let's look at an example.

This approach focuses on the most critical behaviors first and works by replacing ineffective behaviors with more effective ones. It also avoids the common mistake of diving right into abuse history material without first establishing the ability to stay safe and grounded.

 Rhonda began therapy with Sue following a suicide attempt that resulted in hospitalization. "I've taken over-doses before, but this time I guess I almost died. I'm scared to die, but scared to keep living, too," Rhonda said. "I suppose we should really talk about my childhood abuse. If only I could get over that once and for all I'm sure I'd be all right. But every time I try to talk about it I get suicidal again."

After a complete evaluation, Sue told Rhonda that she believed she had both Recurrent Major Depressive Disorder and Borderline Personality Disorder. She reviewed the criteria for each in light of Rhonda's presenting symptoms and history. Rhonda was beginning to come out of her deep depression due to medications initiated in the hospital, but she still suffered intensely. Rhonda and Sue collaborated on a list of behaviors that caused Rhonda pain:

- Overdosing on over-the-counter and prescription medications (about twice per month)
- Labile emotions
- Poor sleep
- Passivity with others, with occasional blow-ups that damaged or ended relationships
- Inability to concentrate at work
- Frequently losing track of time, especially when stressed

Sue described the basics of dialectical behavior therapy (DBT) and suggested they work on building specific skills to target specific ineffective behaviors. Because overdosing was the most life-threatening target behavior, they agreed to work first on developing distress tolerance skills. They agreed that Rhonda would keep a daily diary of both her target and skillful behaviors. They also agreed that they would table any discussion of her abusive childhood until after Rhonda had some practice in using skills to stay safe.

TIP

Teach and practice coping and emotional regulation skills before working to resolve traumatic material. If clients are not prepared and skilled in this area, they can easily be overwhelmed, which can initiate a crisis.

A similar approach can be used with other personality disorders. For example, a client with Avoidant Personality Disorder could learn interpersonal skills to solve a current problem at work. A client with Dependent Personality Disorder could learn interpersonal skills, as well as mindfulness skills to target becoming aware of his or her own likes and dislikes.

In summary, when working with clients with personality disorders:

- Do a thorough evaluation.
- Treat Axis I disorders and medical problems.
- Identify and validate client goals.
- Identify specific behaviors that cause suffering.
- Offer specific skillful behaviors to replace the ineffective ones.
- Avoid processing painful history until the client can tolerate the distress engendered.

Introduction to Dialectical Behavior Therapy

Dialectical behavior therapy is a specific, evidence-based treatment for Borderline Personality Disorder. Developed by Marsha M. Linehan, PhD, of the University of Washington, DBT is based on a unique combination of radical behavioral psychology and the mindfulness tradition of Zen Buddhism. Dialectical behavior therapy uses the methods of behavioral therapy and mindfulness to encourage "dialectical behaviors"—those behaviors of thought, emotion, and action that balance seemingly opposite choices and transform them into new, more helpful behaviors.

Dialectical behavior therapy is most effective when used in several formats simultaneously. New skills are learned and practiced in skills training classes. Individual therapy focuses on applying those skills to specific problems the client experiences. Case management and pharmacotherapy may also be utilized using the DBT model. In addition, DBT mandates regular consultation groups consisting of all providers working with clients using DBT concepts. Consultation groups are used to encourage continued education in the approach, as well as to problem-solve its application with specific clients. The DBT consultation group also "balances the therapist in his or her interactions with the patient" (Linehan, 1993a, p. 424).

Behavior Chain Analysis

Behavior chain analysis is a technique used in DBT to assist client and therapist in understanding how harmful behaviors occur. The therapist actively assists the client in listing the specific events, thoughts, emotions, and actions that lead to the behavior. These events are written down to show the clear chain of events that leads to a target behavior. The chain is then analyzed by the therapist and the client to determine places where, in future similar situations, more skillful behaviors may be substituted. A plan of action is developed to practice these skillful behaviors in real-life situations.

Consider the behavior chain analysis in Rhonda's therapy.

At Rhonda's next session with Sue, Rhonda began by saying, "Well, I did it again. Even though I was feeling better after our last session, 2 days later I overdosed. I did not take as much as the last time, but I woke up the next morning feeling groggy. I think I did want to die. I felt so bad about it that I was afraid to come back to therapy today. But here I am."

After sharing that she was glad that Rhonda had decided to come to the session, Sue suggested that they try to do a behavior chain analysis of this most recent overdose, as decreasing this behavior was a high-priority target. Rhonda agreed, and Sue got out a worksheet. Sue helped Rhonda write down exactly what happened:

- *Precipitating event:* I was relaxing after dinner with a few glasses of wine. I had had a pretty awful day at work, and I had forgotten to take my meds that morning. Then my so-called best friend called. She said some terrible things to me.

- *What I did:* I took 12 over-the-counter antihistamines, along with the 6 sleeping pills I had left; took them at about 11:30 PM, in my bedroom, and immediately went to bed.

- *The consequences:* I did not die. Felt both exhausted and wired the next morning. I called in sick to work, stayed home, and cried all day.

  The chain (**E** = Event; **T** = Thought; **F** = Feeling; **A** = Action):

  E: The phone rang.

  A: I answered the phone.

  E: Sally started telling me what a terrible friend I am because I forgot to meet her for lunch that day.

  T: I am a terrible friend.

  F: Guilty.

  A: I apologized.

  E: Sally continued to berate me, and then suddenly hung up.

  A: I tried to call her back—no answer.

  T: Well, I have lost another friend.

  T: I am a failure.

  F: Self-hatred.

  T: I should have died last time, because then I would not have to be dealing with these situations.

  F: Angry.

  T: I will show her!

  F: Angry.

  A: Drank two more glasses of wine.

  A: Went to the kitchen to get all the meds I could find.

  T: I might as well get it over with.

  T: If I do not do it this time, I am just a coward.

  F: Resigned to the idea that I will kill myself.

  A: Took a handful of meds with another glass of wine.

  A: Went to my bedroom and laid down.

  T: I hope it works this time.

  F: Sad and defeated.

  T: I will just go to sleep and see what happens.

A: I went to sleep.

A: I woke up at 3 AM.

T: Damn it.

F: Angry.

A: Got out of bed and went to the living room to watch TV. Slept on and off on the couch until 8 AM.

T: I cannot go to work like this.

F: Guilty.

A: Called in sick. Cried on the couch.

T: I cannot tell Sue about this. She will think I am a bad client.

Rhonda and Sue then looked at the behavior chain to see if any different behaviors could lead to a different outcome. They identified four main points of action:

1. When I drink wine after dinner, I tend to get emotional, sad, and impulsive.

   Plan: Go for a walk after dinner instead. Do crossword puzzles if I get bored. Rent movies to watch. Get some of my favorite fruit juice to drink instead.

2. When someone attacks me, I tend to blame myself and then feel self-hatred.

   Plan: Use caller ID and do not answer the phone if I think the person calling is going to be blaming. If I do talk to the person, listen carefully, say I am sorry once (if I did something that violates my own values), and then get off the phone if the person continues to attack. Write down three positive affirmations and say them immediately (keep the list by the phone and in my purse).

3. When I start to think about overdosing, I think I have to do it or else I am a coward.

   Plan: Write a list of "10 Things to Do Instead of Overdosing." Keep the list in the kitchen and bedroom. As soon as I notice a thought about overdosing, I will go to the list and do three of the things on the list. If I am still thinking about

overdosing, I will do three more. If I am still thinking about it, I will call the crisis line to talk about
safety options.

4. When I have overdosed, I want to keep it a secret.

   Plan: If I am thinking about overdosing, I will call Sue.
   I will leave a voice mail saying, "I am thinking
   about overdosing. I will be doing the things on my
   list to keep myself safe. We will need to talk about
   this at our next session. I will call the crisis line if
   I think I cannot keep myself safe." I will also write
   in my journal about my thoughts and feelings and
   bring it to my next session with Sue.

Rhonda and Sue agreed to review the plan at every session for a while to see how it is working. Sue agreed to
teach Rhonda some behavioral skills that will fit into the
plan and Rhonda agreed to practice them, especially
when she is not thinking about overdosing. Sue made a
copy of the behavior chain analysis and gave Rhonda the
original to take home.

Mindfulness

Mindfulness practice is central to DBT treatment. Mindfulness
can be described as focused awareness in the present moment
without judgment. Linehan (1993b) teaches mindfulness by
breaking it down into specific steps, which can be practiced sepa-
rately and together, and without any religious or spiritual focus:

Wise Mind (A Dialectical Balance between "Emotional Mind" and "Rational Mind")

The "What" Skills
- Observe (just notice)
- Describe (put words on experiences)
- Participate (be in the moment you are in)

The "How" Skills
- Nonjudgmentally (with interest and curiosity, but without
  judging as "good" or "bad")

- One-mindfully (directing your attention to one thing at a time)
- Effectively (doing the most helpful thing to do in the moment)

Teaching mindfulness skills to clients with a history of mood instability, trauma, or even episodes of dissociation can be a gentle way to move focus away from intolerable feelings and thoughts and toward an accepting experience of the present moment.

Dialectical Behavior Therapy and Trauma

The DBT skills can be helpful for any client with a history of trauma. Clients with a long history of trauma often feel as though they have a huge suitcase full of traumatic memories. This suitcase weighs them down and may get heavier every year. Traumatized clients often want to open up this suitcase in therapy, spilling out its contents in an effort to somehow resolve all past hurts. If a client does not have skills for coping with the contents in a healthy way, though, this is often followed by self-harming behaviors and abrupt termination of therapy.

An alternative to this pattern is to gently and respectfully put the suitcase in a safe place for a while and focus therapy on building skills. Learning the DBT skills of mindfulness, interpersonal effectiveness, emotion regulation, and distress tolerance can help the client begin to live skillfully in the present moment. As clients learn to cope more effectively with the small traumas of everyday life, many find that their trauma suitcase has begun to feel lighter. Some clients will later be motivated to open up their trauma histories for further examination (using skills to remain safe); others may find that this desire to understand the past fades. Clients may prefer to leave the past in the past and to put their energy into living skillfully in the present. (See Chapter 12 for more about working with forgiveness and acceptance.)

Summing Up

In this chapter we examined some of the challenges of working with clients with chemical dependency and personality disorders. Refer to this chapter for tips when you have clients whose symptoms don't seem to improve with standard therapy techniques.

In these cases, you may find a concurrent problem with substance use or a long-standing personality disorder that is masked by their more obvious mental health diagnoses.

EXERCISES

1. What do you think your role as a mental health therapist should be regarding substance abuse in the following situations?
   - A depressed young man reveals that he smokes cannabis daily.
   - A young mother confides that she's been using methamphetamines occasionally to help her get everything done.
   - An elderly man tells you that he's been falling recently in the evenings. He says he has "one or two" drinks a day.
   - A college student says she gets Adderall from the school heath center to help her stay up all night studying.
   - A 35-year-old man with generalized anxiety and panic attacks tells you he's been getting Valium (which he takes 5 or 6 times per day) off the Internet because his doctor won't prescribe them for him anymore.
2. Do you use the AUDIT or another tool to detect alcohol abuse as part of your initial evaluation? Why or why not?
3. Do you feel comfortable treating clients with Borderline Personality Disorder? Why or why not?
4. How would you identify a client with Dependent Personality Disorder?
5. What approach do you think works best with clients with personality disorders?
6. Practice doing a behavior chain analysis with a colleague, using the following scenarios:
   - A 14-year-old girl comes in with bandages on her forearms.
   - A college student reports an alcohol binge.

(Continued)

- A woman struggling with anorexia tells you she hasn't eaten anything for 2 days.
- A 10-year-old boy gets into a fight at school.
- An elderly woman has been arrested for stalking her neighbor.

7. What different skills or behaviors would you want to teach each of these clients?

8. Do you practice any sort of mindfulness or meditation? What is the difference between mindfulness and meditation? Have you taught any mindfulness skills to clients? How do you approach mindfulness with clients?

9. How do you approach clients with severe, extensive trauma histories? What are your first steps in working with a client like this?

14

Managing Adverse Events

What You Will Learn
- How to respond effectively to a client crisis
- When to recommend that your client be hospitalized
- The risk factors for suicide
- What questions to ask a client who expresses suicidal thoughts
- How to create a safety plan with suicidal clients
- How to explore the meaning and function of suicidal ideation
- The importance of postsuicide review

As therapists, we all like to think that we can avert every crisis and help each client to achieve a good quality of life. However, in real practice, adverse events are common enough that we must be prepared for them. In this chapter we discuss the basics of crisis intervention, client hospitalization, and suicide prevention and response.

Crisis Intervention

Crisis intervention skills are an important part of a therapist's toolbox. Some of your clients may come to you without the pressure of a current crisis, but many others will be motivated to begin therapy only while in the midst of a crisis. This can make the evaluation and treatment planning phase of therapy more challenging, as you must address the crisis sufficiently to move into the treatment phase.

A crisis may also arise during an ongoing episode of psychotherapy. A client crisis is marked by a sense of urgency, at least for the client. Rapid speech, high anxiety, and poor judgment often occur during a crisis. Encourage slowing down the process to understand whether any action needs to be taken immediately. One way to do this is to slow the pace of your voice, while acknowledging the seriousness of the crisis. The client will often unconsciously match your voice pace, which creates a physiologically calming effect.

Your tasks in crisis intervention include:

- Calming the client with voice pacing and validation.
- Understanding the crisis by asking questions. (Who, what, where, when, and why are good places to start.)
- Determining if action needs to be taken, and by whom.
- Developing a plan of action.

Let's look at an example of crisis intervention.

Jerry has been in therapy with Susan for several months, working on his severe anxiety, which has been interfering with his relationships and his job. On this day, he comes into the session out of breath and clearly fearful. In a rush of words, he tells Susan, "I think I've lost my job! I sent my boss an e-mail about my concerns with the project, and he e-mailed back and said we needed to talk right away! He said that if I could not get the project done on schedule, he might need to replace me! This was my chance to get back on his good side, and I've blown it again. I don't know what I'm going to do! I told him I had a headache and needed to go home, and said we could meet tomorrow morning. I just don't know what I'm going to do if I lose this job!"

Using a calm, slightly slower voice, Susan says, "Let's see if we can figure this out together. You sound pretty out of breath right now. Would you be willing to practice some relaxing breathing with me for a few minutes?" She guides him through a skill she has been teaching him, and he visibly relaxes. "I can see your shoulders sinking back down, and your breath has slowed. Let's review what's happening in your job and see what you can do about it."

Susan (still using a slow and steady tone of voice) asks Jerry to remember what concerns he had about the project, how he expressed this in his e-mail, and whether he thinks he can get the project done. Together they make a list of specific problems and possible solutions. Susan asks Jerry if he needs to take any specific actions. They agree that he will:

- Spend the evening writing out a summary of the problems and solutions he sees in the project
- Take a 15-minute relaxation and breath work break during the evening
- Take a short walk in the morning before work
- Go to the boss's office in the morning and ask for a meeting
- Share the summary of problems and solutions for getting the project back on track, acting as confidently and calmly as possible (including slowing his breath and speech)
- Listen to his boss's feedback about his plan
- Use breath and relaxation skills after the meeting to clear his mind

When Jerry returns the next week, he reports that the plan was successful; he and his boss have developed a common understanding of the challenges of the project and have agreed on a set of solutions that will enable him to complete the project on time. He became more aware of his own ability to calm himself with the relaxation tools Susan has taught him. Susan and Jerry are then able to return to the work they've been doing to understand the cognitive distortions that tend to contribute to his anxiety around relationships.

In this example, the therapist used voice pacing to help calm the client, asked probing questions to clarify the problem, and helped the client develop a successful plan of action. By working through the crisis, the therapist was able to reinforce some of the relaxation training they had been working on and help the client shift negative cognitions effectively. A crisis can become an opportunity for the client to practice new skills and behaviors in a real-world situation.

Hospitalization

Hospitalization is necessary when clients are a danger to themselves or others, or are so gravely disabled that they cannot otherwise be safe. Familiarize yourself with local and regional mental health hospitalization options. Know what kind of services they provide, what level of security they have, and the patient ages they accept. Establish a good working relationship with hospital social workers, who can help bridge services when you have a patient hospitalized. Always be truthful when interacting with hospital staff. Their ability to trust you can pay big dividends later. If a client has the potential for violence, let them know. Issues such as these can determine the appropriate hospital milieu. Another placement may be more appropriate.

TIP

"Gravely disabled" is a term that refers to the state a person may be in when, due to a mental illness, he cannot take care of his basic needs, such as providing for his own safety, proper nutrition, health, and shelter.

Each state has its own laws and procedures regarding involuntary hospitalization. Learn what they are in your state and how they are implemented locally. Involuntary hospitalization temporarily takes away a client's civil rights, so it should be treated as a serious step. Convincing a client to accept voluntary hospitalization can be a delicate matter.

The decision to recommend hospitalization is based on several factors:

- Your evaluation of the client's clear and present risk of suicide or serious assault of others (using both established risk factors and your own intuition). (See Chapter 3 for more on legal issues regarding risk to others.)

- Your evaluation of the client's psychosis (i.e., hearing voices telling him to harm himself or others).
- Your evaluation of the client's natural supports (family and friends who can help the client stay safe during outpatient treatment).
- Your evaluation of the risks versus benefits of hospitalization.
- Your evaluation of whether medication initiation or changes can only be made safely in the hospital.

Your recommendation is not likely to be the only determining factor. Be aware of your responsibilities and limitations when hospitalization is considered. You have a responsibility to recognize the risk; to make a recommendation to the client, family, and hospital staff; and to notify and cooperate with involuntary hospitalization laws and local procedures. Other factors may be out of your control, such as hospital bed availability, your client's preferences, insurance coverage, financial and employment costs, and legal issues. Always document thoroughly every communication you have with your client and others about a potential hospitalization.

After your client has been hospitalized, be sure to keep in touch with the hospital social worker about your client's progress. Be sure to see your client soon after discharge, preferably within a week, to reengage him or her in outpatient treatment. Make sure your client has a clear relapse prevention plan and knows what resources can be of use if a crisis recurs. (See Chapter 11 for "The 10 Lessons of Relapse.")

Suicidal Ideation and Intent

Suicide is the 11th leading cause of death in the United States. For men it is the eighth leading cause; for women it is the 16th. For children (ages 10 to 14), adolescents (ages 15 to 19), and young adults (ages 20 to 24), suicide is the third leading cause of death. There are gender differences as well, with almost 4 times as many adolescent males as females committing suicide. More than 6 times the number of young adult males commit suicide in comparison to females (Centers for Disease Control and Prevention, n.d., based on 2004 data).

The National Institute of Mental Health (n.d.) lists the following suicide risk factors:

- Depression and other mental disorders, or a substance abuse disorder (often in combination with other mental disorders). More than 90% of people who die by suicide have this risk factor.
- Stressful life events, in combination with other risk factors, such as depression. However, suicide and suicidal behavior are not normal responses to stress; many people have these risk factors but are not suicidal.
- A prior suicide attempt.
- A family history of mental disorder or substance abuse.
- A family history of suicide.
- Family violence, including physical or sexual abuse.
- Firearms in the home, the method used in more than half of suicides.
- Incarceration.
- Exposure to the suicidal behavior of others, such as family members, peers, or media figures.

Suicidal thoughts can be frightening to client and psychotherapist alike. The fear that a client might actually die by suicide can lead new therapists into paralysis or overreaction. While the rate of completed suicide is 10.9 for every 100,000 people (Centers for Disease Control and Prevention, n.d., based on 2004 data), suicidal ideation is much more common. It is estimated that for every suicidal death there are eight to 25 attempts (Moscicki, 2001).

As with other symptoms, a focused evaluation of suicidal ideation is imperative. You will not encourage suicide by asking about it. Suicidal ideation varies from "Gee, wouldn't it be nice to be dead" to "I'm saving my pills so that I can overdose after this session." If the client communicates any level of suicidal ideation, ask for specifics in a calm, caring way, such as:

- What exactly do you think when you think of suicide?
- When did this thinking start?
- How are you feeling just before you start thinking of suicide? After thinking about it for a while?

- How often do you think of suicide? Does it vary by time, day, mood, medications, alcohol or drug use, activities, or sleep quantity and quality?
- When you think of suicide, do you have any specific plans for how you might do it? If so, what are they? Any others? Do you have access to what you would need to carry it out?
- Have you ever tried to kill yourself? What happened?
- Do you think you want to be dead, as opposed to not feeling so much pain?
- Who do you think would be sad if you killed yourself?
- What other reactions do you imagine others might have?
- Have you had any friends or relatives who have attempted or completed suicide?
- What happens if you try to ignore the thoughts?
- What has worked in the past to decrease your suicidal thinking?
- Do you intend to kill yourself? When? How?

Once you have a clear picture of the client's suicidality, you can establish safety and treatment plans. A safety plan consists of specific steps to prevent suicidal behaviors. It may involve immediate hospitalization if the risk is high. It may include significant others who will take responsibility for monitoring the client. It should include whom to contact if suicidal ideation or intent becomes worse. It may involve specific things to do to decrease risk (e.g., using emotion regulation skills, engaging in pleasant activities, increasing social contact, taking medications as prescribed, avoiding alcohol and nonprescribed drugs, and removing guns from the home). You may also include an agreement between therapist and client that the client will not act on suicidal urges. Always write out the plan clearly and make sure both you and the client have a copy. Encourage your client to share the plan with family or friends, if appropriate.

Once safety planning is in place you can address treatment of the suicidal ideation as a symptom or behavior. Certainly, if the suicidal ideation is caused by a serious mental illness, such as major depression, Bipolar Disorder, or a psychotic disorder, a psychiatrist should be consulted. (See Chapter 15 for more on medications and working effectively with prescribers.) Medications may need to be initiated or adjusted. A psychiatrist or primary care physician may also be consulted regarding any medical problems that may be a contributing factor. If the onset of suicidal ideation is abrupt, further medical work-up may be needed to rule out sudden medical problems. (See Chapter 15 for more on medical conditions that have mental health symptoms.)

If suicidal ideation is a recent symptom, examine possible triggers. Are there new stressors in a relationship? Has the client been recently diagnosed with a serious illness? Has the client suffered recent losses, such as death of a friend or family member, loss of a job, loss of a relationship? If any of these questions are answered positively, therapists can use education and problem solving to develop a short-term plan that focuses on safety and coping with the immediate situation.

Some clients use suicidal ideation as a lifelong, but ultimately unsuccessful, way to modulate painful emotions, thoughts, or events. They may have seen suicidality modeled by parents or family members in childhood. They may have been given invalidating, "Do not be" messages. They may see suicide as the ultimate escape hatch if life becomes too unbearable. Suicidal ideation may actually improve mood by reassuring the client that suffering will eventually end, if only by death. Suicide risk can increase when a deeply depressed client starts to feel better.

Marsha Linehan's (1993a) dialectical behavior therapy provides a useful structure for working with clients with chronic suicidal ideation. This therapy balances genuine validation of the client's suffering with active strategies to change thoughts, emotions, and actions to decrease suffering. It also offers psychoeducational and skill-building tools to replace unhelpful behaviors with specific skillful behaviors. Linehan's (1993b) dialectical behavior therapy teaches clients how to measure misery and suicidal ideation on a scale of 1 to 5 and keep a daily Diary Card of both target behaviors and skillful behaviors. In this way, clients learn how cause and effect works in their lives to increase or decrease suffering. Become familiar with DBT resources in your community, learn to use it yourself, and get consultation with skilled DBT therapists when needed. Clients are often hungry for this approach and make exciting gains in overall functioning over time. (See Chapter 13 for more on dialectical behavior therapy.)

Postsuicide Review

Those who are counseling others often work with very despondent, depressed, self-destructive individuals. The likelihood that a practitioner will work with a client who successfully completes suicide is very real. When a client commits suicide, it is an extraordinary event, and it is standard practice to do a postsuicide review, particularly if the therapist is working in an agency or group practice. The review involves gathering as much information as possible about:

- The history of the client.
- The events leading up to the event: Were specific triggers or life circumstances contributing factors? What was the involvement of the spouse, parent, or family in the treatment?

The review committee usually consists of as many of the practitioners who were directly involved with the case as possible. Varying viewpoints and experiences with the client are reviewed. Also included on the committee are peers not directly involved with the client who can give an objective viewpoint of the case and ask pertinent questions. All of these people are then assembled to do a debriefing following this format:

- *Case review:* What was the history of the client and who was involved in the treatment? What were the issues the client was struggling with? What kinds of treatments were given? What was the sequence of events that led to the suicide?
- *Chart review:* Was there proper documentation in the chart? (This is usually done beforehand by a peer.)
- *Quality of care review:* Did the practitioners involved follow proper procedures and protocols given the nature of the client? Was something missed? Was the diagnosis correct? Was a suicide risk factor and assessment done? Were proper safety procedures followed, such as removal of all lethal means?
- *Quality of service review:* This usually involves a delivery system analysis. Was there a breakdown or delay in the on-call system, triage, or communication between practitioners or assignment of the case?

- *Needs assessment:* What are the counseling needs of the client's family? Do they need assistance? What about the practitioners involved? Do they need assistance?

This can be a difficult process for all to undergo, but a lot of valuable information can come out of this type of review, such as answers to the following questions:

- Are there any quality of care issues?
- Are there any quality of service issues?
- Are there any system or care improvements that could be implemented in the future?

Those who were treating the client are not involved in deciding the error rating. The committee makes recommendations for improvement that can be implemented in the agency or practice. If there were violations of standard practice by an individual, further review and sanctions may be in order. The notes from this quality committee are usually free from legal discovery so that there can be a free and impartial review that is private, thus enabling any needed changes to be made. The following is an example of an extraordinary event review form.

Extraordinary Event Review Form

Client name:_____ Date of event:_____
Date of the review:_____ Practitioners involved:_____
Review Committee members:_____

Case review:

Chart review:

Quality of care review:

Quality of service review:

Needs assessment:

Recommendations:
Error Rating

❏ No error occurred in the care process. No harm came to the client.
❏ No error occurred in the care process; however, an adverse event did occur.
❏ An event occurred in which there was almost an error (action or medication), but it was identified and corrected before it was completed.
❏ An error occurred, but the client experienced no harm.
❏ An error did occur in the care process, and harm came to the client as a result.

Summing Up

Responding skillfully and effectively to a client crisis is one of the most important functions of a psychotherapist. In the moment of crisis you may not have much time to mull over options, so having some practice in crisis intervention is essential. Seek out opportunities for training and supervision in working with adverse events. Learn to recognize when your client may need to be hospitalized, and know the resources available in your community. Be alert to any signs of suicidal ideation, planning, or intent, and be prepared to take clear steps to ensure your client's safety. Coping with the tragedy of a client's suicide is something we all hope to avoid, but it is a real risk in this profession. Be sure you have consultation and support available to you in case you ever have this unfortunate experience.

EXERCISES

1. How do you respond to crisis in your personal life? Does this differ from how you respond to it with clients?
2. What are the four main tasks in any crisis intervention?
3. Discuss a reasonable approach to the following client scenarios:
   - A client calls your office at 5 PM stating that he just wants to say good-bye, as he plans to shoot himself tonight.
   - A client comes to session distraught over finding out that her son is using heroin again.
   - A client calls you for an emergency appointment because he's been arrested for driving drunk.
4. Have you ever had to suggest hospitalization to a client? What factors go into a decision to hospitalize a client?
5. How do you work with a client who has just been discharged from a psychiatric hospital?
6. Role-play an assessment of a client who presents with suicidal ideation.
7. What would you include in a safety plan for a suicidal client?
8. Have you ever been involved in a postsuicide review? How did it affect you personally?

Resources

Klott, J., & Jongsma, A. E., Jr. (2004). *The suicide and homicide risk assessment and prevention treatment planner*. Hoboken, NJ: Wiley.

15

Understanding Medications and the Role of Medical Conditions

What You Will Learn

- Why it is important to know about medications your clients may take
- The function of the four major neurotransmitters
- The different kinds of antidepressants, mood stabilizers, anti-anxiety medications, psychostimulants, and antipsychotic medications
- How to work effectively with medication prescribers
- How to recognize common medication emergencies
- How to reconcile the role of mind and body in mental disorders and wellness
- How certain medical disorders may cause mental health symptoms

We have focused primarily on the interactional aspects of psychotherapy in this book, but it is also necessary to be aware of the client's total experience. The use of medications may enhance therapy or cause side effects that can interfere with therapy. Physical problems may be a topic of discussion or the source of the client's symptoms. In this chapter we focus on understanding medications and the role of medical conditions on mental health symptoms.

Understanding Medications

Many clients you see will be on medications; others may need them. Part of your initial treatment plan may be talking with your client about the use of medications. Before discussing the various classes of psychiatric medications with clients, it is important that you:

- Know the expected benefits of medications
- Recognize common side effects
- Know the standard dosage ranges
- Are aware of potential interactions between medications
- Know how to consult with prescribers about a client's response to medication
- Know how to coach clients about how to communicate effectively with prescribers
- Recognize medication emergencies

Many mental health disorders can be treated without medication. Often, at the beginning of a treatment episode, you may not have historical information about symptoms or how the client will respond to psychotherapy alone. If you have strong beliefs about either the benefit or harm of medications, be sure to be clear about this with yourself and your client. Your client must ultimately make the choice about whether to consider adding, continuing, or stopping medication during an episode of care.

At the beginning of treatment, always ask about current and prior medications and the client's response to those medications. Be sure to consider drugs being prescribed for medical conditions that may have an effect on mental health symptoms. For example, a client taking prednisone for an asthma flare-up may experience heightened anxiety, sleeplessness, or even hallucinations. In addition, take note of any possible street drugs that may impact mental health symptoms. Caffeine and alcohol can exaggerate or inhibit response to medications. For example, a client with severe daily anxiety may be taking an anti-anxiety medication—along with a pot or two of coffee each day! If you have any initial concerns about the effects of medications, or think that a client may benefit from medication, discuss this during your first few sessions.

At times, a client's symptoms are so severe that he or she cannot fully benefit from talk therapy. The fatigue and lack of concentration during depressive periods may make it difficult for the client to participate in the cognitive demands of therapy. Medication may provide enough symptom relief for the client to become more engaged in the therapy process. For some, adding a medication can make psychotherapy more effective. You may want to encourage your client to talk with his or her doctor about adding or reviewing medications. Asking for a release of information so that you can consult with the prescriber can improve care coordination.

Many psychiatric medications are marketed directly to the public through television and print advertisements. These are often the newest and most expensive medications and may have side effects that are not yet known. Generic medications are often just as effective and less costly. Encourage clients to discuss possible options with their prescriber and to take advertisements with a grain of salt.

Nontraditional treatments such as nutritional supplements, herbal treatments, and alternative medical treatments may also be heavily marketed. Again, if you have strong beliefs about the benefit or harm of these approaches, be honest with yourself and your client about your opinions. Be wary of making suggestions without knowing every drug the client is already taking. For example, suggesting that a client take valerian root to help with sleep may cause a toxic load on the liver for a client who is already taking Depakote. Encourage your client to get information from a variety of sources and to discuss options with his or her prescriber or primary care provider before adding a new herbal treatment or over-the-counter medication, as these may interact with other medications the client is taking.

If you do not know much about psychiatric medications, take a class or workshop and get a resource book with details on the various classes of medications. Much of this information is now available online. You will also be able to learn a great deal from experiences with your clients over time. Take every opportunity to continue to learn more, as medications and the understanding of how they affect human neurobiology are constantly evolving and changing. Each person's unique body chemistry can affect his or her response to a particular medication, so what may work for one person may not for another.

Neurotransmitters

Understanding the common neurotransmitters and their effects in the brain will help you to understand the effects and side effects of various medications. Neurotransmitters are chemicals that are used to relay, amplify, and modulate electrical signals between a neuron and another cell. Neuroscientists continue to discover more about how the brain works, opening new doors for research into better treatments. Let us take a brief look at some major neurotransmitters.

Serotonin is probably the best known of the neurotransmitters. Interestingly, 60% to 90% of the serotonin in the body is synthesized in the gastrointestinal tract (Gaginella & Galligan, 1995). It is also present in a variety of fruits and vegetables such as mushrooms, walnuts and hickory nuts, plantains, pineapple, banana, kiwi, plums, and tomatoes (J. M. Feldman & Lee, 1985). It has been associated with the regulation of anger and aggression, mood changes, sleep, sexuality, and appetite. Its deficiency is believed to be involved in anxiety disorders, eating disorders, Obsessive-Compulsive Disorder, and mood disorders.

Norepinephrine is a hormone released by the adrenal glands that also acts as a neurotransmitter. It is involved in the flight-or-fight response, where it increases heart rate and prepares the muscles for action. Lack of energy and poor concentration can signal a deficiency. For medicinal purposes, it is used to increase alertness and arousal. It can be helpful for treating attentional problems as well as depression.

Dopamine is involved in the pleasure/reward system in the brain, which can motivate a person to repeat behaviors that are pleasurable, such as eating and sex. The use of cocaine or amphetamines can increase dopamine. The intense drive to repeat this experience can lead to addiction. Dopamine also increases arousal, goal-directed behaviors, and latent inhibition (the inability to shut out incoming stimuli). An excess of dopamine is associated with both psychosis and creativity. Dopamine is also involved in movement disorders such as Parkinson's disease, in which there is a deficiency, and Tourette's Syndrome, in which there is an excess.

Gamma-aminobutyric acid (GABA) has an inhibitory effect on the firing rate of a neuron and can have a balancing effect on mood. It often induces sleep and relaxation. Recent research shows an increasing relationship between GABA levels and Panic Disorder (Goddard et al., 2001).

Types of Medications

Most psychiatric medications fall into one of five types.

Antidepressants

Antidepressants fall into several subcategories, depending on the type of neurotransmitter targeted. Typically, these are taken for a period of 6 to 9 months to alleviate symptoms; however, it is not unusual for individuals to take antidepressants for extended periods, especially when there are repeated episodes of illness. Antidepressants are used to treat a current illness as well as prevent the reoccurrence of one. The neurotransmitters that are targeted to treat depression are also involved in other processes, such as sleeping, pain, and eating.

Selective serotonin reuptake inhibiters (SSRIs) predominantly target one neurotransmitter, serotonin, whereas other antidepressants target several. There is some thought that this is why there are fewer side effects in SSRIs compared to other types of antidepressants. The SSRIs act by inhibiting the reuptake of serotonin into

TIP

While on patent, a medication is typically called by its brand name (e.g., Prozac). The production of a medication is limited to the company that developed it, and its cost is controlled by them. A generic medication is one that is produced without patent protection. Brand-name drugs can cost several dollars a pill, while generics are considerably cheaper. This is why insurance companies push so hard for use of generics.

the neuroreceptors, thus keeping it in the synapse longer (although this is just a small part of their action). They are useful in treating both anxiety disorders and depression. The most common medications in this category are fluoxetine (Prozac), paroxetine (Paxil), sertraline (Zoloft), citalopram (Celexa), and escitalopram (Lexapro). Typical side effects are gastrointestinal problems, nervousness, insomnia, headache, and sexual problems.

Tricyclic antidepressants predate the use of the SSRIs and typically target two neurotransmitters, serotonin and norepinephrine. They are called tricyclic because of the three components of their molecular structure. Besides being used as an antidepressant, these medications are sometimes used for pain control. Some of the common generic medications in this category are amitriptyline, imipramine, doxepin, desipramine, and nortriptyline. Typical side effects are dry mouth, blurred vision, constipation, difficulty urinating, worsening of glaucoma, impaired thinking, and fatigue. They can also affect blood pressure and heart rate. Overdoses of these medications are usually more serious than for SSRIs because of their adverse cardiac effects.

Monoamine oxidase inhibitors (MAOIs) target serotonin, norepinephrine, and dopamine, which are collectively known as the monoamines. The drug causes a buildup of these substances, which helps alleviate depression, but as they do, they also increase tyramine, which can cause a dramatic increase in blood pressure that can be fatal. Clients who take MAOIs need to restrict their diet from aged foods that can cause an increase in tyramine. Severe headaches can also occur because of increased blood pressure. Because of the dietary restrictions and the adverse effects from the interaction with other medications, MAOIs are rarely prescribed. They need to be monitored closely, and the client must be very compliant with the dietary restrictions. They can be very effective with some clients for whom nothing else works. Medications in this category are Marplan, Nardil, and Parnate.

Atypical antidepressants include medications such as venlafaxine (Effexor) and Cymbalta. These medications target the reuptake of various combinations of neurotransmitters such as serotonin and norepinephrine or a combination of reuptake inhibitors and a receptor blocker. Examples of these medications are nefazodone (Serzone) and mirtazapine (Remeron). Bupropion (Wellbutrin) targets norepinephrine and dopamine and is also used to ease the symptoms of smoking cessation. One of the atypicals, Trazodone, is often used as a sleep aid for its dramatic sedative effects. The use of these medications is quite common. Each medication can cause a unique set of side effects.

TIP

Medications typically have an active ingredient name, such as fluoxetine, and a brand name, such as Prozac. Practitioners, especially physicians, usually refer to the drug by the active ingredient name. Clients, influenced by advertisements, typically use the brand name.

Mood Stabilizers

Mood stabilizers are a group of medications that can treat both mania and depression, which are common symptoms in fluctuating mood disorders such as Bipolar Disorder. Medications in this category are lithium carbonate, Depakote, lamotrigine (Lamictal), and Tegretol. Some of these medications may cause symptoms of toxicity, such as nausea, vomiting, diarrhea, and ataxia. Blood levels are checked not only to monitor the level of the drug but also to evaluate liver, kidney, and thyroid function, which can impact treatment. Mood stabilizers can be highly effective in treating mania and stabilizing the rapid fluctuation of moods. However, with the exception of lamotrigine, they are not always effective in treating depression. A few psychiatrists and many primary care physicians add an antidepressant to the medication regime for this purpose. Caution is necessary, though, as antidepressants can increase mood cycling in some bipolar patients. The standard of care for psychiatrists is that they often use two mood stabilizers at lower dosages to avoid side effects while also getting the maximum benefits. Atypical antipsychotics are also used as mood stabilizers, and some are FDA-approved for this purpose. Therapists are typically not aware of this level of detail regarding medications, so if you mention your knowledge of this while consulting with psychiatrists, they will be very impressed!

Anti-Anxiety Medications

Anti-anxiety medications, or anxiolitics, are used to treat symptoms of Anxiety and Panic Disorders and also act as a muscle relaxant. There are two subgroups.

Benzodiazepines calm the central nervous system and are effective in the relief of anxiety common to Panic Disorder, Obsessive-Compulsive Disorder, Phobias, and Posttraumatic Stress Disorder as well as Generalized Anxiety Disorder. They are usually used for short-term relief, as they easily become both physically and psychologically habit forming. Side effects are drowsiness and fatigue, so it is recommended that one does not drive or operate machinery while taking these drugs. If used for extended periods, anxiolitics should be tapered gradually. Medications in this category are Ativan, Klonipin, Xanax, and Valium. They are believed to target the neurotransmitter GABA.

Buspar is in a class of its own as a *nonbenzodiazepine* and is less habit forming than the benzodiazepines. It is used to treat chronic and generalized anxiety. It is not useful for Panic Disorder or acute anxiety. It likely works on serotonin receptors, so some psychiatrists add it to an SSRI for its synergistic effects.

Psychostimulants

Psychostimulants activate the central nervous system and can cause an increase in energy and confidence, euphoria, and improved cognitive and psychomotor performance. The common psychostimulants methylphenidate (Ritalin), dextroamphetamine (Dexedrine), and Adderall are used to treat Attention Deficit Disorder. They appear to work by speeding up the transmission of information between the neurons and induce increased alertness and activity. Common side effects are loss of appetite, sleep disturbance, changes in arousal (either overstimulation and anxiety or listlessness and lethargy), and mood changes.

Antipsychotic Medications

Antipsychotic medications are used to treat psychotic disorders such as Schizophrenia and Delusional Disorder. There are two groups of antipsychotic medications. The older, first-generation drugs such as

Mellaril, Thorazine, and Haldol are called neuroleptics because of their severe neurological side effects, including tardive dyskinesia, a repetitive, involuntary movement of the face, lips, legs, and torso.

Some of the common second-generation antipsychotic drugs, called atypicals, are aripiprazole (Abilify), risperidone (Risperdal), quetiapine (Seroquel), and olanzapine (Zyprexa). Atypical agents carry some risk of obesity, diabetes, and increase in lipids as well as a low incidence of movement disorders. The reader is referred to the resource section for FDA patient handouts that list the precautions and common side effects of these medications.

TIP

"Off-label" refers to the use of medications that have not undergone scientific study for a particular condition and thus have not been approved to treat that condition or age group. Practitioners in the field have found that they are effective for a particular condition or diagnosis, so it becomes a standard practice to prescribe for these conditions.

Working Effectively with Prescribers

Clients may be receiving their psychiatric medications from their primary care physician, a psychiatrist, or a psychiatric nurse practitioner. Teaching your clients how to work effectively with prescribers is an important task. Some clients may know quite a bit about medications and their own individual responses to them, but others may not. Help your clients learn how to precisely describe symptoms and measure them over time, if possible. Typically, clients see a prescriber monthly when starting medications, and every 3 to 6 months once they are stable. Sometimes therapists are in a position to observe what the physician cannot because of the frequency of psychotherapy visits. When symptoms have been stable, clients may not see their prescriber very often. If you, as the therapist, are seeing a client regularly and he or she starts to decompensate, you can give valuable and timely feedback to the psychiatrist. It is important to maintain contact with the client's prescriber to collaborate and give feedback regarding relevant issues related to the client you have in common. Help clients develop skills to tell the prescriber which symptoms are most disabling and which side effects may be tolerable or problematic. Consider this example.

 Susan came to see Tom for psychotherapy. She had been feeling depressed for quite a while. She had gone to her primary care provider (PCP) about a year ago. He prescribed Prozac at 20 mg per day. She found that this helped her sleep a bit better, but she felt somewhat groggy during the day, which made her work as a bank teller more difficult. She was not sure how to approach her PCP about this. A friend recommended a few sessions with Tom to help get her on track.

Tom helped Susan make a list of her current symptoms, in order of importance to her:

- Sad mood every day
- Difficulty sleeping (wake up early)
- Fatigue (especially in the morning)
- Feelings of guilt
- Memory problems
- Low appetite

Tom then asked Susan to rate each of these daily for 1 week (e.g., intensity of sadness on a scale of 1 to 10; number of hours sleep; time of awakening; number of meals eaten). When Susan came back the next week, Tom reviewed the data and helped Susan formulate a plan for discussing depression with her PCP using her symptom list and ratings.

The next week, Susan came to her appointment with Tom feeling a bit better. Her PCP had increased her Prozac to 40 mg per day. She felt more hopeful, was sleeping longer, and found she had a better appetite. However, she was noticing an increase in memory problems. She decided to give the change in dosage a few more weeks to determine if the positive and negative effects would continue. During this time, Tom worked with Susan's cognitive style and belief systems, as well as skills for coping with stressful interpersonal events.

After several more weeks, Susan found that her memory problems were worse, though her depressed mood was lifting. She and Tom again worked out a strategy for talking with her PCP; she clarified that her main question was whether a different medication might continue to improve her mood without the side effect of memory problems. Armed with her symptom ratings record, Susan talked with her PCP. Together they decided that a trial of a different class of medication would be appropriate. Susan found that not only did her mood continue to improve but her memory improved significantly. Her sleep and appetite were still problematic, however, so Tom helped Susan establish some behavioral changes that addressed these symptoms adequately.

In this situation, the therapist was able to help the client clarify symptoms, goals, and priorities. Neither medication nor psychotherapy alone was sufficient to help her get relief from her symptoms, but a combination was quite helpful. The therapist provided cognitive and behavioral interventions and helped the client communicate effectively with her prescriber.

Medication Emergencies

A competent psychotherapist must be able to recognize medication emergencies. A client who has recently started an antipsychotic medication and develops stiff muscles and an irresistible urge to move should see a medical provider immediately. A client with a recent increase in lithium dosage who becomes lethargic or ill with diarrhea or vomiting may be developing a serious reaction and should seek medical help right away. A client who is taking both an SSRI antidepressant and migraine medication who begins to feel overheated and anxious may be developing serotonin syndrome and needs immediate medical attention. The psychotherapist's role in each of these situations is to recognize the emergency and help the client to get medical care; depending on circumstances, the client may need to see his or her prescriber or go to the emergency room of a local hospital.

> **TIP**
>
> Serotonin syndrome is used to describe a condition caused by excess serotonin activity in the central nervous system. Symptoms can include confusion, hypomania, sweating, hypertension, and muscle twitching. In severe cases, it can lead to shock.

Mind-Body Interactions

The idea that the mind and body are separate and interactive components is a helpful way to organize complex neurobiological concepts. But where is the separation? In the West, we tend to separate these concepts so that we can make sense of them. We test and analyze by breaking these concepts into their component parts to determine function. Once we understand how the separate parts function, we hope that we can put it all back together to understand the entire person. The Eastern approach is to attempt to bring the mind and body together in harmony to improve optimal functioning. The mental health practitioner should understand both approaches!

Mental health practitioners may have clients with an initial presentation of mental symptoms, but these symptoms may have an underlying physical cause. In these cases, talk therapy interventions may have limited effectiveness. It is important for the practitioner to be aware that a physical cause may be present. Get proper consultation from a medical care provider whenever you have suspicions that your client's mental health symptoms may have a physical cause.

Medical Conditions That Have Mental Health Symptoms

Several medical conditions can initially present with mental health symptoms. A client with sudden fatigue and worsening depression may have undiagnosed diabetes. A client with sudden mood swings may need to be evaluated for a brain tumor and neurological diseases, or may need an urgent medication review by her prescriber. A client with panic attacks and tachycardia may have undiagnosed heart problems or thyroid dysfunction. Other medical causes of mental symptoms are extensive alcohol and street drug use. If the psychiatric symptoms occur as a first episode of someone over 40 years old, this may be a clue to an underlying medical condition. When the response to appropriate mental health treatment is poor, it is time to rethink the diagnosis, reassess, and consider getting consultation from a psychiatrist or other physician.

As you do your initial evaluation with a new client, be sure to ask about medical conditions and any changes in health. Be alert to whether physical symptoms and mental health symptoms began simultaneously. Ask whether the client has seen a physician recently; if any unexplained physical symptoms are present, strongly encourage an appointment soon. Help the client clarify what the symptoms are, when they started, and to what extent they are affecting current functioning. You may want to help the client write this information down so that it can be communicated clearly to the physician. Ask for a release of information and permission to contact the client's PCP if you believe the client may not be able to communicate this information effectively.

If a medical condition has been diagnosed and is being adequately treated and the client continues to have mental health symptoms, you may need to work with the client on skills to help her cope with these symptoms. Clients may need help in developing and following through with daily medical self-care; for example, a newly diagnosed diabetic may need help remembering to test his blood sugar and take his medications, as well as maintaining a healthy diet. Another client may be faced with a life-threatening illness with a poor prognosis; this is likely to bring up end-of-life concerns. Yet another client may need assistance coping with chronic pain or dramatic lifestyle changes. In all of these clinical situations, your role is to help the client manage and cope with mental health symptoms while maintaining appropriate medical care.

Summing Up

In this chapter we reviewed neurotransmitters, psychiatric medications, and the importance of identifying both psychological and medical causes for symptoms. Both new and experienced therapists are encouraged to continue to learn more about these topics, as new research contributes to evolving perspectives. Be sure to consult with medical professionals as needed to provide integrated care for your clients.

══EXERCISES══

1. Do you think you know enough about psychiatric medicines? If not, how could you learn more?
2. Have you ever recommended that a client try medication? Why or why not?
3. Name some of the common neurotransmitters and explain how they are involved in particular diagnoses.
4. Name five types of psychiatric medications and the function of each. Name some of the common side effects.
5. Which type of medication is potentially more fatal when taken in an overdose: a tricyclic antidepressant or an SSRI?
6. What precautions need to be taken by a client when taking MAOIs?
7. Why do prescribers sometimes add an antidepressant to a mood stabilizer? What diagnosis needs a level of caution when taking an antidepressant? What are the signs that this class of medications may be contraindicated?
8. You are treating a very anxious client who is being prescribed a benzodiazepine by her primary care physician. Every time she has a bad day at work or has an argument with her family, you notice that she seems to be escalating her use of the medication. How would you handle this situation?
9. Do you recommend nutritional supplements, herbal treatments, or other alternative treatments to your clients? Why or why not?
10. How could you find out about positive effects and side effects of a particular medication?

(*Continued*)

11. How have you worked with medication prescribers? Do you consult with them directly? Do you coach clients in how to communicate effectively with prescribers?

12. Have you worked with clients with medical illnesses that affect their mental health? How has this been similar to or different from working with other clients?

13. You are treating a 43-year-old man who is having some intermittent episodes of psychotic and paranoid thinking. This has never happened before. He fell off a ladder recently, received some medical attention in the emergency room, and was released. Your treatment approach does not seem to be having much positive effect. How would you handle this situation?

Resources

Preston, J. D., O'Neal, J. H., & Talaga, M. C. (2005). *Handbook of clinical psychopharmacology for therapists* (4th ed.). Oakland, CA: New Harbinger Publications.

The Food and Drug Administration web site lists patient handouts on antipsychotic medication with precautions and common side effects: www.fda.gov/CDER/Drug/infopage/antipsychotics/default.htm.

Medline Plus, a service of the U.S. Library of Medicine and the National Institutes of Health, provides information on the action and side effects of medications, supplements, and herbs: www.nlm.nih.gov/medlineplus/medlineplus.html.

SECTION III

MANAGING PROFESSIONAL GROWTH

16

Professional Growth through Personal Management

What You Will Learn

- How to create your professional identity
- How to identify your four major customers
- How to find a mentor
- How to deal with burnout and vicarious trauma
- How to develop the seven core characteristics of an effective psychotherapist
- How clients influence your personal development
- How to decide whether to be a specialist or a generalist

In what other profession are you faced daily with different and challenging situations where you must use your knowledge, intuition, and skill to help others, while at the same time this process contributes to your own personal development? To be a successful psychotherapist, you need to find ways to develop and change throughout your career. Psychotherapy practitioners have a unique opportunity to grow and to be personally enriched during a lifetime of helping others. In this chapter we examine some of the ways you can manage your practice with purpose in order to promote personal growth.

Creating a Professional Identity

Creating your professional identity is a key element in beginning a psychotherapy practice. The office space, your advertising plan to get referrals, your approach to clients, and your relationship with other professionals will help to establish this professional identity. To have a successful practice it is important to engage in the delicate dance between your vision, core beliefs and the realities of the business world. The expansion of managed care and the proliferation of practitioners has produced an extremely competitive market.

As a psychotherapist in any community, you have several customers. Your first customer is yourself. Practitioners have to find their own way to create personal and professional balance. You will not last long in the field if you ignore your own personal and business ethics. Your second customer is your group of clients; they must leave your office knowing and feeling they have benefited from your interactions. Corporations have spent millions of dollars trying to understand what their customers want in order to satisfy their needs and attract more. Individual practitioners would be well advised to start to establish this mind-set. Your third customer is the community itself. You must present yourself as a valuable resource to medical practitioners, the court system, spiritual leaders, educators, community leaders, and the therapeutic community in order to succeed. Knowing your community's values and clearly communicating how you can support those values will increase your worth. Your fourth, and essential, customer is composed of your payers. Many beginning practitioners concentrate so heavily on the clinical that they neglect the business aspects of their practice. They assume that people will beat a path to their door. No matter how altruistic, you cannot ignore the reality that psychotherapy is also a business. Who will pay you for your work? An agency? Insurance? Your clients? How can you establish your value to them? All practitioners must ask these questions and create their own answers as they develop.

How to Get Referrals: The Mental Health Professional's Guide to Strategic Marketing by Linda L. Lawless and G. Jean Wright (2000) contains a step-by-step process for identifying your practice strengths, needs, and goals. It discusses strategies for understanding various referral sources, including physicians, attorneys, religious leaders, educators, and managed care organizations. Time spent creatively marketing your practice will help you to achieve your personal and professional goals.

Mentorship

As you begin your practice, you are likely to seek out and find experienced therapists who can help you make sense of your vocation. More important, experienced therapists can help you to deepen your understanding of yourself as you are continually impacted by your clients and the work you do with them.

It is difficult to find mentors; fortunately, they usually find you. Experienced therapists gain new perspectives through mentoring younger psychotherapists. It has often been said that the best way to learn something is to teach it! As experienced mentors share how they have grown in their understanding of psychotherapy, their own experiences are deepened. Mentoring occurs when experienced practitioners are at a point in their career where they want to pass on some of their wisdom, and they meet willing new practitioners who are eager to be initiated into the profession. For this to happen, there needs to be the right combination of timing, mutual need, compatibility, rapport, and respect. It does not happen often. That is why, when it does, it is such a treasure.

Dealing with Burnout and Vicarious Trauma

Psychotherapists work with people whose lives are filled with discontent, frustration, emotional crises, experiences of trauma, and tragic circumstances. How does one cope with exposure to all of this suffering? (See Chapter 12 for more about working with forgiveness and acceptance and Chapter 13 for more about working with trauma.) Burnout can be a serious problem for experienced therapists. However, there are several things you can do to prevent (or cope with) burnout and vicarious trauma:

- Continue to develop a strong sense of self—what you like and dislike, what you believe in, what you stand for.
- Attend to and renew your spiritual connections and traditions, whatever they are, as they can keep you grounded.

- Work hard to develop and maintain a sense of optimism and hopefulness in the world—cynicism can be a dangerous thing in a therapist.
- Foster an attitude of "engaged equanimity" (Morgan, 2005, p. 140) in your interactions with your clients. It is important to strive to understand and help your clients, while at the same time to appreciate that you are not in control of the outcome. Accept that clients pretty much do what they want to do.
- Take time for friends, family, and activities that have nothing to do with therapy to create balance in your life.
- When needed, seek out an experienced therapist for yourself or consultation from a colleague about how he or she deals with similar issues.

Developing Core Characteristics

Throughout your career you will have many opportunities to sharpen your skills. These skills will become the core characteristics of your therapy practice and will help you to become more effective and balanced.

Humility

If you do not start out with a degree of humility, you certainly will develop it over time. Just when you have had a series of successes with clients and you are feeling confident in your abilities, a client comes along who shatters all that you thought you knew. Maintaining a certain sense of humility helps keep one from getting overconfident. Overconfidence clouds vision so that important aspects of the situation are missed. Even great successes are rarely due exclusively to our skills. Our clients do the most courageous, difficult work in therapy.

Compassion

Compassion is another essential characteristic of a good psychotherapist. The repeated exposure to tragic circumstances helps one realize that anyone could be in that circumstance. Compassion is the ability to understand another's pain and to wish for an end to suffering. Without compassion, we can easily become critical, judgmental, and even harmful to our clients. As therapists, we must also cultivate compassion toward ourselves. We are not perfect. We experience painful emotions and make mistakes. While we strive to do better, judging ourselves harshly rarely helps.

Concerned Detachment

As mentioned earlier, an attitude of concerned detachment, or engaged equanimity, is a core characteristic of a successful psychotherapist. This sense of detachment comes from a profound understanding of the limits of our influence. While some of the outcome of therapy is due to the therapist's behavior, much of it is due to factors completely out of our control. Our task is to remain concerned, engaged, and deeply caring about the welfare of our clients, at the same time bringing all of our attention and skill to the present moment. We often cannot see the whole picture and know what positive outcomes may occur long after therapy ends. An artist has a completed canvas to represent the fruits of her labors; a construction worker has a completed house. A psychotherapist's rewards are often less tangible; often, we are not even present when they come to fruition. Whenever you get discouraged, think of the movie *Mr. Holland's Opus*, about a music teacher who did not think that he was having much of an impact until many of his students returned and told him what an impact he had on their lives. The fruits of a psychotherapist's labor are living, breathing sculptures who are leading more satisfying and productive lives, causing a ripple effect throughout society.

Respect for Clients

A corollary to compassion is respect for our clients. Clients know when professionals are not respecting them. However, they will rarely tell you when it happens. Clients feel disrespected when the practitioner makes assumptions or does not include them in the process in some way—ignoring their needs or time or not recognizing their efforts. Strive to cultivate an attitude of respect by actively looking for client strengths. For many clients, just coming to a therapy session takes great courage. Respect is often displayed in actions: being on time, awake, aware, and engaged in

If you want others to be happy, practice compassion. If you want to be happy, practice compassion.
—His Holiness, the Dalai Lama

their process. (See Chapter 10 for more about therapist behaviors that interfere with therapy.)

Listening Skills

To listen fully means to pay close attention to what is being said beneath the words. You listen not only to the "music," but to the essence of the person speaking. You listen not only for what someone knows, but for what he or she is. Ears operate at the speed of sound, which is far slower than the speed of light the eyes take in. Generative listening is the art of developing deeper silences in yourself, so you can slow your mind's hearing to your ears' natural speed, and hear beneath the words to their meaning.
—Peter Senge

Listening skills are often the first things taught to beginning psychotherapy students. We all know the "therapist's posture": leaning slightly forward, hands visible and relaxed, head slightly tilted, with a gentle and engaging smile. Psychotherapists must learn to listen for both spoken and unspoken elements of the client's communication. Effective listening includes sharing your understanding of the client's words and asking clarifying questions. Listening involves being truly awake and mindful of your client in each moment. Sharpen your listening skills by noticing others who listen well to you; identify what they do that indicates that they are hearing you accurately.

Observation Skills

Part of effective listening is careful observation. Picking up on body language, tone of voice, even eye movements can give you a great deal of added information. Learn to notice small cues given by the client.

Observation also includes noticing how you react to clients. If you notice strong emotions during a session, look for elements in the client's words and behavior that may be triggering these, or examine your own issues that may be involved. (See Chapter 10 for more on countertransference.)

Becoming a Psychological Detective

One of the most enjoyable aspects of psychotherapy is being a psychological detective, looking for clues to the client's problems and possible solutions. Knowing what questions to ask and how to put together seemingly unrelated evidence to develop a deeper understanding of the client is an art that you can continue to develop throughout your career.

Clients' Influence on Your Development

Client and therapist profoundly affect each other. Allow yourself to be receptive to this. Each client teaches you about human nature, about the processes of stagnation and change, and about your response to the world. Some clients challenge you to reflect on your competency as a therapist. Be brutally honest with yourself at these moments: Ask yourself how *you* are being asked to change. At the same time, maintain your own balance and sense of self through your personal relationships, beliefs, and passions. It is within the dialectical balance between your personal history and the challenges clients bring to you that you will create growth.

Finding Your Niche: Generalist or Specialist?

As you develop your practice, you will have the opportunity to identify yourself as a specialist in a particular area. For instance, if you have training and experience in eye movement desensitization and reprocessing, you may become a specialist in Posttraumatic Stress Disorder; if you have worked in a community mental health setting, you may become a specialist in severe and persistent mental illnesses. Most therapists will develop one or two specialties at some point in their careers. Be cautious, though, in promoting yourself as a specialist—you may find that you are inundated with a particular kind of client. If you eventually find you don't enjoy seeing these clients every day, it may be difficult to change to a more general practice. (See Chapter 5 for more on developing specialties.)

As a generalist, you will see a variety of clients and be challenged to develop myriad skills. However, if you are practicing in a crowded field, with many other practitioners vying for a limited number of clients (and insurance panel memberships), you may need to specialize in order to stand out from the pack. Managed care companies often choose therapists based on their business need; for example, if they have a need for therapists to treat adolescents with Bipolar Disorder, they may not choose therapists who are generalists without any specific interest in treating adolescents. Look at market conditions, as well as your preferences, before committing to a specialty.

In *Getting Started in Private Practice: The Complete Guide to Building Your Mental Health Practice*, Chris E. Stout and Laurie Cope Grand (2005, p. 164) explain why it's important to have a niche:

> Whether you choose solo practice or join a group, you should have at least one market niche—an area in which you have special expertise and interest. Having an area of specialization gives clients and referral sources a reason to choose you rather than the dozens of other therapists available in your area.

The important thing is not to stop questioning. Curiosity has its own reason for existing. One cannot help but be in awe when he contemplates the mysteries of eternity, of life, of the marvelous structure of reality. It is enough if one tries merely to comprehend a little of this mystery every day. Never lose a holy curiosity.

—Albert Einstein

Think carefully about your particular interests and talents before selecting a specialty. Your practice's success may depend on an astute evaluation of both yourself and the market in which you are working. As your career develops, you may find you must change and adapt your specialties to respond effectively to market changes.

Summing Up

The challenges and rewards of a psychotherapy career are countless. Your own personal experience will shape your interactions with your clients, and your clients will in turn shape you. Strive to become and remain aware of your growth as you move through your career. It is this reflective capacity that will enable you to integrate your experiences into a meaningful and valuable life.

EXERCISES

1. Who are your customers? How do they influence the growth and health of your practice?
2. Analyze your customers as specifically as possible in these four areas:
   - Yourself (your values, ethics, and goals)
   - Your clients (past, present, and future)
   - Your community (values and resources)
   - Your payers (private, insurance, other sources)
3. Who has mentored you in your psychotherapy practice? Who have you mentored? How did you find a mentor?
4. What is your plan for how you will maintain your own psychological health? How do you balance your own needs with the demands of your clients?
5. Which of the seven core characteristics discussed in this chapter do you feel are your strengths currently? Which would you like to strengthen?
6. Do you prefer to practice as a generalist or a specialist? What specialties interest you? Is there a market for these specialties in your community? What additional training do you need?

Resources

Kase, L. (2005). *The successful therapist: Your guide to building the career you've always wanted*. Hoboken, NJ: Wiley.

Kottler, J. A. (1993). *On being a therapist* (Rev. ed.). San Francisco: Jossey-Bass.

Lawless, L. L., & Wright, G. J. (2000). *How to get referrals: The mental health professional's guide to strategic marketing*. New York: Wiley.

Pipher, M. (2003). *Letters to a young therapist*. New York: Basic Books.

Stout, C. E., & Cope Grand, L. (2005). *Getting started in private practice: The complete guide to building your mental health practice*. Hoboken, NJ: Wiley.

Yalom, I. D. (2003). *The gift of therapy: An open letter to a new generation of therapists and their patients*. New York: HarperCollins.

References

American Counseling Association. (1995). *Codes of ethics and standards of practice: A.6—Dual relationships*. Retrieved September 1, 2007, from http://ethics.iit.edu/codes/coe/amer.couns.assoc.html.

The American heritage dictionary of the English language (4th ed.). Retrieved February 22, 2008, from Dictionary.com web site: http://dictionary.reference.com/browse/psychopathology.

American Psychiatric Association. (2000). *Diagnostic and statistical manual of mental disorders* (4th ed., text rev.). Washington, DC.

American Psychological Association. (2003). *Ethical principles of psychologists and code of conduct*. (Section 10.10: Terminating Therapy). Retrieved September 1, 2007, from www.apa.org/ethics/code2002.html#10_10.

Arkowitz, H., Westra, H. A., Miller, W. R., & Rollnick, S. (Eds.). (2008). *Motivational interviewing in the treatment of psychological problems*. New York: Guilford Press.

Babor, T. F., Higgins-Biddle, J .C., Saunders, J. B., & Montiero, M. G. (2001). *The Alcohol Use Disorders Identification Test. Guidelines for use in primary care* (2nd ed.). Geneva, Switzerland: World Health Organization, Department of Mental Health and Substance Dependence. Retrieved February 26, 2008, from http://whqlibdoc.who.int/hq/2001/WHO_MSD_MSB_01.6a.pdf.

Baldick, T. L. (1980, April). Ethical discrimination ability of intern psychologists: A function of training in ethics. *Professional Psychology*, 276–282.

Bavonese, J. (n.d.). *What is marketing?* Retrieved June 17, 2007, from Uncommon Practices web site: www.uncommon-practices.com/marketing.html.

Bernard, J. L., & Jara, C. S. (1986). The failure of clinical psychology graduate students to apply understood ethical principles. *Professional Psychology: Research and Practice, 17*(4), 313–315.

Bernstein, B. E., & Hartsell, T. L. (2000). *The portable ethicist for mental health professionals: An A–Z guide to responsible practice*. New York: Wiley.

Bernstein, B. E., & Hartsell, T. L. (2004). *The portable lawyer for mental health professionals: An A–Z guide to protecting your clients, your practice, and yourself* (2nd ed.). Hoboken, NJ: Wiley.

Bernstein, B. E., & Hartsell, T. L. (2005). *The portable guide to testifying in court for mental health professionals: An A–Z guide to being an effective witness*. Hoboken, NJ: Wiley.

Bradley, K. A., McDonell, M. B., Bush, K., Kivlahan, D. R., Diehr, P., & Fihn, S. D. (1998). The AUDIT alcohol consumption questions: Reliability, validity, and responsiveness to change in older male primary care patients. *Alcoholism: Clinical and Experimental Research, 22*(8), 1842–1849.

Brown, A. J. (2007). *Core beliefs psychotherapy* (2nd ed.). Plymouth, MI: Core Healing Center.

Brown, J., Dris, S., & Nace, D. K. (2006). What really makes a difference in psychotherapy outcome? Why does managed care want to know? In M. A. Hubble, B. L. Duncan, & S. D. Miller (Eds.), *The heart and soul of change: What works in therapy* (pp. 389–406). Washington, DC: American Psychological Association.

Burns, D. (1993). *Ten days to self-esteem*. New York: Morrow.

Caudill, B. (n.d.). *Malpractice and licensing pitfalls for therapists: A defense attorney's list*. Retrieved May 2, 2007, from www.kspope.com/ethics/malpractice.php.

Centers for Disease Control and Prevention, National Center for Injury Prevention and Control. (n.d.). *Web-Based Injury Statistics Query and Reporting System*. Retrieved September 19, 2007, from www.cdc.gov/ncipc/wisqars/.

Cohen-Posey, K. (2000). *Brief therapy client handouts*. New York: Wiley.

Condor, B. (2007, April 30). Living well: Gender differences about alcohol are sobering. *Seattle Post-Intelligencer*. Retrieved July 15, 2007, from http://seattlepi.nwsource.com/health/313508_condor30.html.

Cope Grand, L. (2002a). *The therapist's advertising and marketing kit*. Hoboken, NJ: Wiley.

Cope Grand, L. (2002b). *The therapist's newsletter kit*. New York: Wiley.

Daniels, N. (1986). Sounding board: Why saying no to patients in the United States is so hard. *New England Journal of Medicine, 314*(21), 1380–1383.

Davis, T., & Ritchie, M. (1993, September). Confidentiality and the school counselor: A challenge for the 1990s. *School Counselor, 41*(1), 23–30.

Debate over the importance of self-esteem, from the Harvard Mental Health Letter. (n.d.). *Medical News Today* (Mental Health section). Retrieved August 29, 2007, from Medical News Today web site: www.medicalnewstoday.com/articles/71917.php.

de Shazer, S. (1985). *Keys to solution in brief therapy*. New York: Norton.

de Shazer, S. (1988). *Clues: Investigating solutions in brief therapy*. New York: Norton.

de Shazer, S. (1991). *Putting difference to work*. New York: Norton.

Edwards, C. E., & Murdock, N. L. (1994). Characteristics of therapist disclosure in the counseling process. *Journal of Counseling and Development, 72*, 384–389.

The ethical mind: A conversation with psychologist Howard Gardiner. (2007, March). *Harvard Business Review*, 51–56.

Farber, B. A. (2003). Self-disclosure in psychotherapy practice and supervision: An introduction. *Journal of Clinical Psychology: In Session, 59*(5), 525–528.

Feedback to therapists about client progress improves response to therapy. (2005, June). *Clinician's Research Digest*, 5.

Feldman, J. M., & Lee, E. M. (1985). Serotonin content of foods: Effect on urinary excretion of 5-hydroxyindoleacetic acid. *American Journal of Clinical Nutrition, 42*(4), 639–643. Retrieved June 5, 2007, from American Journal of Clinical Nutrition web site: www.ajcn.org/cgi/reprint/42/4/639.pdf.

Feldman, S. (2001). *How to stay out of trouble with everyone: A handbook of law and ethics for the mental health professional*. Seattle, WA: Still River Foundation Press.

Froetschel, S. (2007, February 19). *Globalization forces a health check of U.S. auto industry*. Retrieved July 29, 2007, from Yale Global web site: http://yaleglobal.yale.edu/display.article?id=8785.

Gaginella, T. S., & Galligan, J. J. (1995). *Serotonin and gastrointestinal functioning*. Boca Raton, FL: CRC Press

Gallo, F. P. (1999). *Energy psychology: Explorations at the interface of energy, cognition, behavior, and health*. Boca Raton, FL: CRC Press.

Gaston, L., Thompson, L., Gallagher, D., Cournoyer, L. G., & Gagnon, R. (1998). Alliance, technique, and their interactions in predicting outcome of behavioral, cognitive, and brief dynamic therapy. *Psychotherapy Research, 8*(2), 190–209.

Geller, J. D., & Farber, B. A. (1997, August). *Why therapists do and don't disclose*. Paper presented at the annual meeting of the American Psychological Association, Chicago.

Gelso, C. J., & Hayes, J. A. (2002). The management of countertransference. In J. C. Norcross (Ed.), *Psychotherapy relationships that work: Therapist contributions and responsiveness to patients* (pp. 267–283). New York: Oxford University Press.

Germer, C. K., Siegel, R. D., & Fulton, P. R. (Eds.). (2005). *Mindfulness and psychotherapy*. New York: Guilford Press.

Goddard, A. W., Mason, G. F., Almai, A., Rothman, D. L., Behar, K. L., Petroff, O. A. C., et al. (2001). Reductions in the occipital cortex GABA levels in panic disorder detected with H-magnetic resonance spectroscopy. *Archive of General Psychiatry, 58,* 556–561.

Green, R. G., Baskind, F. R., Mustian, B. E., Reed, L. N., & Taylor, H. R. (2007). Professional education and private practice: Is there a disconnect? *Social Work Journal, 52*(2), 151–159.

Greenwald, H. (1977). *Humour in psychotherapy.* In A. Chapman & H. Foot (Eds.), *It's a funny thing, humour.* Oxford, England: Pergamon Press.

Grodzki, L. (2000). *Building your ideal private practice: A guide for therapists and other healing professionals.* New York: Norton.

Grodzki, L. (2000). *12 months to your ideal private practice: A workbook.* New York: Norton.

Group Health Cooperative. (2007). *Understanding the effects of alcohol* [Brochure]. Seattle, WA.

GSC Home Study Courses. (2006). *2074: Ethical codes of conduct and standards in professional documentation of clinical records* (pp. 1–29). Sacramento, CA.

Hammond, M. (2006, January/February). Mental wellness and how to help your clients find it. *Social Work Today,* 41–43.

Handelsman, M. M. (1986). Problems with ethics training by "osmosis." *Professional Psychology: Research and Practice, 17*(4), 371–372.

Hass, L. J., Malouf, J. L., & Mayerson, N. H. (1986). Ethical dilemmas in psychological practice: Results of a national survey. *Professional Psychology: Research and Practice, 17*(4), 316–321.

Hill, C. E., & Knox, S. (2002). Self-disclosure. In J. C. Norcross (Ed.), *Psychotherapy relationships that work: Therapist contributions and responsiveness to patients* (pp. 255–265). New York: Oxford University Press.

Hill, C. E., & Lambert, M. J. (in press). Methodological issues in studying psychotherapy processes and outcomes. In M. J. Lambert (Ed.), *Handbook of psychotherapy and behavior change* (5th ed.). Hoboken, NJ: Wiley.

Jongsma, Jr., A. E., Peterson, L. M., & Bruce, T. J. (Contributing Ed.). (2006). *The complete adult psychotherapy treatment planner* (4th ed.). Hoboken, NJ: Wiley.

Kaplan, H. B. (2006). Understanding the concept of resilience. In S. Goldstein & R. Brooks (Eds.), *The handbook of resilience in children* (pp. 39–48). New York: Springer.

Kase, L. (2005). *The successful therapist: Your guide to building the career you've always wanted.* Hoboken, NJ: Wiley.

Katz, R. S. (2006). The journey inside: Examining countertransference and its implications for end-of-life care. In R. S. Katz & T. A. Johnson (Eds.), *When professionals weep: Emotional and countertransference responses in end-of-life care.* New York: Routledge.

Katz, R. S. (2007, April). *How we define quality: The impact of professionals' emotional responses*. Workshop lecture presented at Defining Quality at End of Life: A Multidisciplinary Conference for Health Professionals, Bellingham, WA.

Kaye, E. (1997). Lolita comes again. *Esquire, 127*(2), 50–52.

Keith-Spiegel, P., & Koocher, G. P. (1985). *Ethics in psychology: Professional standards and cases*. New York: Random House.

Klott, J., & Jongsma, A. E., Jr. (2004). *The suicide and homicide risk assessment and prevention treatment planner*. Hoboken, NJ: Wiley.

Kottler, J. A. (1993). *On being a therapist*. (Rev. ed.). San Francisco: Jossey-Bass.

LaBare, K. M. (n.d.). *A closer look at Carl Rogers*. Retrieved April 29, 2007, from http://facultyweb.cortland.edu/andersmd/ROGERS/rogers.html.

Lambert, M. J., & Okiishi, J. C. (1997). The effects of the individual therapist and implications for further research. *Clinical Psychology: Science and Practice, 4*(1), 66–75.

Lambert, M. J., Whipple, J. L., Hawkins, E. J., Vermeersh, D. A., Nielson, S. L., & Smart, D. W. (2003). Is it time for clinicians to routinely track patient outcome? A meta-analysis. *Clinical Psychology: Science and Practice, 10*, 288–301.

Lane, J., Farber, B., & Geller, J. (2001, June). *What therapists do and do not disclose to their patients*. Paper presented at the annual conference of the Society for Psychotherapy Research, Montevideo, Uruguay.

Lawless, L. L. (1997). *How to build and market your mental health practice*. New York: Wiley.

Lawless, L. L., & Wright, G. J. (2000). *How to get referrals: The mental health professional's guide to strategic marketing*. New York: Wiley.

Learning Point Associates. (1998). *Duty to warn*. Retrieved June 23, 2006, from Pathways to School Improvement web site: http:ncrel.org/sdrs/areas/issues/envrnmnt/css/cs3lk1.htm. (Part of the publication *Critical issue: Addressing confidentiality concerns in school-linked integrated service efforts*: http:ncrel.org/sdrs/areas/issues/envrnmnt/css/cs300.htm)

Lilienfeld, S. O. (2007). Psychological treatments that cause harm. *Perspectives on Psychological Science, 2*(1), 53–70.

Linehan, M. M. (1993a). *Cognitive behavioral treatment of borderline personality disorder*. New York: Guilford Press.

Linehan, M. M. (1993b). *Skills training manual for borderline personality disorder*. New York: Guilford Press.

Lutz, W. (2002). Patient-focused psychotherapy research and individual treatment progress as scientific groundwork for an empirically based clinical practice. *Psychotherapy Research, 12*(3), 251–272.

Maslow, A. (1961). *Toward a psychology of being*. Princeton, NJ: Van Nostrand.

McWhinney, M., Haskins-Herkenham, D., & Hare, I. (1992). *The school social worker and confidentiality* (Position Statement of the National Association of Social Workers, Commission on Education). Washington, DC: National Association of Social Workers.

Meichenbaum, D. (2005, October). *ENRAGED! Addressing violent behavior toward self and others in adult psychiatric patients*. Handout presented at the Institute for the Advancement of Human Behavior Workshop, Bellingham, WA.

Miller, D. M. (2008). *The correlation between sense of humor and mental health*. Retrieved February 28, 2008, from Missouri Western State University web site: http://clearinghouse.missouriwestern.edu/manuscripts/405.asp.

Miller, W. R., & Rollnick, S. (1991). *Motivational interviewing: Preparing people to change addictive behavior*. New York: Guilford Press.

Miller, W. R., & Rollnick, S. (2002). *Motivational interviewing: Preparing people for change*. New York: Guilford Press.

Moran, M. (2003). Antidepressants don't cause rapid cycling, study finds. *Psychiatric News, 38*(21), 36. Retrieved December 1, 2007, from http://pn.psychiatryonline.org/cgi/content/full/38/21/36?etoc/.

More studies validate AUDIT as alcohol screen. (2007, November). *Brown University digest of addiction theory and application, 2–3.*

Morgan, S. P. (2005). Depression: Turning toward life. In C. K. Germer & R. D. Seigel (Eds.), *Mindfulness in psychotherapy* (pp. 130–151). New York: Guilford Press.

Moscicki, E. K. (2001). Epidemiology of completed and attempted suicide: Toward a framework for prevention. *Clinical Neuroscience Research, 1,* 310–323.

National Association of Social Workers Code of Ethics. (1999a). *Section 1.08(a): Access to records*. Retrieved August 28, 2007, from www.socialworkers.org/pubs/code/code.asp.

National Association of Social Workers Code of Ethics. (1999b). *Section 1.16(c): Termination of services*. Retrieved August 28, 2007, from www.socialworkers.org/pubs/code/code.asp.

National Institute of Mental Health. (n.d.). *Suicide in the U.S.: Statistics and prevention*. Retrieved November 16, 2007, from www.nimh.nih.gov/health/publications/suicide-in-the-us-statistics-and-prevention.shtml#Cog-Therapy.

Nelson, Portia (1993). *There's a hole in my sidewalk*. Hillsboro, OR: Beyond Words Publishing.

Norcross, J. C. (2002). *Psychotherapy relationships that work: Therapist contributions and responsiveness to patients*. New York: Oxford University Press.

Norcross, J. C. (2004). Empirically supported therapy relationships. *Clinical Psychologist, 57*(3), 19–24.

Norcross, J. C. (2007, May). *Tailoring the therapeutic relationship to the individual patient: Evidence based practices.* Workshop sponsored by Group Health Cooperative, Seattle, WA.

Orlinsky, D. E., & Rønnestad, M. H. (2005). *How psychotherapists develop: A study of therapeutic work and professional growth.* Washington, DC: American Psychological Association.

Peterson, C., Maier, S. F., & Seligman, M. E. P. (1993). *Learned helplessness: A theory for the age of personal control.* New York: Oxford University Press.

Pipher, M. (2003). *Letters to a young therapist.* New York: Basic Books.

Pope, K. S., Tabachnick, B. G., & Keith-Spiegel, P. (1987). Ethics of practice: The beliefs and behaviors of psychologists as therapists. *American Psychologist, 42*(11), 993–1006.

Pope, K. S., & Vasquez, M. J. T. (1998). *Ethics in psychotherapy and counseling: A practical guide* (2nd ed.). San Francisco: Jossey-Bass.

Pope, K. S., & Vetter, V. A. (1992). Ethical dilemmas encountered by members of the American Psychological Association: A national survey. *American Psychologist, 47*(3), 397–411.

Preston, J. D., O'Neal, J. H., & Talaga, M. C. (2005). *Handbook of clinical psychopharmacology for therapists* (4th ed.). Oakland, CA: New Harbinger.

Prochaska, J. O. (1979). *Systems of psychotherapy: A transtheoretical analysis.* Chicago: Dorsey.

Prochaska, J. O., DiClemente, C. C., & Norcross, J. C. (1992). In search of how people change. *American Psychologist, 47*(9), 1102–1114.

Prochaska, J. O., Norcross, J. C., & DiClemente, C. C. (1994). *Changing for good: A revolutionary six-stage program for overcoming bad habits and moving your life positively forward.* New York: HarperCollins.

Psychopathology. (n.d.). *The American heritage dictionary of the English language* (4th ed.). Retrieved February 22, 2008, from Dictionary.com website: http://dictionary.reference.com/browse/psychopathology.

Reamer, F. G. (2006, January/February). Clients' rights. *Social Work Today,* 14–15.

Redlich, F. C., & Pope, K. S. (1980). Ethics of mental heath training. *Journal of Nervous and Mental Disease, 168*(12), 709–714.

Revich, K., Gillham J. E., Chaplin, T. M., & Seligman, M. E. P. (2006). From helplessness to optimism: The role of resiliency in treating and preventing depression in youth. In S. Goldstein & R. B. Brooks (Eds.), *The handbook of resilience in children* (pp. 223–237). New York: Springer Science & Business Media.

Revised Code of Washington statute 26.44.030, Reports—Duty and authority to make—Duty of receiving agency—Duty to notify—Case planning and consultation—Penalty for unauthorized exchange of information—Filing dependency petitions—Interviews of children—Records—Risk assessment process. (Effective until October 1, 2008). Retrieved February 18, 2008, from http://apps.leg.wa.gov/RCW/default.aspx?cite=26.44.030/.

Revised Code of Washington statute 26.44.040, Reports—Oral, written—Contents. Retrieved February 18, 2008, from http://apps.leg.wa.gov/RCW/default.aspx?cite=26.44.040/.

Revised Code of Washington statute 71.05.120, Exemptions from liability (2). Retrieved February 18, 2008, from http://apps.leg.wa.gov/RCW/default.aspx?cite=71.05.120/.

Revised Code of Washington statute 71.34.530 (formerly 71.34.030). Age of consent—Outpatient treatment of minors. Retrieved February 22, 2008, from http://apps.leg.wa.gov/rcw/default.aspx?cite=71.34.530/.

Rogers, C. R. (1961). *On becoming a person.* Boston: Houghton Mifflin.

Rogers, C. R. (1975). *Carl Rogers: The man and his ideas.* New York: Dutton.

Rogers, C. R. (1980). *A way of being.* Boston: Houghton Mifflin.

Rotter, J. B. (1966). Generalized-expectancies for internal versus external control of reinforcement. *Psychological Monographs, 80*(1, Whole No. 609).

Sabin, J. E, & Daniels, N. (1994). Determining "medical necessity" in mental health practice. *Hastings Center Report 24*(6), 5–13.

Schmidt, N. B., & Woolaway-Bickel, K. (2000). The effects of treatment compliance on outcome in cognitive-behavioral therapy for panic disorder: Quality vs. quantity. *Journal of Consulting and Clinical Psychology, 68*(1), 13–18.

Schwartz, J., & Weiner, M. B. (2003, July). Finding meaning in medical necessity. *Social Work, 48*(3), 392–400.

Scott, E. (n.d.). *The stress management and health benefits of laughter.* Retrieved April 9, 2007, from http://stress.about.com/od/stresshealth/a/laughter.html.

Seligman, M. E. P. (with Reivich, K., Jaycox, L., & Gillham, J.). (1995). *The optimistic child: A proven program to safeguard children against depression and build lifelong resilience.* Boston: Houghton Mifflin.

Simon, J. C. (1990). Criteria for therapist self-disclosure. In G. Stricker & M. Fisher (Eds.), *Self-disclosure in the therapy relationship* (pp. 207–225). New York: Plenum Press.

Sommerfeld, J., & Berens, M. J. (2006, April 24). License to harm. *Seattle Times,* pp. 1, 6.

Stern, G. M. (2006, September 13). Re-examining business ethics. *USA Weekend,* 12.

Stoesen, L. (2007, November). New Internet tools changing practice. *National Association of Social Workers News, 52*(10), 4.

Stout, C. E., & Cope Grand, L. (2005). *Getting started in private practice: The complete guide to building your mental health practice*. Hoboken, NJ: Wiley.

Strean, H. (Ed.). (1994). *The use of humor in psychotherapy*. Northvale, NJ: Aronson.

Sultanoff, S. M. (1992). *The impact of humor in the counseling relationship*. Retrieved February 28, 2008, from www.humormatters.com/articles/ therapy2.htm. (Original work published by Publication of the American Association for Therapeutic Humor, *Laugh It Up*, July/August, 1992, 1)

Swick, K. J., & Graves, D. B. (1986). Locus of control and interpersonal support as related to parenting. *Childhood Education, 63*(1), 41–50.

Szalavitz, M. (2007, April 11). When the cure is not worth the cost. *New York Times*. Retrieved April 11, 2007, from www.nytimes .com/2007/04/11/opinion/11szalavitz.html?_r=2&oref=slogin/.

Tarasoff v. Regents of University of California, 17 Cal. 3d 425, 551 P.2d 334, 131 Cal. Rptr. 14 (Cal. 1976). Retrieved February 18, 2008, from LSU Law Center's Medical and Public Health Law web site: http:// biotech.law.lsu.edu/cases/privacy/tarasoff.htm.

The top 10: The most influential therapists of the past quarter-century. (2007, March/April). *Psychotherapy Networker*, 24–37, 68.

Travis, C. S. (2007, October). *Is it anxiety disorder or maladaptive coping? The functionality of anxiety and depression*. Brochure presented at the Cross Country Education Workshop, Benton, WA.

Tryon, G. S. (1985). The engagement quotient: One index of a basic counseling task. *Journal of College Student Personnel, 26*, 351–354.

Tryon, G. S., & Tryon, W. W. (1986). Factors associated with clinical practicum trainees' engagement of clients in counseling. *Professional Psychology: Research and Practice, 17*(6), 586–589.

U.S. Department of Health and Human Services. (2003, May). *OCR privacy brief: Summary of the HIPAA privacy rule*. Retrieved February 18, 2008, from www.hhs.gov/ocr/privacysummary.pdf.

Veryard, R. (n.d.). *Reframing: Reframing in NLP*. Retrieved August 4, 2007, from Veryard Projects: Innovation for Demanding Change web site: www.users.globalnet.co.uk/~rxv/demcha/reframe.htm.

Wagner, C. C., & Conners, W. (n.d.). *Motivational interviewing (resources for clinicians, researchers, and trainers): Interaction techniques*. Retrieved April 26, 2007, from the Motivational Interviewing web site: www .motivationalinterview.org/clinical/interaction.html.

Washington Administrative Code 246-809-035, Record keeping and retention, 1 (a–g). Retrieved February 20, 2008, from http://apps.leg .wa.gov/WAC/default.aspx?cite=246-809-035/.

Washington Administrative Code 246-809-035, Record keeping and retention, 2 (a-e), 3. Retrieved February 20, 2008,from http://apps .leg.wa.gov/WAC/default.aspx?cite=246-809-035/.

Wiger, D. E. (1998). *The psychotherapy documentation primer.* New York: Wiley.

Wiger, D. E. (2005). *The clinical documentation sourcebook: The complete paperwork resource for your mental health practice* (3rd ed.). Hoboken, NJ: Wiley.

Wiger, D. E. (2007). *The well managed mental health practice: Your guide to building and managing a successful practice, group or clinic.* Hoboken, NJ: Wiley.

Wubbolding, R. E., & Brickell, J. J. (1998). Qualities of the reality therapist. *International Journal of Reality Therapy, 17*(2), 47–49.

Yalom, I. D. (2003). *The gift of therapy: An open letter to a new generation of therapists and their patients.* New York: HarperCollins.

Subject Index

Author Index